C-2704

THIS IS YOUR **PASSBOOK**® FOR ...

SENIOR COURT CLERK

NATIONAL LEARNING CORPORATION®
passbooks.com

PASSBOOK® SERIES

THE *PASSBOOK® SERIES* has been created to prepare applicants and candidates for the ultimate academic battlefield – the examination room.

At some time in our lives, each and every one of us may be required to take an examination – for validation, matriculation, admission, qualification, registration, certification, or licensure.

Based on the assumption that every applicant or candidate has met the basic formal educational standards, has taken the required number of courses, and read the necessary texts, the *PASSBOOK® SERIES* furnishes the one special preparation which may assure passing with confidence, instead of failing with insecurity. Examination questions – together with answers – are furnished as the basic vehicle for study so that the mysteries of the examination and its compounding difficulties may be eliminated or diminished by a sure method.

This book is meant to help you pass your examination provided that you qualify and are serious in your objective.

The entire field is reviewed through the huge store of content information which is succinctly presented through a provocative and challenging approach – the question-and-answer method.

A climate of success is established by furnishing the correct answers at the end of each test.

You soon learn to recognize types of questions, forms of questions, and patterns of questioning. You may even begin to anticipate expected outcomes.

You perceive that many questions are repeated or adapted so that you can gain acute insights, which may enable you to score many sure points.

You learn how to confront new questions, or types of questions, and to attack them confidently and work out the correct answers.

You note objectives and emphases, and recognize pitfalls and dangers, so that you may make positive educational adjustments.

Moreover, you are kept fully informed in relation to new concepts, methods, practices, and directions in the field.

You discover that you arre actually taking the examination all the time: you are preparing for the examination by "taking" an examination, not by reading extraneous and/or supererogatory textbooks.

In short, this PASSBOOK®, used directedly, should be an important factor in helping you to pass your test.

SENIOR COURT CLERK

DUTIES:

Senior Court Clerks serve as part clerks swearing witnesses, polling jurors, maintaining custody of exhibits and keeping court minutes in individual assignment system and other parts. As part clerks, Senior Court Clerks are responsible for the supervision of uniformed court personnel who have peace officer status and who guard prisoners and maintain security in the courtroom. Senior Court Clerks also work in court offices where they supervise Court Assistants and other court personnel engaged in processing prisoner correspondence, reviewing calendaring decisions, motions for sufficiency and preference, and orders for conformance with decisions. Senior Court Clerks may also supervise a full-time branch office of a court staffed by Court Assistants, be designated to act in the absence of the Chief Clerk or Commissioner of Jurors, and perform other related duties.

EXAMPLES OF DUTIES:

Accepts and tallies bail, filing fees and fines from the public, attorneys, and litigants, maintains records of said transactions; examines court documents to ensure their accuracy, completeness and legal sufficiency; maintains personnel records for court employees; compiles statistical information such as the number of cases bending, the number of cases handled by a particular court term or part, calendar entries, and fines paid; prepares orders, warrants, decrees, summonses, conditional discharges, violations of probation, and other court forms to be submitted to the Judge for signature; prepares, calls and annotates the court calendar; takes juror attendance, polls jurors, swears in jurors, and witnesses, and retains custody of exhibits; responds to oral and written inquiries from the public and lawyers concerning the scheduling of cases and court procedures and practices; maintains permanent court records of all court proceedings; assigns responsibilities to court assistants, office assistants, typists and stenographers, and court interpreters; communicates with outside agencies such as the police, probation, defense attorneys, and mental health clinics in order to coordinate the court's activities with said agencies; interprets orders, decisions, judgments, pleadings, and motions to determine the directives of judges and the reliefs sought by attorneys and litigants; advises the central jury room as to jury requirements; records challenges to the jury during jury selection; and performs related duties.

SCOPE OF THE EXAMINATION

This written examination will be multiple-choice to assess knowledge of legal terminology, statutes, rules and procedures in effect in the New York State Unified Court Systems as set forth in:

1. **Civil Practice Laws and Rules** - Articles 1, 2, 3, 4, 5, 6, 9, 10, 11, 12, 20, 21, 22, 23, 24, 30, 32, 34, 40, 41, 42, 44, 50, 52, 55, 63, 70, 78 and 80 and any other statutes, rules and court procedures referred to therein;

2. **Criminal Procedure Law** - Articles 1,10, 30, 100, 110, 120, 160, 170, 180, 190, 195, 200, 210, 216, 220, 260, 270, 280, 300, 310, 320, 330, 350, 360, 380, 390, 410, 420, 430, 500, 720, 725 and 730 and any other statutes, rules and court procedures referred to therein;

3. **Penal Law** - Articles 10, 55 and 80 and any other statutes, rules and court procedures referred to therein;

4. **Family Court Act** - Articles 1 (Parts 1, 5, 6, 7), 2, 3 (Parts 1, 2, 4, 5, 6, 7, 8), 4, 5, 5A, 5B, 6, 7, 8, 10, 10A and 11 and any other statutes, rules and court procedures referred to therein;

5. **Other laws and statutes including:**
   a. Uniform Rules for the New York State Trial Courts - Parts130.1(Sub A), 200 (Sections 1-9), 202 (Sections 2, 3, 5, 6, 8, 9, 12,13 ,21, 22, 26, 27, 28, 42, 44, 48, 56, 67), and 205;
   b. Real Property Actions and Proceedings Law - Article 7;
   c. Domestic Relations Law - Article 5-A;
   d. Social Services Law - Section 384B;
   e. Vehicle and Traffic Law - Sections 1192 and 1193.

HOW TO TAKE A TEST

I. YOU MUST PASS AN EXAMINATION

A. WHAT EVERY CANDIDATE SHOULD KNOW

Examination applicants often ask us for help in preparing for the written test. What can I study in advance? What kinds of questions will be asked? How will the test be given? How will the papers be graded?

As an applicant for a civil service examination, you may be wondering about some of these things. Our purpose here is to suggest effective methods of advance study and to describe civil service examinations.

Your chances for success on this examination can be increased if you know how to prepare. Those "pre-examination jitters" can be reduced if you know what to expect. You can even experience an adventure in good citizenship if you know why civil service exams are given.

B. WHY ARE CIVIL SERVICE EXAMINATIONS GIVEN?

Civil service examinations are important to you in two ways. As a citizen, you want public jobs filled by employees who know how to do their work. As a job seeker, you want a fair chance to compete for that job on an equal footing with other candidates. The best-known means of accomplishing this two-fold goal is the competitive examination.

Exams are widely publicized throughout the nation. They may be administered for jobs in federal, state, city, municipal, town or village governments or agencies.

Any citizen may apply, with some limitations, such as the age or residence of applicants. Your experience and education may be reviewed to see whether you meet the requirements for the particular examination. When these requirements exist, they are reasonable and applied consistently to all applicants. Thus, a competitive examination may cause you some uneasiness now, but it is your privilege and safeguard.

C. HOW ARE CIVIL SERVICE EXAMS DEVELOPED?

Examinations are carefully written by trained technicians who are specialists in the field known as "psychological measurement," in consultation with recognized authorities in the field of work that the test will cover. These experts recommend the subject matter areas or skills to be tested; only those knowledges or skills important to your success on the job are included. The most reliable books and source materials available are used as references. Together, the experts and technicians judge the difficulty level of the questions.

Test technicians know how to phrase questions so that the problem is clearly stated. Their ethics do not permit "trick" or "catch" questions. Questions may have been tried out on sample groups, or subjected to statistical analysis, to determine their usefulness.

Written tests are often used in combination with performance tests, ratings of training and experience, and oral interviews. All of these measures combine to form the best-known means of finding the right person for the right job.

II. HOW TO PASS THE WRITTEN TEST

A. NATURE OF THE EXAMINATION

To prepare intelligently for civil service examinations, you should know how they differ from school examinations you have taken. In school you were assigned certain definite pages to read or subjects to cover. The examination questions were quite detailed and usually emphasized memory. Civil service exams, on the other hand, try to discover your present ability to perform the duties of a position, plus your potentiality to learn these duties. In other words, a civil service exam attempts to predict how successful you will be. Questions cover such a broad area that they cannot be as minute and detailed as school exam questions.

In the public service similar kinds of work, or positions, are grouped together in one "class." This process is known as *position-classification*. All the positions in a class are paid according to the salary range for that class. One class title covers all of these positions, and they are all tested by the same examination.

B. FOUR BASIC STEPS

1) Study the announcement

How, then, can you know what subjects to study? Our best answer is: "Learn as much as possible about the class of positions for which you've applied." The exam will test the knowledge, skills and abilities needed to do the work.

Your most valuable source of information about the position you want is the official exam announcement. This announcement lists the training and experience qualifications. Check these standards and apply only if you come reasonably close to meeting them.

The brief description of the position in the examination announcement offers some clues to the subjects which will be tested. Think about the job itself. Review the duties in your mind. Can you perform them, or are there some in which you are rusty? Fill in the blank spots in your preparation.

Many jurisdictions preview the written test in the exam announcement by including a section called "Knowledge and Abilities Required," "Scope of the Examination," or some similar heading. Here you will find out specifically what fields will be tested.

2) Review your own background

Once you learn in general what the position is all about, and what you need to know to do the work, ask yourself which subjects you already know fairly well and which need improvement. You may wonder whether to concentrate on improving your strong areas or on building some background in your fields of weakness. When the announcement has specified "some knowledge" or "considerable knowledge," or has used adjectives like "beginning principles of…" or "advanced … methods," you can get a clue as to the number and difficulty of questions to be asked in any given field. More questions, and hence broader coverage, would be included for those subjects which are more important in the work. Now weigh your strengths and weaknesses against the job requirements and prepare accordingly.

3) Determine the level of the position

Another way to tell how intensively you should prepare is to understand the level of the job for which you are applying. Is it the entering level? In other words, is this the position in which beginners in a field of work are hired? Or is it an intermediate or advanced level? Sometimes this is indicated by such words as "Junior" or "Senior" in the class title. Other jurisdictions use Roman numerals to designate the level – Clerk I, Clerk II, for example. The word "Supervisor" sometimes appears in the title. If the level is not indicated by the title, check the description of duties. Will you be working under very close supervision, or will you have responsibility for independent decisions in this work?

4) Choose appropriate study materials

Now that you know the subjects to be examined and the relative amount of each subject to be covered, you can choose suitable study materials. For beginning level jobs, or even advanced ones, if you have a pronounced weakness in some aspect of your training, read a modern, standard textbook in that field. Be sure it is up to date and has general coverage. Such books are normally available at your library, and the librarian will be glad to help you locate one. For entry-level positions, questions of appropriate difficulty are chosen – neither highly advanced questions, nor those too simple. Such questions require careful thought but not advanced training.

If the position for which you are applying is technical or advanced, you will read more advanced, specialized material. If you are already familiar with the basic principles of your field, elementary textbooks would waste your time. Concentrate on advanced textbooks and technical periodicals. Think through the concepts and review difficult problems in your field.

These are all general sources. You can get more ideas on your own initiative, following these leads. For example, training manuals and publications of the government agency which employs workers in your field can be useful, particularly for technical and professional positions. A letter or visit to the government department involved may result in more specific study suggestions, and certainly will provide you with a more definite idea of the exact nature of the position you are seeking.

III. KINDS OF TESTS

Tests are used for purposes other than measuring knowledge and ability to perform specified duties. For some positions, it is equally important to test ability to make adjustments to new situations or to profit from training. In others, basic mental abilities not dependent on information are essential. Questions which test these things may not appear as pertinent to the duties of the position as those which test for knowledge and information. Yet they are often highly important parts of a fair examination. For very general questions, it is almost impossible to help you direct your study efforts. What we can do is to point out some of the more common of these general abilities needed in public service positions and describe some typical questions.

1) General information

Broad, general information has been found useful for predicting job success in some kinds of work. This is tested in a variety of ways, from vocabulary lists to questions about current events. Basic background in some field of work, such as sociology or economics, may be sampled in a group of questions. Often these are principles which have become familiar to most persons through exposure rather than through formal training. It is difficult to advise you how to study for these questions; being alert to the world around you is our best suggestion.

2) Verbal ability

An example of an ability needed in many positions is verbal or language ability. Verbal ability is, in brief, the ability to use and understand words. Vocabulary and grammar tests are typical measures of this ability. Reading comprehension or paragraph interpretation questions are common in many kinds of civil service tests. You are given a paragraph of written material and asked to find its central meaning.

3) Numerical ability

Number skills can be tested by the familiar arithmetic problem, by checking paired lists of numbers to see which are alike and which are different, or by interpreting charts and graphs. In the latter test, a graph may be printed in the test booklet which you are asked to use as the basis for answering questions.

4) Observation

A popular test for law-enforcement positions is the observation test. A picture is shown to you for several minutes, then taken away. Questions about the picture test your ability to observe both details and larger elements.

5) Following directions

In many positions in the public service, the employee must be able to carry out written instructions dependably and accurately. You may be given a chart with several columns, each column listing a variety of information. The questions require you to carry out directions involving the information given in the chart.

6) Skills and aptitudes

Performance tests effectively measure some manual skills and aptitudes. When the skill is one in which you are trained, such as typing or shorthand, you can practice. These tests are often very much like those given in business school or high school courses. For many of the other skills and aptitudes, however, no short-time preparation can be made. Skills and abilities natural to you or that you have developed throughout your lifetime are being tested.

Many of the general questions just described provide all the data needed to answer the questions and ask you to use your reasoning ability to find the answers. Your best preparation for these tests, as well as for tests of facts and ideas, is to be at your physical and mental best. You, no doubt, have your own methods of getting into an exam-taking mood and keeping "in shape." The next section lists some ideas on this subject.

IV. KINDS OF QUESTIONS

Only rarely is the "essay" question, which you answer in narrative form, used in civil service tests. Civil service tests are usually of the short-answer type. Full instructions for answering these questions will be given to you at the examination. But in case this is your first experience with short-answer questions and separate answer sheets, here is what you need to know:

1) Multiple-choice Questions

Most popular of the short-answer questions is the "multiple choice" or "best answer" question. It can be used, for example, to test for factual knowledge, ability to solve problems or judgment in meeting situations found at work.

A multiple-choice question is normally one of three types—

- It can begin with an incomplete statement followed by several possible endings. You are to find the one ending which *best* completes the statement, although some of the others may not be entirely wrong.
- It can also be a complete statement in the form of a question which is answered by choosing one of the statements listed.
- It can be in the form of a problem – again you select the best answer.

Here is an example of a multiple-choice question with a discussion which should give you some clues as to the method for choosing the right answer:

When an employee has a complaint about his assignment, the action which will *best* help him overcome his difficulty is to
- A. discuss his difficulty with his coworkers
- B. take the problem to the head of the organization
- C. take the problem to the person who gave him the assignment
- D. say nothing to anyone about his complaint

In answering this question, you should study each of the choices to find which is best. Consider choice "A" – Certainly an employee may discuss his complaint with fellow employees, but no change or improvement can result, and the complaint remains unresolved. Choice "B" is a poor choice since the head of the organization probably does not know what assignment you have been given, and taking your problem to him is known as "going over the head" of the supervisor. The supervisor, or person who made the assignment, is the person who can clarify it or correct any injustice. Choice "C" is, therefore, correct. To say nothing, as in choice "D," is unwise. Supervisors have and interest in knowing the problems employees are facing, and the employee is seeking a solution to his problem.

2) True/False Questions

The "true/false" or "right/wrong" form of question is sometimes used. Here a complete statement is given. Your job is to decide whether the statement is right or wrong.

SAMPLE: A roaming cell-phone call to a nearby city costs less than a non-roaming call to a distant city.

This statement is wrong, or false, since roaming calls are more expensive.

This is not a complete list of all possible question forms, although most of the others are variations of these common types. You will always get complete directions for answering questions. Be sure you understand *how* to mark your answers – ask questions until you do.

V. RECORDING YOUR ANSWERS

Computer terminals are used more and more today for many different kinds of exams.

For an examination with very few applicants, you may be told to record your answers in the test booklet itself. Separate answer sheets are much more common. If this separate answer sheet is to be scored by machine – and this is often the case – it is highly important that you mark your answers correctly in order to get credit.

An electronic scoring machine is often used in civil service offices because of the speed with which papers can be scored. Machine-scored answer sheets must be marked with a pencil, which will be given to you. This pencil has a high graphite content which responds to the electronic scoring machine. As a matter of fact, stray dots may register as answers, so do not let your pencil rest on the answer sheet while you are pondering the correct answer. Also, if your pencil lead breaks or is otherwise defective, ask for another.

Since the answer sheet will be dropped in a slot in the scoring machine, be careful not to bend the corners or get the paper crumpled.

The answer sheet normally has five vertical columns of numbers, with 30 numbers to a column. These numbers correspond to the question numbers in your test booklet. After each number, going across the page are four or five pairs of dotted lines. These short dotted lines have small letters or numbers above them. The first two pairs may also have a "T" or "F" above the letters. This indicates that the first two pairs only are to be used if the questions are of the true-false type. If the questions are multiple choice, disregard the "T" and "F" and pay attention only to the small letters or numbers.

Answer your questions in the manner of the sample that follows:

32. The largest city in the United States is
    A. Washington, D.C.
    B. New York City
    C. Chicago
    D. Detroit
    E. San Francisco

1) Choose the answer you think is best. (New York City is the largest, so "B" is correct.)
2) Find the row of dotted lines numbered the same as the question you are answering. (Find row number 32)
3) Find the pair of dotted lines corresponding to the answer. (Find the pair of lines under the mark "B.")
4) Make a solid black mark between the dotted lines.

VI. BEFORE THE TEST

Common sense will help you find procedures to follow to get ready for an examination. Too many of us, however, overlook these sensible measures. Indeed, nervousness and fatigue have been found to be the most serious reasons why applicants fail to do their best on civil service tests. Here is a list of reminders:

- Begin your preparation early – Don't wait until the last minute to go scurrying around for books and materials or to find out what the position is all about.
- Prepare continuously – An hour a night for a week is better than an all-night cram session. This has been definitely established. What is more, a night a week for a month will return better dividends than crowding your study into a shorter period of time.
- Locate the place of the exam – You have been sent a notice telling you when and where to report for the examination. If the location is in a different town or otherwise unfamiliar to you, it would be well to inquire the best route and learn something about the building.
- Relax the night before the test – Allow your mind to rest. Do not study at all that night. Plan some mild recreation or diversion; then go to bed early and get a good night's sleep.
- Get up early enough to make a leisurely trip to the place for the test – This way unforeseen events, traffic snarls, unfamiliar buildings, etc. will not upset you.
- Dress comfortably – A written test is not a fashion show. You will be known by number and not by name, so wear something comfortable.
- Leave excess paraphernalia at home – Shopping bags and odd bundles will get in your way. You need bring only the items mentioned in the official notice you received; usually everything you need is provided. Do not bring reference books to the exam. They will only confuse those last minutes and be taken away from you when in the test room.
- Arrive somewhat ahead of time – If because of transportation schedules you must get there very early, bring a newspaper or magazine to take your mind off yourself while waiting.
- Locate the examination room – When you have found the proper room, you will be directed to the seat or part of the room where you will sit. Sometimes you are given a sheet of instructions to read while you are waiting. Do not fill out any forms until you are told to do so; just read them and be prepared.
- Relax and prepare to listen to the instructions
- If you have any physical problem that may keep you from doing your best, be sure to tell the test administrator. If you are sick or in poor health, you really cannot do your best on the exam. You can come back and take the test some other time.

VII. AT THE TEST

The day of the test is here and you have the test booklet in your hand. The temptation to get going is very strong. Caution! There is more to success than knowing the right answers. You must know how to identify your papers and understand variations in the type of short-answer question used in this particular examination. Follow these suggestions for maximum results from your efforts:

1) Cooperate with the monitor

The test administrator has a duty to create a situation in which you can be as much at ease as possible. He will give instructions, tell you when to begin, check to see that you are marking your answer sheet correctly, and so on. He is not there to guard you, although he will see that your competitors do not take unfair advantage. He wants to help you do your best.

2) Listen to all instructions

Don't jump the gun! Wait until you understand all directions. In most civil service tests you get more time than you need to answer the questions. So don't be in a hurry. Read each word of instructions until you clearly understand the meaning. Study the examples, listen to all announcements and follow directions. Ask questions if you do not understand what to do.

3) Identify your papers

Civil service exams are usually identified by number only. You will be assigned a number; you must not put your name on your test papers. Be sure to copy your number correctly. Since more than one exam may be given, copy your exact examination title.

4) Plan your time

Unless you are told that a test is a "speed" or "rate of work" test, speed itself is usually not important. Time enough to answer all the questions will be provided, but this does not mean that you have all day. An overall time limit has been set. Divide the total time (in minutes) by the number of questions to determine the approximate time you have for each question.

5) Do not linger over difficult questions

If you come across a difficult question, mark it with a paper clip (useful to have along) and come back to it when you have been through the booklet. One caution if you do this – be sure to skip a number on your answer sheet as well. Check often to be sure that you have not lost your place and that you are marking in the row numbered the same as the question you are answering.

6) Read the questions

Be sure you know what the question asks! Many capable people are unsuccessful because they failed to *read* the questions correctly.

7) Answer all questions

Unless you have been instructed that a penalty will be deducted for incorrect answers, it is better to guess than to omit a question.

8) Speed tests

It is often better NOT to guess on speed tests. It has been found that on timed tests people are tempted to spend the last few seconds before time is called in marking answers at random – without even reading them – in the hope of picking up a few extra points. To discourage this practice, the instructions may warn you that your score will be "corrected" for guessing. That is, a penalty will be applied. The incorrect answers will be deducted from the correct ones, or some other penalty formula will be used.

9) Review your answers

If you finish before time is called, go back to the questions you guessed or omitted to give them further thought. Review other answers if you have time.

10) Return your test materials

If you are ready to leave before others have finished or time is called, take ALL your materials to the monitor and leave quietly. Never take any test material with you. The monitor can discover whose papers are not complete, and taking a test booklet may be grounds for disqualification.

VIII. EXAMINATION TECHNIQUES

1) Read the general instructions carefully. These are usually printed on the first page of the exam booklet. As a rule, these instructions refer to the timing of the examination; the fact that you should not start work until the signal and must stop work at a signal, etc. If there are any *special* instructions, such as a choice of questions to be answered, make sure that you note this instruction carefully.

2) When you are ready to start work on the examination, that is as soon as the signal has been given, read the instructions to each question booklet, underline any key words or phrases, such as *least, best, outline, describe* and the like. In this way you will tend to answer as requested rather than discover on reviewing your paper that you *listed without describing*, that you selected the *worst* choice rather than the *best* choice, etc.

3) If the examination is of the objective or multiple-choice type – that is, each question will also give a series of possible answers: A, B, C or D, and you are called upon to select the best answer and write the letter next to that answer on your answer paper – it is advisable to start answering each question in turn. There may be anywhere from 50 to 100 such questions in the three or four hours allotted and you can see how much time would be taken if you read through all the questions before beginning to answer any. Furthermore, if you come across a question or group of questions which you know would be difficult to answer, it would undoubtedly affect your handling of all the other questions.

4) If the examination is of the essay type and contains but a few questions, it is a moot point as to whether you should read all the questions before starting to answer any one. Of course, if you are given a choice – say five out of seven and the like – then it is essential to read all the questions so you can eliminate the two that are most difficult. If, however, you are asked to answer all the questions, there may be danger in trying to answer the easiest one first because you may find that you will spend too much time on it. The best technique is to answer the first question, then proceed to the second, etc.

5) Time your answers. Before the exam begins, write down the time it started, then add the time allowed for the examination and write down the time it must be completed, then divide the time available somewhat as follows:

- If 3-1/2 hours are allowed, that would be 210 minutes. If you have 80 objective-type questions, that would be an average of 2-1/2 minutes per question. Allow yourself no more than 2 minutes per question, or a total of 160 minutes, which will permit about 50 minutes to review.
- If for the time allotment of 210 minutes there are 7 essay questions to answer, that would average about 30 minutes a question. Give yourself only 25 minutes per question so that you have about 35 minutes to review.

6) The most important instruction is to *read each question* and make sure you know what is wanted. The second most important instruction is to *time yourself properly* so that you answer every question. The third most important instruction is to *answer every question*. Guess if you have to but include something for each question. Remember that you will receive no credit for a blank and will probably receive some credit if you write something in answer to an essay question. If you guess a letter – say "B" for a multiple-choice question – you may have guessed right. If you leave a blank as an answer to a multiple-choice question, the examiners may respect your feelings but it will not add a point to your score. Some exams may penalize you for wrong answers, so in such cases *only*, you may not want to guess unless you have some basis for your answer.

7) Suggestions
   a. Objective-type questions
      1. Examine the question booklet for proper sequence of pages and questions
      2. Read all instructions carefully
      3. Skip any question which seems too difficult; return to it after all other questions have been answered
      4. Apportion your time properly; do not spend too much time on any single question or group of questions
      5. Note and underline key words – *all, most, fewest, least, best, worst, same, opposite,* etc.
      6. Pay particular attention to negatives
      7. Note unusual option, e.g., unduly long, short, complex, different or similar in content to the body of the question
      8. Observe the use of "hedging" words – *probably, may, most likely,* etc.
      9. Make sure that your answer is put next to the same number as the question
      10. Do not second-guess unless you have good reason to believe the second answer is definitely more correct
      11. Cross out original answer if you decide another answer is more accurate; do not erase until you are ready to hand your paper in
      12. Answer all questions; guess unless instructed otherwise
      13. Leave time for review

   b. Essay questions
      1. Read each question carefully
      2. Determine exactly what is wanted. Underline key words or phrases.
      3. Decide on outline or paragraph answer

4. Include many different points and elements unless asked to develop any one or two points or elements
5. Show impartiality by giving pros and cons unless directed to select one side only
6. Make and write down any assumptions you find necessary to answer the questions
7. Watch your English, grammar, punctuation and choice of words
8. Time your answers; don't crowd material

8) Answering the essay question

Most essay questions can be answered by framing the specific response around several key words or ideas. Here are a few such key words or ideas:

M's: manpower, materials, methods, money, management
P's: purpose, program, policy, plan, procedure, practice, problems, pitfalls, personnel, public relations
   a. Six basic steps in handling problems:
     1. Preliminary plan and background development
     2. Collect information, data and facts
     3. Analyze and interpret information, data and facts
     4. Analyze and develop solutions as well as make recommendations
     5. Prepare report and sell recommendations
     6. Install recommendations and follow up effectiveness

   b. Pitfalls to avoid
     1. *Taking things for granted* – A statement of the situation does not necessarily imply that each of the elements is necessarily true; for example, a complaint may be invalid and biased so that all that can be taken for granted is that a complaint has been registered
     2. *Considering only one side of a situation* – Wherever possible, indicate several alternatives and then point out the reasons you selected the best one
     3. *Failing to indicate follow up* – Whenever your answer indicates action on your part, make certain that you will take proper follow-up action to see how successful your recommendations, procedures or actions turn out to be
     4. *Taking too long in answering any single question* – Remember to time your answers properly

IX. AFTER THE TEST

Scoring procedures differ in detail among civil service jurisdictions although the general principles are the same. Whether the papers are hand-scored or graded by machine we have described, they are nearly always graded by number. That is, the person who marks the paper knows only the number – never the name – of the applicant. Not until all the papers have been graded will they be matched with names. If other tests, such as training and experience or oral interview ratings have been given, scores will be combined. Different parts of the examination usually have different weights. For example, the written test might count 60 percent of the final grade, and a rating of training and experience 40 percent. In many jurisdictions, veterans will have a certain number of points added to their grades.

After the final grade has been determined, the names are placed in grade order and an eligible list is established. There are various methods for resolving ties between those who get the same final grade – probably the most common is to place first the name of the person whose application was received first. Job offers are made from the eligible list in the order the names appear on it. You will be notified of your grade and your rank as soon as all these computations have been made. This will be done as rapidly as possible.

People who are found to meet the requirements in the announcement are called "eligibles." Their names are put on a list of eligible candidates. An eligible's chances of getting a job depend on how high he stands on this list and how fast agencies are filling jobs from the list.

When a job is to be filled from a list of eligibles, the agency asks for the names of people on the list of eligibles for that job. When the civil service commission receives this request, it sends to the agency the names of the three people highest on this list. Or, if the job to be filled has specialized requirements, the office sends the agency the names of the top three persons who meet these requirements from the general list.

The appointing officer makes a choice from among the three people whose names were sent to him. If the selected person accepts the appointment, the names of the others are put back on the list to be considered for future openings.

That is the rule in hiring from all kinds of eligible lists, whether they are for typist, carpenter, chemist, or something else. For every vacancy, the appointing officer has his choice of any one of the top three eligibles on the list. This explains why the person whose name is on top of the list sometimes does not get an appointment when some of the persons lower on the list do. If the appointing officer chooses the second or third eligible, the No. 1 eligible does not get a job at once, but stays on the list until he is appointed or the list is terminated.

X. HOW TO PASS THE INTERVIEW TEST

The examination for which you applied requires an oral interview test. You have already taken the written test and you are now being called for the interview test – the final part of the formal examination.

You may think that it is not possible to prepare for an interview test and that there are no procedures to follow during an interview. Our purpose is to point out some things you can do in advance that will help you and some good rules to follow and pitfalls to avoid while you are being interviewed.

What is an interview supposed to test?
The written examination is designed to test the technical knowledge and competence of the candidate; the oral is designed to evaluate intangible qualities, not readily measured otherwise, and to establish a list showing the relative fitness of each candidate – as measured against his competitors – for the position sought. Scoring is not on the basis of "right" and "wrong," but on a sliding scale of values ranging from "not passable" to "outstanding." As a matter of fact, it is possible to achieve a relatively low score without a single "incorrect" answer because of evident weakness in the qualities being measured.

Occasionally, an examination may consist entirely of an oral test – either an individual or a group oral. In such cases, information is sought concerning the technical knowledges and abilities of the candidate, since there has been no written examination for this purpose. More commonly, however, an oral test is used to supplement a written examination.

Who conducts interviews?

The composition of oral boards varies among different jurisdictions. In nearly all, a representative of the personnel department serves as chairman. One of the members of the board may be a representative of the department in which the candidate would work. In some cases, "outside experts" are used, and, frequently, a businessman or some other representative of the general public is asked to serve. Labor and management or other special groups may be represented. The aim is to secure the services of experts in the appropriate field.

However the board is composed, it is a good idea (and not at all improper or unethical) to ascertain in advance of the interview who the members are and what groups they represent. When you are introduced to them, you will have some idea of their backgrounds and interests, and at least you will not stutter and stammer over their names.

What should be done before the interview?

While knowledge about the board members is useful and takes some of the surprise element out of the interview, there is other preparation which is more substantive. It *is* possible to prepare for an oral interview – in several ways:

1) Keep a copy of your application and review it carefully before the interview

This may be the only document before the oral board, and the starting point of the interview. Know what education and experience you have listed there, and the sequence and dates of all of it. Sometimes the board will ask you to review the highlights of your experience for them; you should not have to hem and haw doing it.

2) Study the class specification and the examination announcement

Usually, the oral board has one or both of these to guide them. The qualities, characteristics or knowledges required by the position sought are stated in these documents. They offer valuable clues as to the nature of the oral interview. For example, if the job involves supervisory responsibilities, the announcement will usually indicate that knowledge of modern supervisory methods and the qualifications of the candidate as a supervisor will be tested. If so, you can expect such questions, frequently in the form of a hypothetical situation which you are expected to solve. NEVER go into an oral without knowledge of the duties and responsibilities of the job you seek.

3) Think through each qualification required

Try to visualize the kind of questions you would ask if you were a board member. How well could you answer them? Try especially to appraise your own knowledge and background in each area, *measured against the job sought*, and identify any areas in which you are weak. Be critical and realistic – do not flatter yourself.

4) Do some general reading in areas in which you feel you may be weak

For example, if the job involves supervision and your past experience has NOT, some general reading in supervisory methods and practices, particularly in the field of human relations, might be useful. Do NOT study agency procedures or detailed manuals. The oral board will be testing your understanding and capacity, not your memory.

5) Get a good night's sleep and watch your general health and mental attitude

You will want a clear head at the interview. Take care of a cold or any other minor ailment, and of course, no hangovers.

What should be done on the day of the interview?

Now comes the day of the interview itself. Give yourself plenty of time to get there. Plan to arrive somewhat ahead of the scheduled time, particularly if your appointment is in the fore part of the day. If a previous candidate fails to appear, the board might be ready for you a bit early. By early afternoon an oral board is almost invariably behind schedule if there are many candidates, and you may have to wait. Take along a book or magazine to read, or your application to review, but leave any extraneous material in the waiting room when you go in for your interview. In any event, relax and compose yourself.

The matter of dress is important. The board is forming impressions about you – from your experience, your manners, your attitude, and your appearance. Give your personal appearance careful attention. Dress your best, but not your flashiest. Choose conservative, appropriate clothing, and be sure it is immaculate. This is a business interview, and your appearance should indicate that you regard it as such. Besides, being well groomed and properly dressed will help boost your confidence.

Sooner or later, someone will call your name and escort you into the interview room. *This is it.* From here on you are on your own. It is too late for any more preparation. But remember, you asked for this opportunity to prove your fitness, and you are here because your request was granted.

What happens when you go in?

The usual sequence of events will be as follows: The clerk (who is often the board stenographer) will introduce you to the chairman of the oral board, who will introduce you to the other members of the board. Acknowledge the introductions before you sit down. Do not be surprised if you find a microphone facing you or a stenotypist sitting by. Oral interviews are usually recorded in the event of an appeal or other review.

Usually the chairman of the board will open the interview by reviewing the highlights of your education and work experience from your application – primarily for the benefit of the other members of the board, as well as to get the material into the record. Do not interrupt or comment unless there is an error or significant misinterpretation; if that is the case, do not hesitate. But do not quibble about insignificant matters. Also, he will usually ask you some question about your education, experience or your present job – partly to get you to start talking and to establish the interviewing "rapport." He may start the actual questioning, or turn it over to one of the other members. Frequently, each member undertakes the questioning on a particular area, one in which he is perhaps most competent, so you can expect each member to participate in the examination. Because time is limited, you may also expect some rather abrupt switches in the direction the questioning takes, so do not be upset by it. Normally, a board member will not pursue a single line of questioning unless he discovers a particular strength or weakness.

After each member has participated, the chairman will usually ask whether any member has any further questions, then will ask you if you have anything you wish to add. Unless you are expecting this question, it may floor you. Worse, it may start you off on an extended, extemporaneous speech. The board is not usually seeking more information. The question is principally to offer you a last opportunity to present further qualifications or to indicate that you have nothing to add. So, if you feel that a significant qualification or characteristic has been overlooked, it is proper to point it out in a sentence or so. Do not compliment the board on the thoroughness of their examination – they have been sketchy, and you know it. If you wish, merely say, "No thank you, I have nothing further to add." This is a point where you can "talk yourself out" of a good impression or fail to present an important bit of information. Remember, *you close the interview yourself.*

The chairman will then say, "That is all, Mr. _____, thank you." Do not be startled; the interview is over, and quicker than you think. Thank him, gather your belongings and take your leave. Save your sigh of relief for the other side of the door.

How to put your best foot forward

Throughout this entire process, you may feel that the board individually and collectively is trying to pierce your defenses, seek out your hidden weaknesses and embarrass and confuse you. Actually, this is not true. They are obliged to make an appraisal of your qualifications for the job you are seeking, and they want to see you in your best light. Remember, they must interview all candidates and a non-cooperative candidate may become a failure in spite of their best efforts to bring out his qualifications. Here are 15 suggestions that will help you:

1) Be natural – Keep your attitude confident, not cocky

If you are not confident that you can do the job, do not expect the board to be. Do not apologize for your weaknesses, try to bring out your strong points. The board is interested in a positive, not negative, presentation. Cockiness will antagonize any board member and make him wonder if you are covering up a weakness by a false show of strength.

2) Get comfortable, but don't lounge or sprawl

Sit erectly but not stiffly. A careless posture may lead the board to conclude that you are careless in other things, or at least that you are not impressed by the importance of the occasion. Either conclusion is natural, even if incorrect. Do not fuss with your clothing, a pencil or an ashtray. Your hands may occasionally be useful to emphasize a point; do not let them become a point of distraction.

3) Do not wisecrack or make small talk

This is a serious situation, and your attitude should show that you consider it as such. Further, the time of the board is limited – they do not want to waste it, and neither should you.

4) Do not exaggerate your experience or abilities

In the first place, from information in the application or other interviews and sources, the board may know more about you than you think. Secondly, you probably will not get away with it. An experienced board is rather adept at spotting such a situation, so do not take the chance.

5) If you know a board member, do not make a point of it, yet do not hide it

Certainly you are not fooling him, and probably not the other members of the board. Do not try to take advantage of your acquaintanceship – it will probably do you little good.

6) Do not dominate the interview

Let the board do that. They will give you the clues – do not assume that you have to do all the talking. Realize that the board has a number of questions to ask you, and do not try to take up all the interview time by showing off your extensive knowledge of the answer to the first one.

7) Be attentive

You only have 20 minutes or so, and you should keep your attention at its sharpest throughout. When a member is addressing a problem or question to you, give him your undivided attention. Address your reply principally to him, but do not exclude the other board members.

8) Do not interrupt

A board member may be stating a problem for you to analyze. He will ask you a question when the time comes. Let him state the problem, and wait for the question.

9) Make sure you understand the question

Do not try to answer until you are sure what the question is. If it is not clear, restate it in your own words or ask the board member to clarify it for you. However, do not haggle about minor elements.

10) Reply promptly but not hastily

A common entry on oral board rating sheets is "candidate responded readily," or "candidate hesitated in replies." Respond as promptly and quickly as you can, but do not jump to a hasty, ill-considered answer.

11) Do not be peremptory in your answers

A brief answer is proper – but do not fire your answer back. That is a losing game from your point of view. The board member can probably ask questions much faster than you can answer them.

12) Do not try to create the answer you think the board member wants

He is interested in what kind of mind you have and how it works – not in playing games. Furthermore, he can usually spot this practice and will actually grade you down on it.

13) Do not switch sides in your reply merely to agree with a board member

Frequently, a member will take a contrary position merely to draw you out and to see if you are willing and able to defend your point of view. Do not start a debate, yet do not surrender a good position. If a position is worth taking, it is worth defending.

14) Do not be afraid to admit an error in judgment if you are shown to be wrong

The board knows that you are forced to reply without any opportunity for careful consideration. Your answer may be demonstrably wrong. If so, admit it and get on with the interview.

15) Do not dwell at length on your present job

The opening question may relate to your present assignment. Answer the question but do not go into an extended discussion. You are being examined for a *new* job, not your present one. As a matter of fact, try to phrase ALL your answers in terms of the job for which you are being examined.

Basis of Rating

Probably you will forget most of these "do's" and "don'ts" when you walk into the oral interview room. Even remembering them all will not ensure you a passing grade. Perhaps you did not have the qualifications in the first place. But remembering them will help you to put your best foot forward, without treading on the toes of the board members.

Rumor and popular opinion to the contrary notwithstanding, an oral board wants you to make the best appearance possible. They know you are under pressure – but they also want to see how you respond to it as a guide to what your reaction would be under the pressures of the job you seek. They will be influenced by the degree of poise you display, the personal traits you show and the manner in which you respond.

ABOUT THIS BOOK

This book contains tests divided into Examination Sections. Go through each test, answering every question in the margin. At the end of each test look at the answer key and check your answers. On the ones you got wrong, look at the right answer choice and learn. Do not fill in the answers first. Do not memorize the questions and answers, but understand the answer and principles involved. On your test, the questions will likely be different from the samples. Questions are changed and new ones added. If you understand these past questions you should have success with any changes that arise. Tests may consist of several types of questions. We have additional books on each subject should more study be advisable or necessary for you. Finally, the more you study, the better prepared you will be. This book is intended to be the last thing you study before you walk into the examination room. Prior study of relevant texts is also recommended. NLC publishes some of these in our Fundamental Series. Knowledge and good sense are important factors in passing your exam. Good luck also helps. So now study this Passbook, absorb the material contained within and take that knowledge into the examination. Then do your best to pass that exam.

EXAMINATION SECTION

EXAMINATION SECTION
TEST 1

DIRECTIONS: Each question or incomplete statement is followed by several suggested answers or completions. Select the one that BEST answers the question or completes the statement. *PRINT THE LETTER OF THE CORRECT ANSWER IN THE SPACE AT THE RIGHT.*

1. The rules contained in the Civil Practice Law and Rules (CPLR) MAY be amended ONLY by the
    I. Appellate Divisions
    II. Judicial Conference
    III. Legislature
    IV. Court of Appeals
The CORRECT answer is:

  A. I *only*   B. II *only*   C. I, IV   D. II, III

1.____

2. The procedure in civil judicial proceedings in all courts of the state is

  A. governed by the CPLR unless the procedure is regulated by an inconsistent statute
  B. governed by the CPLR when there is an inconsistent statute
  C. governed by the Civil Practice Act
  D. always governed by the CPLR

2.____

3. Which of the following statements is(are) CORRECT?
    I. Procedural requirements under the CPLR should be strictly construed.
    II. The words *special proceeding* include an action.
    III. Except where otherwise prescribed by law, procedure in special proceedings shall be the same as in actions.
    IV. If a court has obtained jurisdiction over the parties, a civil judicial proceeding can still be dismissed SOLELY because it is not brought in the proper form.
    V. Under the CPLR, the word *judgment* means only a final judgment.
The CORRECT answer is:

  A. I, II, III, IV, V   B. I, II, III, IV
  C. I, II, IV, V   D. III *only*

3.____

4. Which of the following are CORRECT?
The person prosecuting a civil action or proceeding may be called
    I. petitioner
    II. poor person
    III. plaintiff
    IV. respondent
    V. defendant
The CORRECT answer is:

  A. I, II, III   B. II, III, V   C. IV, V   D. II, III

4.____

5. A special proceeding may BEST be described as   5.___

    A. an important civil judicial proceeding
    B. a civil judicial proceeding wherein prosecution in the form of a special proceeding is authorized
    C. all civil judicial proceedings which are not designated *actions* in the CPLR
    D. a civil judicial proceeding relating solely to election matters

6. A civil action is commenced by the service of a   6.___

    A. subpoena   B. subpoena duces tecum
    C. summons   D. complaint

7. Which of the following, if any, are necessary parties who MUST be joined in an action?   7.___
Persons
    I. who ought to be parties if complete relief is to be accorded between the parties who are parties to the action
    II. who assert a right of joint relief arising out of the same transaction involved in the complaint where there is a common question of law or of fact
    III. designated by the court in an order to show cause
    IV. who, if not joined, might be inequitably affected by a judgment
The CORRECT answer is:

    A. None of the above   B. All of the above
    C. II, III   D. I, IV

8. Which of the following statements is(are) INCORRECT?   8.___
    I. The difference between permissive joinder and necessary joinder is that permissive joinder means that parties may be joined in an action only when they consent.
    II. An action may continue without joinder of necessary parties but only by permission of the court when justice requires and when jurisdiction cannot be obtained over the necessary party except by his consent or appearance.
    III. When a person who should be a plaintiff refuses to join the action, he may be made a third-party defendant.
    IV. When a person who should be a plaintiff refuses to join the action as such, he may be made a defendant.
    V. An action may never continue without joinder of necessary parties.
The CORRECT answer is:

    A. V *only*   B. I, II, IV   C. II, IV   D. I, III, V

9. In determining whether to permit an action to proceed without the joinder of a necessary   9.___
party, the court should consider whether
    I. the guardian of an infant may be made a party
    II. jurisdiction may be obtained by substituted service
    III. the plaintiff has an effective remedy in case the action is dismissed on account of the nonjoinder
    IV. an effective judgment may be rendered in the absence of a person who is not joined
The CORRECT answer is:

    A. I, II, III   B. II, III, IV   C. I, II   D. III, IV

10. Which of the following statements is (are) INCORRECT? 10._____
    I. Misjoinder of parties may be a ground for dismissal of an action.
    II. The court may order the addition or deletion of a party only on a motion by one of the parties.
    III. A guardian of an infant's property may be sued without joining the infant as a party.
    IV. An action may never be dismissed for nonjoinder of a necessary party.
    The CORRECT answer is:

    E. III *only*   F. I, II   G. I, II, III   H. I, II, III, IV

11. An action in which there is a common question of interest to many persons may be brought in the form of a(n) 11._____

    A. motion for leave to intervene
    B. successive third-party complaint
    C. class action
    D. interpleader action

12. Which of the following statements, if any, is(are) INCORRECT? 12._____
    I. The Attorney-General must be notified by the court when the constitutionality of a state statute is involved in the action.
    II. The Attorney-General may be permitted to intervene in the discretion of the court when public retirement benefits are at issue.
    III. A person shall be permitted to intervene as of right when the representation of that person's interest by the parties already in the action may be inadequate provided a timely motion is made.
    IV. A person shall be permitted to intervene in an action as of right at any time prior to final judgment.
    The CORRECT answer is:

    A. I, III   B. I *only*   C. II, III   D. II, IV

13. Which of the following statements, if any, is(are) INCORRECT? 13._____
    I. The stakeholder may be discharged of his liability for a liquidated claim by conceding the liability and paying the fund or the object of the claim into court.
    II. Interpleader is a procedure whereby a person who is called a stakeholder may be brought into an action in which there are adverse claimants to the same fund.
    III. Intervention is a procedure whereby a person who is called a stakeholder may be brought into an action in which there are adverse claimants to the same fund.
    IV. Intervention is a procedure by which a person not a party to an action enters that action for the purpose of protecting his rights.
    The CORRECT answer is:

    A. I, IV   B. II *only*   C. I *only*   D. II, III

14. John Doe has been held in contempt for his refusal to call off an illegal strike against his   14._____
employer. Doe has been arrested and is lodged in the civil jail.
Doe may be kept in jail

    A. not more than three months
    B. not more than six months
    C. until he posts bail
    D. until he calls off the strike

15. In executing an order of civil arrest, the LEAST desirable place to make the arrest is   15._____

    A. the defendant's place of business
    B. in a public place
    C. on the street outside the defendant's home
    D. the defendant's home

16. An order of civil arrest has been issued for an Orthodox Jew.   16._____
On which of the following days is he immune from arrest?

    A. Only on Saturday
    B. Only on Sunday
    C. On both Saturday and Sunday
    D. Neither on Saturday nor on Sunday

17. Of the following persons, the one who is NOT immune from civil arrest is a(n)   17._____

    A. ordained clergyman
    B. maid who works at the French Ambassador's home
    C. fireman on duty
    D. marine on active duty

18. After an order of civil arrest has been signed, it   18._____

    A. may not be withdrawn without a court order
    B. must be executed within ten days
    C. must be filed in the county clerk's office
    D. may be withdrawn by the plaintiff's attorney anytime before it is executed

19. Even though the defendant is known to be in New York, the one of the following which   19._____
need NOT be personally served upon him is a(n)

    A. order preliminarily enjoining the defendant
    B. order temporarily restraining the defendant
    C. subpoena duces tecum commanding defendant to deliver books
    D. summons

20. The provisional remedy of civil arrest is available in an action for   20._____

    A. trespass to a chattel
    B. ejectment
    C. specific performance of a contract to convey land located outside the state
    D. specific performance of a contract to convey land located in the state

KEY (CORRECT ANSWERS)

1.	D	11.	C
2.	A	12.	D
3.	D	13.	D
4.	A	14.	D
5.	B	15.	D
6.	C	16.	C
7.	D	17.	A
8.	D	18.	D
9.	D	19.	A
10.	C	20.	C

TEST 2

DIRECTIONS: Each question or incomplete statement is followed by several suggested answers or completions. Select the one that BEST answers the question or completes the statement. *PRINT THE LETTER OF THE CORRECT ANSWER IN THE SPACE AT THE RIGHT.*

1. The FIRST paper served in a civil action in the Supreme Court is a   1.___

   A. subpoena   B. injunction   C. summons   D. complaint

2. The books containing the decisions of the New York courts are known as   2.___

   A. framed issues   B. citations
   C. reports   D. references

3. The term applied to a person appointed to represent an infant in an action in the   3.___
   Supreme Court is:

   A. Testamentary guardian   B. Guardian ad litem
   C. Referee   D. Guardian of the person

4. The statute of limitations is a law limiting the   4.___

   A. sentence that may be imposed upon conviction for a particular crime
   B. courts in which an action may be brought
   C. amount of money that may be awarded in a civil action
   D. time within which criminal prosecution or civil action must be commenced

5. A guardian ad litem is a guardian for   5.___

   A. the purpose of conserving real property
   B. the purpose of representing a corporation
   C. a particular lawsuit
   D. all purposes

6. In an ex parte proceeding,   6.___

   A. special relief is sought by both parties in judge's chambers
   B. only one side is heard without notice to the other side
   C. each side is heard separately before the court on different days
   D. both sides are heard before a court without a jury

7. 29 N.Y.S. 2d 53 means, in part,   7.___

   A. 53rd volume   B. 29th page
   C. second volume   D. 2d series

8. When a court refers to *McKinney's,* it means the   8.___

   A. rules of evidence
   B. local ordinances
   C. consolidated laws of New York State
   D. federal rules

9. A poor person is a(n)

    A. infant whose father has less than $300 in property
    B. person who has been adjudicated an incompetent
    C. person who is unable to pay the costs, fees, and expenses necessary to prosecute or defend the action
    D. person who has less than $300 in real or personal property

9.____

10. Which of the following statements are CORRECT?

    I. A motion for the appointment of a guardian ad litem may be made at any stage of the action.
    II. The court may direct the appearance of an adult who is incapable of adequately prosecuting or defending his rights by a guardian ad litem even if that adult has not been judicially declared incompetent.
    III. An infant must always appear in an action by a guardian ad litem.
    IV. Where an infant is over 14 years of age, it is not necessary to serve a copy of a notice of motion for the appointment of a guardian ad litem on anyone other than the infant.
    V. A default judgment may never be entered against an infant or a person judicially declared to be an incompetent.
    VI. A controversy involving an adult incapable of adequately protecting his rights may be submitted to arbitration without a court order.

The CORRECT answer is:

    A. I, IV, V   B. I, II, III   C. I, II, IV   D. I, II, VI

10.____

11. New York courts do NOT acquire jurisdiction over a nonresident under the *long-arm* statute when the cause of action arises out of

    A. the commission of a tort in New York
    B. solicitation of business within New York by the circulation of catalogues
    C. entering into a contract in New York
    D. possession of real property in New York

11.____

12. An article 78 proceeding may be brought against a public official or body

    A. to review capricious acts
    B. to enjoin such a body from proceeding where it is claimed that the action is unauthorized
    C. to compel the performance of a duty required by law
    D. for all of the above

12.____

13. A motion for summary judgment in lieu of a complaint is available in an action

    A. on account stated
    B. to recover payments pursuant to a separation agreement
    C. other than a matrimonial action if the moving papers establish a prima facie case and there is no real defense
    D. based upon a judgment

13.____

14. In which of the following provisional remedies, granted before a summons is served, must jurisdiction be acquired over the defendant or his property within a certain time limit or else the provisional remedy becomes void?
Attachment

    A. and arrest
    B. and lis pendens (notice of pendency)
    C. arrest, and receivership
    D. injunction, and lis pendens (notice of pendency)

14.____

15. The sheriff has properly delivered an income execution to D's employer. The employer has refused to honor the execution.
The plaintiff's lawyer should NOW serve

    A. motion papers on the employer to punish him for contempt
    B. a notice of petition and a petition to obtain a judgment against the employer
    C. motion papers on the employer, to obtain an order directing payment
    D. a subpoena upon the employer restraining him from paying D

15.____

16. An order of civil arrest has been signed against Doe in an action for fraud. The action has not yet been commenced.
The summons MUST be served

    A. within 48 hours after Doe is arrested
    B. within 30 days after the arrest order is signed or the arrest order will become void
    C. at the time the deputy sheriff arrests Doe
    D. at a time not specified by any of the foregoing

16.____

17. The date on which a summons is prepared in a civil action

    A. is the date upon which the statute of limitations stops running
    B. is the date from which the defendant measures his time in which to appear
    C. must be typed on the face of the summons
    D. has no legal significance

17.____

18. An attorney has delivered an execution to the sheriff's office.
A levy may thereafter be made under this execution within sixty days

    A. or else the execution becomes void and cannot be extended
    B. unless the period is extended (by a maximum of one sixty-day increment) in writing by the plaintiff's attorney
    C. unless the period is extended by court order
    D. unless the period is extended by successive sixty-day periods in writing by the plaintiff's attorney

18.____

19. John Doe, a judgment debtor, has personal property stored in a warehouse owned by X. X has issued to Doe a negotiable warehouse receipt for the property.
A PROPER way to levy upon this property is to

    A. go to the warehouse and seize the property
    B. seize the warehouse receipt from Doe
    C. go to the warehouse and leave the execution with X
    D. do none of the foregoing

19.____

20. A and B, two individuals, are partners in a finance company known as Ace Finance. A judgment has been entered against B for his negligence in driving his family automobile on a pleasure trip to Miami.
This judgment may be executed by levying upon

    A. B's desk in the office of Ace Finance
    B. B's interest in the partnership
    C. a bank account maintained in the name of Ace Finance
    D. B's Timex watch, worth $25.00

20.____

KEY (CORRECT ANSWERS)

1.	C	11.	B
2.	C	12.	D
3.	B	13.	D
4.	D	14.	B
5.	C	15.	B
6.	B	16.	C
7.	D	17.	D
8.	C	18.	D
9.	C	19.	B
10.	D	20.	B

9

TEST 3

DIRECTIONS: Each question or incomplete statement is followed by several suggested answers or completions. Select the one that BEST answers the question or completes the statement. *PRINT THE LETTER OF TEE CORRECT ANSWER IN THE SPACE AT THE RIGHT.*

1. Escheat is a legal term meaning that

    A. a fraud has been committed
    B. property has reverted to the state
    C. an agent's license has been revoked
    D. property under a trust deed may be reconveyed

1._____

2. A contract of sale passes

    A. the full fee simple title to the purchaser
    B. only an equitable title
    C. the legal title
    D. an estate for years

2._____

3. The instrument used to remove the lien of a trust deed from record is called a

    A. satisfaction
    B. release
    C. deed of reconveyance
    D. certificate of redemption

3._____

4. A power of attorney is terminated by

    A. an express revocation by the principal
    B. the death of the principal
    C. incapability of the principal to contract
    D. any of the above

4._____

5. For negotiating the sale of a business opportunity business without a license, a person may be prosecuted by a(n)

    A. jury
    B. judge of a superior court
    C. district attorney
    D. attorney general

5._____

6. A married woman is legally capable of contracting at the minimum age of

    A. seventeen   B. eighteen   C. twenty   D. twenty-one

6._____

7. In searching the records at the county recorder's office, you can usually distinguish a second trust deed from the first trust deed by the

    A. heading of the recorded documents
    B. information contained in the note
    C. recorder's declaration
    D. time and date of recordation

7._____

8. The MINIMUM time which must run after publication of a notice to creditors, under the provisions of the Uniform Commercial Code pertaining to bulk sales before consummation of the sale, is _____ days.

    A. 5   B. 10   C. 15   D. 20

8._____

9. To be valid, a bill of sale MUST be   9._____

    A. dated   B. signed   C. notarized   D. witnessed

10. Property held in joint tenancy, upon the death of one of the tenants, passes to the   10._____

    A. landlord   B. state
    C. county assessor   D. surviving joint tenant

11. Alienation expresses a meaning MOST completely opposite to   11._____

    A. acquisition   B. ad valorem
    C. acceleration   D. amortization

12. Anything that is fastened or attached to real property permanently is considered to be   12._____
    _____ property.

    A. personal   B. real   C. private   D. separate

13. The instrument used to secure a loan on personal property is called a   13._____

    A. bill of sale   B. trust deed
    C. security agreement   D. bill of exchange

14. A promissory note that provides for payment of interest only during the term of the note   14._____
    would be a(n) _____ note.

    A. installment   B. straight
    C. amortized   D. non-negotiable

15. Community property is property owned by   15._____

    A. churches   B. husband and wife
    C. the municipality   D. the community

16. The seller is sometimes called the   16._____

    A. vendee   B. vendor   C. lessee   D. lessor

17. A contract based on an illegal consideration is   17._____

    A. valid   B. void   C. legal   D. enforceable

18. A check that has been altered or raised by a person other than the maker is   18._____

    A. valid   B. invalid   C. cancelled   D. dishonorable

19. A valid bill of sale MUST contain   19._____

    A. a date   B. an acknowledgment
    C. the seller's signature   D. a verification

20. A security agreement is USUALLY given in connection with   20._____

    A. real property   B. agricultural property
    C. rentals   D. personal property

21. Title to fixtures, shelves, counters, and merchandise is transferred or conveyed by   21._____

    A. deed   B. bill of sale
    C. security agreement   D. escrow

22. Involuntary alienation of an estate means: 22.____

    A. Estate cannot be transferred without the consent of the owner
    B. Aliens are forbidden to own estates in fee simple in the state
    C. Ownership of estates may be transferred by operation of law
    D. No one can be compelled to transfer title without his consent

23. When a broker receives a deposit on a business which he has listed, the money   23.____
becomes the property of the

    A. seller   B. broker
    C. escrow company   D. prospective buyers

24. A financing statement may be released from the records by   24.____

    A. payment in full
    B. a reconveyance
    C. filing a release statement
    D. death of the mortgagor

25. The stock and fixtures that are to be transferred with the sale of a business are usually   25.____
enumerated in a(n)

    A. contract of sale   B. inventory
    C. deed   D. appraisal

KEY (CORRECT ANSWERS)

1.	B		11.	A
2.	C		12.	B
3.	A		13.	C
4.	D		14.	B
5.	C		15.	B
6.	B		16.	B
7.	B		17.	B
8.	A		18.	B
9.	B		19.	C
10.	D		20.	D

21.	A
22.	C
23.	A
24.	A
25.	B

EXAMINATION SECTION

TEST 1

DIRECTIONS: Each question or incomplete statement is followed by several suggested answers or completions. Select the one that BEST answers the question or completes the statement. *PRINT THE LETTER OF THE CORRECT ANSWER IN THE SPACE AT THE RIGHT.*

1. Which statement about the Rules from the CPLR is CORRECT?　　　　　　　1.＿＿＿
   A. Any rule may be adopted.
   B. Any rule may be rescinded.
   C. Additional civil practice rules may be adopted, not inconsistent with the Constitution, by act of the legislature.
   D. All of the above

2. All civil judicial proceedings shall be prosecuted in the form of a(n)　　　　　2.＿＿＿
   A. action
   B. special proceeding
   C. action except where prosecution in the form of a special proceeding is authorized
   D. mediation

3. The word *infant* as used in these rules means a person who has not attained　　3.＿＿＿
   the age of ＿＿＿＿ years.
   A. 16　　　　　　B. 17　　　　　　C. 18　　　　　　D. 21

4. An action for which no limitation is specifically prescribed by law must be　　4.＿＿＿
   commenced within ＿＿＿＿ years.
   A. 4　　　　　　B. 6　　　　　　C. 10　　　　　　D. 20

5. Proof of service shall NOT specify　　　　　　　　　　　　　　　　　　　5.＿＿＿
   A. the papers served
   B. the person who was served
   C. the date, time, address or, in the event there is no address, place and manner of service
   D. witnesses who will be present

6. The court shall not stay or dismiss any action on the ground of inconvenient　　6.＿＿＿
   forum, where the action arises out of or relates to a
   A. contract, agreement or undertaking, and the parties to the contract have agreed that the law of this state shall govern their rights or duties in whole or in part
   B. tort, and the parties have agreed that the law of this state shall govern their rights or duties in whole or in part
   C. personal injury matter
   D. part civil and part criminal matter

7. Which of the following is NOT a prerequisite to a class action?   7.____
   A. The class is so numerous that joinder of all members, whether otherwise required for permitted, is impracticable.
   B. There are questions of law or fact common to the class which predominate over any questions affecting only individual members.
   C. The claims or defenses of the representative parties are typical of the claims or defenses of the class.
   D. A class action is inferior to other available methods for the fair and efficient adjudication of the controversy.

8. Which of the following situations is descriptive of a time when parties need   8.____
   NOT be joined?
   A. When the plaintiff has another effective remedy in case the action is dismissed on account of the nonjoinder
   B. When prejudice may not in the future be avoided
   C. The non-feasibility of a protective provision by order of the court or in the judgment
   D. When an effective judgment may not be rendered in the absence of the person who is not joined

9. A motion to proceed as a poor person need NOT include a(n)   9.____
   A. affidavit   B. certificate   C. notice   D. fee

10. A guardian ad litem may NOT be suggested to the court by   10.____
    A. an infant party if he is more than fourteen years of age
    B. a relative, friend or a guardian, committee of the property, or conservator
    C. any person not a party to the action
    D. any other party to the action if a motion has not been made under paragraph one or two within ten days after completion of service

11. Which of the following professionals may NOT file an affirmation in lieu of   11.____
    and with the same force and effect as an affidavit?
    A. Physician   B. Osteopath   C. Dentist   D. Psychologist

12. A notice of motion and supporting affidavits shall be served AT LEAST   12.____
    _____ days before the time at which the motion is noticed to be heard.
    A. six   B. seven   C. eight   D. ten

13. Answering affidavits shall be served AT LEAST _____ day(s) before the   13.____
    motion is noticed to be heard.
    A. one   B. two   C. three   D. four

14. Answering affidavits and any notice of cross-motion, with supporting papers,   14.____
    if any, shall be served AT LEAST _____ days before the motion is noticed to
    be heard if a notice served AT LEAST _____ days before such time so
    demands.
    A. seven; fifteen   B. seven; sixteen
    C. eight; fifteen   D. eight; sixteen

15. Failure to comply with a subpoena issued by any of the following EXCEPT _____ shall be punishable as a contempt of court.

    A. judge   B. clerk
    C. officer of the court   D. witness

15._____

16. Subpoenas may be issued without a court order by all of the following EXCEPT

    A. the clerk of the court or a judge where there is no clerk
    B. the attorney general, an attorney of record for a party to an action
    C. an arbitrator, a referee, or any member of a board, commission or committee authorized by law to hear
    D. a witness

16._____

17. A person for whose benefit an undertaking has been given to a _____ of the state may move, on notice to persons interested in the disposition of the proceeds, for leave to bring an action in his own name for breach of a condition.

    A. public officer, board or municipal corporation
    B. teacher, board, or municipal corporation
    C. CEO, teacher, or board
    D. accountant, teacher or board

17._____

18. A subpoenaed person who fails to comply with a court-ordered subpoena shall be liable to the person on whose behalf the subpoena was issued for a penalty not exceeding _____ and damages sustained by reason of the failure to comply.

    A. $50   B. $100   C. $150   D. $200

18._____

19. A subpoenaed person who fails to comply with a subpoena not returnable in court shall be liable to the person on whose behalf the subpoena was issued for a penalty not exceeding _____ and damages sustained by reason of the failure to comply.

    A. $50   B. $100   C. $150   D. $200

19._____

20. A _____ is a statement under oath that the pleading is true to the knowledge of the deponent, except to matters alleged on information and belief, and that as to those matters he believes to be true.

    A. verification   B. pleading
    C. notification   D. none of the above

20._____

21. The plaintiff may seek a default judgment against the defendant when

    A. the defendant failed to appear
    B. the defendant pleads or proceeds to trial of an action reached and called for trial
    C. the court orders a dismissal for any other neglect to proceed
    D. all of the above

21._____

15

22. If the plaintiff's claim is for a sum certain or for a sum which can by computation be made certain, application may be made to the clerk within _____ after a default.
    A. 6 months   B. 1 year   C. 2 years   D. 3 years

22._____

23. Except in a matrimonial action, at any time not later than _____ days before trial, any party against whom a claim is asserted, and against whom a separate judgment may be taken, may serve upon the claimant a written offer to allow judgment to be taken against him for a sum or property or to the effect therein specified, which costs then accrued.
    A. 5   B. 10   C. 15   D. 30

23._____

24. In every dental, podiatric or medical malpractice action, the court shall hold a mandatory settlement conference within _____ days after the filing of the note of issue and certificate or readiness or, if a party moves to vacate the note of issue and certificate of readiness, within _____ days after the denial of such motion.
    A. forty-five; forty-five   B. forty-five; thirty
    C. thirty; thirty   D. thirty; forty-five

24._____

25. A jury shall be composed of _____ persons.
    A. six   B. nine   C. ten   D. twelve

25._____

KEY (CORRECT ANSWERS)

1.	D		11.	D
2.	C		12.	C
3.	C		13.	B
4.	B		14.	B
5.	D		15.	D
6.	A		16.	D
7.	D		17.	A
8.	A		18.	C
9.	D		19.	A
10.	C		20.	A

21.	D
22.	B
23.	B
24.	A
25.	A

EXAMINATION SECTION

TEST 1

DIRECTIONS: Each question or incomplete statement is followed by several suggested answers or completions. Select the one that BEST answers the question or completes the statement. *PRINT THE LETTER OF THE CORRECT ANSWER IN THE SPACE AT THE RIGHT.*

1. Which of the following is NOT a prerequisite to filing a class action lawsuit?   1.____
   A. The class is so numerous that joinder of all members is impracticable.
   B. All members of the class are approximately the same age, gender, or ethnicity.
   C. The claims or defenses of the representative parties are typical of the claims or defenses of the class.
   D. The representative parties will fairly and adequately protect the interests of the class.

2. After the filing of a class action, may the court limit or otherwise exclude   2.____
   members of the class?
   A. Yes, the court may limit the class to those members who do not request exclusion within a specified time after notice.
   B. Yes, if the class appeals to exclude certain members of the action
   C. No, under no circumstances may the court exclude members of the class
   D. No,, however if one of the class members dies he or she may be excluded by default

3. Jason prevailed on his motion to proceed in his lawsuit as a poor person.   3.____
   Jason also prevails in his lawsuit.
   Does Jason have to pay any of the court costs or fees, such as filing fees?
   A. No, because he prevailed on his motion to proceed as a poor person
   B. No, but he can choose to pay court costs and fees now that he has prevailed in his lawsuit
   C. Yes, the court may direct him to pay all or part of the costs and fees out of his recovery
   D. Yes he must revert all of his recovery over to the court

4. When Liz started her job as a stockbroker, she signed an employment contract   4.____
   which, in part, stated that all employment related disputes would be heard in
   Orange County, New York. Liz lives in Albany and her employer is based in
   Nassau County. Liz has since quit her job and sued her former employer.
   Where will Liz's trial MOST likely take place?
   A. Orange County   B. Nassau County
   C. Albany County   D. Kings County

5. The proper or most convenient location for trial of a case is also known as   5.____
   A. res ipsa   B. jurisdiction   C. venue   D. locale

6. When a defendant has failed to appear, plead or proceed to trial of an action
    reached and called for trial, the plaintiff may seek a(n) _____ against him or her.
    A. detainee judgment   B. indictment
    C. default judgment   D. restitution

    6.____

7. Kevin borrowed money from Rich and alleges that the contract he signed
    with the repayment terms—which Rich drafted—was materially altered after
    Kevin signed it.
    Instead of a complaint, Kevin may serve Rich with notice of motion for _____
    supporting papers along with a summons.
    A. summary judgment and   B. default judgment and
    C. subpoena and record with   D. a complaint with

    7.____

8. Under what conditions may a temporary restraining order be granted without
    notice?
    The plaintiff must show that
    A. immediate and irreparable injury, loss or damages will result
    B. harm is likely to occur if a temporary restraining order is not granted
    C. a likelihood of death is more probable than not if a temporary restraining
       order is not granted
    D. injury to personal or real property is a certainty if a temporary restraining
       order is not granted

    8.____

9. Michelle lives in Connecticut. She was served with a subpoena to appear for
    an examination before trial in New York.
    Is Michelle entitled to money for her attendance at the examination before trial?
    A. No, because she was served with a subpoena
    B. No, unless the examination before trial exceeds three hours in duration
    C. No, unless the examination before trial exceeds six hours in duration
    D. Yes

    9.____

10. A judgment which declares the rights of the parties without ordering anything
    be done by either party is also known as a
    A. summons   B. declaratory judgment
    C. default judgment   D. summary judgment

    10.____

11. What must be included in every complaint, counterclaim, cross-claim,
    interpleader complaint, and third party complaint?
    A. Demand for relief   B. Monetary relief
    C. Answer   D. Address of the respondent

    11.____

12. In a wrongful death suit, the complaint must contain a _____ but shall not
    contain _____.
    A. prayer for relief; the amount of damages sought
    B. demand for answers; the amount of punitive damages sought
    C. name of the deceased; the amount of nominal damages recovered
    D. name of the deceased; the amount of damages sought

    12.____

13. Suzanne wants to sue her dentist for malpractice.
    What document must accompany her complaint that is unique to medical,
    dental, and podiatric malpractice actions?
    - A. Subpoena for the dental office's assistant
    - B. Certificate of merit
    - C. Certificate of summons
    - D. A demand for specific relief

13.____

14. Assume the same facts as Question 13.
    Who must prepare the document identified in the above question?
    - A. Attorney for the plaintiff
    - B. Court clerk where the action is filed
    - C. The plaintiff
    - D. The respondent's attorney

14.____

15. In response to a complaint filed by her insurance company against her, Amy
    wants to respond to each allegation separately.
    Which of the following is NOT a proper response to each allegation or
    statement in the complaint?
    - A. Deny the statements known or believed to be untrue
    - B. Assert certain statements may be true
    - C. Specify which statements Amy does not have knowledge or information
      sufficient to form a belief
    - D. Admit to the allegations

15.____

16. The Latin term "res ipsa loquitor" is applicable in which of the following
    circumstances?
    - A. A pre-meditated homicide
    - B. An accident where negligence is inferred
    - C. A petty larceny that is committed by two or more conspiring minors
    - D. A robbery that occurs during a felony trespass

16.____

17. Statements in a pleading are required to be asserted with
    - A. certainty
    - B. honesty
    - C. specificity
    - D. particularity

17.____

18. When is an index number assigned?
    - A. The filing of a summons and complaint
    - B. Summons with notice or petition
    - C. When the proceeding is commenced in supreme or county court
    - D. All of the above

18.____

19. If personal service is completed by mail, how must the service be mailed?
    - A. Priority mail
    - B. Regular mail
    - C. First class mail
    - D. E-mail

19.____

20. Which of the following is a ground for removal?
    A. By supreme court for mistake in choice of court
    B. From court of limited jurisdiction
    C. On consent to court of limited jurisdiction
    D. All of the above
    20.____

21. Can personal service be completed upon an infant?
    A. No
    B. No, unless the child is emancipated
    C. No, unless the infant is old enough to sign the complaint and can attest they have been personally served
    D. Yes
    21.____

22. A person whom the court has determined because of physical or mental limitation requires another individual to handle his or her affairs is known as a
    A. conservator   B. guardian
    C. guardian ad litem   D. conservatee
    22.____

23. Mike and John both want to sue their former employer, Ace Enterprises. Mike alleges that he was discriminated against and fired because of his age. John alleges that he was discriminated against because of his religion and retaliated against for filing a complaint against his boss with Ace's Human Resource Department. After filing their complaint, the court decides that each claim should be litigated separately.
    The court will order a _____ of the claims.
    A. separation   B. severance   C. disjoinder   D. joinder
    23.____

24. If triable issues of fact are raised in a dispute and the parties do not demand a jury trial to decide those issues, at what point is the right to a jury trial deemed waived?
    A. The start of the trial
    B. At the start of opening argument
    C. At the conclusion of closing arguments
    D. At appeal
    24.____

25. An attorney of record may _____ or be changed by order of the court in which the action is pending, upon _____ on such notice.
    A. withdraw; notice   B. recant; motion
    C. recant; notice   D. withdraw; motion
    25.____

KEY (CORRECT ANSWERS)

1.	B		11.	A
2.	A		12.	A
3.	C		13.	B
4.	A		14.	A
5.	C		15.	B
6.	C		16.	B
7.	A		17.	D
8.	A		18.	D
9.	D		19.	C
10.	B		20.	D

21.	D
22.	D
23.	B
24.	A
25.	D

TEST 2

DIRECTIONS: Each question or incomplete statement is followed by several suggested answers or completions. Select the one that BEST answers the question or completes the statement. *PRINT THE LETTER OF THE CORRECT ANSWER IN THE SPACE AT THE RIGHT.*

1. Kim's attorney died in the middle of her trial. What is the legal result of her attorney's death?
   A. Kim will need to stand trial without representation.
   B. Kim's rights are unaltered by the death.
   C. Kim has five days to find another attorney or continue with the trial without representation.
   D. Kim has fourteen business days to find another attorney or continue with the trial without representation.

1.____

2. How does a lawsuit typically commence?
   A. By the filing of a subpoena
   B. By the return of an indictment
   C. By the filing of a summons and complaint
   D. By acknowledgement of the wrongful act

2.____

3. A court may exercise jurisdiction over a person, property, or
   A. chattel   B. status
   C. remaindermen   D. entitlement

3.____

4. A&B Corporation is a Kentucky-based business that sells personal fans that have a "I love New York" logo on the product. The company only sells these products in the State of New York. One of the company's fans has caught fire and the purchasing customer, Michelle, wants to sue the company. Can a New York court exercise jurisdiction over A&B Corp.?
   A. Yes, because the company transacts business within the state
   B. No, because the company is based in Kentucky
   C. No, because the product was not intended to hurt anyone
   D. No, because the company has not availed themselves of New York jurisdiction

4.____

5. A person who owes a debt to a judgment debtor, or a person other than the judgment debtor who has property in his possession or custody in which a judgment debtor has an interest is known as a
   A. lien holder   B. garnishee   C. beneficiary   D. debtor

5.____

6. Which of the following qualifies as "real property"?
   A. Daniel's home in Nassau County
   B. Kim's jewelry gifted from her mother
   C. Tom's car which he purchased using credit
   D. Tanya's bank account, worth $5,600

6.____

7. A complaint and answer are known as

   A. pleadings   B. responses   C. demands   D. interrogatories

7._____

8. The individual or individuals who replace a juror who has died, become ill or otherwise cannot serve are known as _____ jurors.

   A. replacement   B. rescinded   C. alternate   D. substitute

8._____

9. A trial without a jury is also known as a _____ trial.

   A. de novo   B. bench   C. demand   D. benchmarked

9._____

10. Every court in which a special proceeding to enforce a money judgment may be commenced shall have power to punish a contempt of _____ committed with respect to an enforcement procedure.

    A. court   B. issue   C. punishment   D. authority

10._____

11. According to Civil Practice Laws and Rules, the interest rate is _____ per annum.

    A. 4%   B. 5%   C. 6%   D. 9%

11._____

12. Jake and Sam have settled their contract dispute after months of discovery. As the settling defendant, how many days does Sam have to pay Jake?

    A. Ten   B. Twenty-one   C. Thirty   D. Ninety

12._____

13. Assume the same facts as in Question 12, except assume that Sam never paid Jake after the settlement.
    What legal recourse can Jake pursue against Sam?
    Jake may

    A. enter a judgment against Sam and demand interest from the date the stipulation discounting action were tendered
    B. enter a summary judgment against Sam
    C. enter a discourse judgment against Sam
    D. return an indictment against Sam

13._____

14. What is the difference between cross-claims versus a counterclaim?

    A. A counterclaim is a claim against an individual who may be involved in the claims at issue.
    B. A cross-claim is a claim against one or more individuals who may be involved in the claims at issue.
    C. A counterclaim is a direct claim against the person who initiated the lawsuit, whereas a cross-claim is a suit against a co-defendant or co-plaintiff.
    D. A counterclaim and cross-claim are interchangeable terms.

14._____

15. Personal service upon a court consisting of three or more judges may be made by

    A. delivering the summons to the court clerk's office
    B. e-mailing any one of the judges
    C. delivering the summons to any one of them
    D. delivering the summons to any one of the judge's clerk(s)

15._____

16. If an action does not have a limitation specifically prescribed by law then the limitation to commence an action is _____ years.
    A. five   B. six   C. eight   D. ten

16.____

17. Which of the following actions have a limitation of six years to commence?
    A. An action upon a sealed instrument
    B. An action based upon mistake
    C. An action based on fraud
    D. All of the above

17.____

18. Which of the following actions must be commenced within ten years?
    A. To redeem from a mortgage
    B. An action based on fraud
    C. An action upon a sealed instrument
    D. An action based on mistake

18.____

19. Can civil and criminal actions be merged together?
    A. Yes, if the actions concern the same individual
    B. Yes, but the civil action must be heard before the criminal action can commence
    C. Yes, but the criminal action must be heard before the civil action can commence
    D. No

19.____

20. If a party dies and the claim for or against him is not thereby extinguished, the court shall order substitution of the proper parties.
    An example of a substitute party is
    A. the estate of the deceased
    B. the sibling of the deceased
    C. the spouse of the deceased
    D. any of the above are possible substituted parties

20.____

21. Kate casually dated a man who introduced himself as Danny. After seeing one another for two weeks, Danny stole all of Kate's credit cards and began to open up credit cards in her name without her authorization. Kate never discovered Danny's last name.
    If Kate does not know the name or the identity of someone who should be named as a party in her lawsuit, may she commence the suit?
    A. Yes, as the filings can be amended accordingly
    B. No because she must know Danny's last name to commence a suit against him
    C. No, because Kate should have known that Danny would steal from her
    D. No, unless Danny can be located and prove his legal name in a sworn and written statement

21.____

22. A defendant's or lawyer's objection to a proposed juror, made without needing to give a reason, is also known as a
    A. peremptory challenge   B. juror challenge
    C. stare decisis   D. en banc challenge

22.____

23. Must a jury be unanimous to return a decision in a trial?   23.____
    A. Yes, a jury must be unanimous
    B. Yes, unless an alternate juror is substituted for a juror that died during the trial
    C. No, unless an alternate juror is substituted for a juror that died during the trial
    D. No

24. Michelle is a potential juror in a shareholder derivative suit. Ed is suing   24.____
    the Bank of Apple, a public company. Michelle holds stock in the Bank of
    Apple and discloses this fact in the voir dire process.
    What is the likely outcome of Michelle's disclosure?
    Michelle will
    A. be dismissed as a potential juror for cause
    B. be chosen as an alternate juror
    C. likely be chosen as a juror despite her disclosure
    D. likely be questioned by the judge and identified as a bias juror

25. At the close of the evidence in a trial, either the plaintiff or the defense may   25.____
    file a written request to the judge that the court instruct the jury on _____ as set
    forth in the respective written requests.
    A. the law
    B. the facts
    C. the weight that should be applied to the evidence
    D. none of the above

———————

KEY (CORRECT ANSWERS)

1.	B		11.	D
2.	C		12.	B
3.	B		13.	A
4.	A		14.	C
5.	B		15.	C
6.	A		16.	B
7.	A		17.	D
8.	C		18.	A
9.	B		19.	D
10.	A		20.	D

21.	A
22.	A
23.	D
24.	A
25.	A

EXAMINATION SECTION
TEST 1

DIRECTIONS: Each question or incomplete statement is followed by several suggested answers or completions. Select the one that BEST answers the question or completes the statement. *PRINT THE LETTER OF THE CORRECT ANSWER IN THE SPACE AT THE RIGHT.*

Questions 1-12.

DIRECTIONS: Questions 1 through 12 are based on the Criminal Procedure Law. Each question consists of two statements. Mark your answer.
- A. if only sentence I is correct
- B. if only sentence II is correct
- C. if sentences I and II are correct
- D. if neither sentence I nor II is correct

1.   I. Except as otherwise provided in the Criminal Procedure Law, a prosecution for a misdemeanor must be commenced within three years after the commission thereof.

    II. Except as otherwise provided in the Criminal Procedure Law, a prosecution for a petty offense must be commenced within two years after the commission thereof.

1.____

2.   I. A person may not be prosecuted twice for the same offense.

    II. A defendant may not be convicted of any offense upon the testimony of an accomplice unsupported by corroborative evidence tending to connect the defendant with the commission of such offense.

2.____

3.   I. A defendant may testify in his own behalf, but his failure to do so is not a factor from which any inference unfavorable to him may be drawn.

    II. A child less than twelve years old may not testify under oath in a criminal proceeding in a court of law.

3.____

4.   I. A person may be convicted of an offense solely upon evidence of a valid confession or admission made by him without additional proof that the offense charged has been committed.

    II. Evidence of a written or oral confession, admission, or other statement made by a defendant with respect to his participation or lack of participation in the offense charged may not be received in evidence against him in a criminal proceeding if such statement was involuntarily made.

4.____

5.   I. A summons may be served by a police officer, or by a complainant at least eighteen years of age, or by any other person at least eighteen years old designated by the court.

    II. A summons may be served anywhere in the county of issuance or anywhere in an adjoining county in the state.

5.____

6.   I. Any person may arrest another person for a felony anywhere in the state when the latter has in fact committed such felony.

    II. Any person may arrest another person for any offense other than a felony when the latter has in fact committed such offense in his presence, provided that the arrest is made only in the county in which such offense was committed.

6.____

7. I. A search warrant must be executed not more than three days after the date and
        time of issuance and it must thereafter be returned to the court without unnecessary delay.
    II. No search warrant may be executed unless the police officer gives notice of his
        authority and purpose to the occupant of the premises or vehicle to be searched.
        In addition, the police officer must serve a copy of the warrant upon the occupant
        of said premises or vehicle.

7.____

8. I. An appearance ticket may be issued by a police officer following an arrest without a
        warrant if the arrest was for a Class B misdemeanor but not if the arrest was for a
        Class A misdemeanor.
    II. An appearance ticket may, at the discretion of the police officer or other public
        servant authorized to issue appearance tickets, be served either personally or by
        registered or certified mail, return receipt requested.

8.____

9. I. Under the *Youthful Offender Treatment* article of the Criminal Procedure Law (Article 720), *youth* means a person charged with a crime who was at least sixteen
        years old and less than nineteen years old at the time of his alleged commission of
        such crime.
    II. When an individual has been adjudged eligible for youthful offender treatment,
        he may be found guilty by reason of a preponderance of the evidence rather than
        guilty based upon proof beyond a reasonable doubt.

9.____

10. I. A police officer may arrest a person without a warrant for any offense, other than
        for a petty offense, when he has reasonable cause to believe that such person has
        committed such offense, whether in his presence or otherwise.
    II. A police officer may arrest a person for a petty offense without a warrant when
        such offense was committed in the officer's presence, within the geographical
        area of such police officer's employment, and such arrest is made in the county
        where such offense was committed.

10.____

11. I. A police officer may stop a person in a public place located within the geographical
        area of such officer's employment when he reasonably suspects that such person
        is committing, has committed or is about to commit either (a) a felony or (b) any
        misdemeanor as defined in the penal law, and may demand of him his name,
        address, occupation, the name and address of his employer, and an explanation of
        his conduct.
    II. Whenever a police officer stops a person in a public place for temporary questioning, he may search such person for a deadly weapon or any instrument, article or substance readily capable of causing serious physical injury and of a sort
        not ordinarily carried in public places by law-abiding persons.

11.____

12. I. A defendant in any criminal action who is less than eighteen years old may refuse
        to permit himself to be fingerprinted unless accompanied by a parent or legal
        guardian.
    II. A police officer who is executing an arrest warrant need not have the warrant in
        his possession; if he has not, he must show it to the defendant upon request as
        soon after the arrest as possible.

12.____

Questions 13-24.

DIRECTIONS: Questions 13 through 24 are to be answered SOLELY on the basis of the Penal Law.

13. A person is guilty of grand larceny in the first degree when he steals property which   13._____

    A.   consists of personal property valued at more than $1500
    B.   is obtained by instilling in the victim a fear that that the victim's membership in a subversive organization will be revealed
    C.   consists of goods valued in excess of $250
    D.   is obtained by instilling in the victim a fear that an antique vase which he owns will be damaged

14. Using or threatening the immediate use of a dangerous instrument is an element of all of   14._____
the following offenses EXCEPT _____ in the _____ degree.

    A.   robbery; first
    C.   robbery; second

    B.   burglary; first
    D.   burglary; second

15. Which of the following describes a person guilty of escape in the first degree?   15._____

    A.   A person convicted of a felony escapes from a detention facility.
    B.   A person just convicted of a misdemeanor escapes from a courtroom by impersonating a police officer.
    C.   A person escapes from a police officer's custody by causing serious physical injury to the officer.
    D.   After committing a felony, a person escapes from the scene of the crime by using or threatening the immediate use of a deadly weapon.

16. A person who wantonly and recklessly fires a rifle into a crowd of people without any spe-   16._____
cific intent to injure or kill would NOT be guilty of

    A.   murder if death results
    B.   assault in the first degree if serious physical injury results
    C.   assault in the second degree if physical injury results
    D.   reckless endangerment in the first degree if no injury results

17. Each of the following choices states an offense involving the forcible stealing of property,   17._____
and certain additional facts.
In which choice would the defendant be guilty of the offense stated, based SOLELY on the facts given in the choice? Robbery in the

    A.   first degree - defendant robs a bank while carrying two sticks of dynamite, which cannot be seen under his jacket
    B.   second degree - while defendant and his partner are fleeing from a store they have just robbed, the partner pushes a bystander to the ground, thereby causing a painful bruise to bystander's shoulder
    C.   first degree - while robbing a bank, defendant threatens to kidnap and kill the manager's wife unless the manager gives him all the money in the vault
    D.   second degree - defendant robs a jewelry store, while his partner waits in a get-away car parked around the corner

18. A person is ALWAYS guilty of a felony if he unlawfully possesses   18._____

    A. any loaded firearm in a vehicle
    B. any deadly weapon and is not a citizen of the United States
    C. any dagger or razor with intent to use the same unlawfully against another
    D. a shotgun in a building used for educational purposes

19. Knowing that Jones intends to rob a bank, Smith gives Jones a rifle to use during the   19._____
    robbery. However, the day before the robbery is supposed to occur, the police arrest
    Jones on an old charge, thereby preventing the robbery.
    Based on these facts, it would be CORRECT to state that Smith is

    A. *not guilty* of any crime
    B. *guilty* of conspiracy in the second degree and criminal facilitation in the second
       degree
    C. *guilty* of criminal facilitation in the second degree but is not guilty of conspiracy in
       the second degree
    D. *guilty* of conspiracy in the second degree but is not guilty of criminal facilitation in
       the second degree

20. Each of the following choices states an offense involving the death of a person, and cer-   20._____
    tain additional facts.
    In which choice would the defendant NOT be guilty of the offense stated, based-
    SOLELY on the facts given in the choice?

    A. Manslaughter in the second degree - when the defendant intentionally causes or
       aids another person to commit suicide
    B. Murder - when the defendant and two other persons attempt to commit escape in
       the second degree, and one of the participants causes the death of a person other
       than one of the participants
    C. Manslaughter in the first degree - when with intent to cause serious physical injury
       to another person, the defendant causes the death of a third person
    D. Murder - when the defendant engages in conduct which creates a grave risk of
       death of another person, and thereby causes the death of another person

21. Which of the following elements would raise the crime of custodial interference from the   21._____
    second degree to the first degree?

    A. The intent to hold a child permanently or for a protracted period
    B. Exposure of the person taken to a risk that his health will be materially impaired
    C. The taking of a child less than sixteen years old from his lawful custodian
    D. Enticement of an incompetent person from lawful custody

22. Which one of the following elements must ALWAYS be present for a person to be guilty of   22._____
    arson in the first degree?

    A. The presence in the building at the time of another person who is not a participant
       in the crime
    B. Intentional damage to a building caused by a fire
    C. Knowledge by the person that another person not a participant in the crime is
       present in the building
    D. Circumstances which render the presence in the building of another person not a
       participant in the crime a reasonable possibility

23. For which of the following crimes is it a necessary element that a person knowingly enter   23.____
or remain unlawfully in a dwelling, as the word *dwelling* is defined in the Penal Law?

    A.   Criminal trespass in the first and second degree
    B.   Criminal trespass in the second degree and burglary in the first degree
    C.   Criminal trespass in the first degree and burglary in the second degree
    D.   Burglary in the first and second degree

24. Assume that the police stop a car in which three men are riding. Ward is the driver, and   24.____
Jones and King are passengers. During a lawful search, the police find one-quarter
ounce of morphine concealed in King's coat. Based SOLELY on these facts, it would be
CORRECT to state that

    A.   King, Jones, and Ward are all guilty of criminal possession of a dangerous drug
    B.   a presumption of knowingly possessing the morphine applies to Ward but not to
Jones
    C.   King is guilty of criminal possession of a dangerous drug and Ward is guilty of con-
spiracy
    D.   King is guilty of criminal possession of a dangerous drug but Ward and Jones are
not

KEY (CORRECT ANSWERS)

1.	D		11.	D
2.	A		12.	B
3.	C		13.	D
4.	B		14.	C
5.	C		15.	A
6.	C		16.	C
7.	D		17.	B
8.	D		18.	A
9.	A		19.	A
10.	C		20.	D

21.	B
22.	A
23.	B
24.	D

TEST 2

DIRECTIONS: Each question or incomplete statement is followed by several suggested answers or completions. Select the one that BEST answers the question or completes the statement. *PRINT THE LETTER OF THE CORRECT ANSWER IN THE SPACE AT THE RIGHT.*

1. Which of the following statements is(are) CORRECT?
   The Criminal Procedure Law (CPL) applies to
   I.   all criminal actions and proceedings commenced on or after September 1, 1971, and appeals and other post-judgment proceedings relating thereto.
   II. criminal actions and proceedings commenced before September 1, 1971 but pending thereafter
   III. appeals and other post-judgment proceedings commenced on or after September 1, 1971 which relate to criminal actions and proceedings commenced or concluded prior thereto, provided that, where application of CPL would not be feasible or would work injustice, the former Code of Criminal Procedure shall apply
   IV. criminal procedure matters occurring on or after September 1, 1971 which are not a part of any particular action or case
   The CORRECT answer is:

   A. All of the above   B. I *only*
   C. I, II, III   D. II, III, IV

   1.____

2. Which of the following is hearsay?
   A(n)

   A. written statement by a person not present at the court hearing where the statement is submitted as proof of an occurrence
   B. oral statement in court by a witness of what he saw
   C. written statement of what he saw by a witness present in court
   D. re-enactment by a witness in court of what he saw

   2.____

3. In a criminal case, a statement by a person not present in court is

   A. *acceptable* evidence if not objected to by the prosecutor
   B. *acceptable* evidence if not objected to by the defense lawyer
   C. *not acceptable* evidence except in certain well-settled circumstances
   D. *not acceptable* evidence under any circumstances

   3.____

4. The rule on hearsay is founded on the belief that

   A. proving someone said an act occurred is not proof that the act did occur
   B. a person who has knowledge about a case should be willing to appear in court
   C. persons not present in court are likely to be unreliable witnesses
   D. permitting persons to testify without appearing in court will lead to a disrespect for law

   4.____

5. One reason for the general rule that a witness in a criminal case MUST give his testimony in court is that

   A. a witness may be influenced by threats to make untrue statements
   B. the opposite side is then permitted to question him
   C. the court provides protection for a witness against unfair questioning
   D. the adversary system is designed to prevent a miscarriage of justice.

   5.____

6. An appeal MAY be taken from a 6.____

    A. verdict   B. judgment
    C. decision   D. conviction

7. Jury trial commences 7.____

    A. with the selection of a jury
    B. when the defendant makes opening address
    C. when the first opening address is made
    D. when the first witness is sworn

8. Adjective criminal law is governed PRIMARILY by the 8.____

    A. Penal Law
    B. Civil Practice Law and Rules
    C. Criminal Procedure Law
    D. Code of Criminal Procedure

9. Which of the following contain(s) references included in the definition of *warrant of arrest?* 9.____
    I. Process of local criminal court to produce defendant for arraignment
    II. Produce defendant for arraignment upon filed accusatory instrument
    III. Addressed to peace officer to produce defendant for arraignment
    IV. Process of any criminal court requiring defendant to appear before it for arraignment on a prosecutor's information

The CORRECT answer is:

    A. I, II, III, IV   B. III *only*
    C. I, II, III   D. I, II, IV

10. Superior courts have jurisdiction in the following areas: 10.____
    I. Unlimited trial jurisdiction of all offenses
    II. Exclusive trial jurisdiction of felonies
    III. Concurrent trial jurisdiction of misdemeanors
    IV. Preliminary jurisdiction of all offenses, exercised only through grand juries

The CORRECT answer is:

    A. I *only*   B. I, II
    C. I, II, III   D. II, III, IV

11. Petty offense means 11.____

    A. all violations and traffic infractions
    B. some misdemeanors and all violations
    C. only conduct which is not a traffic infraction and is punishable by imprisonment for not more than 15 days
    D. a class B misdemeanor only

12. An offense committed near a boundary between two adjoining counties of this state may be prosecuted in either of such counties.
The MAXIMUM distance from a county border is

    A. 1,000 feet   B. 1,000 yards   C. 500 feet   D. 500 yards

12.____

13. A felony is committed on the Hudson River south of the northern boundary of New York City.
The county or counties having jurisdiction to try the case is(are)

    A. New York, Richmond, Bronx, Kings, and Queens Counties
    B. New York, Richmond, and Bronx Counties
    C. New York and Richmond Counties only
    D. New York County only

13.____

14. A crime is committed on a bus regularly carrying passengers from Nassau County to Manhattan by way of Queens. At the time of the occurrence, the bus is in Nassau on its way to its terminal point – Manhattan. The victim is a Queens resident. The alleged perpetrator is a resident of Manhattan.
The county or counties having jurisdiction in this case is(are)

    A. Nassau or New York   B. Nassau or Queens
    C. Nassau, Queens, or Manhattan   D. Nassau only

14.____

15. Prosecution of a crime MUST be commenced within

    A. one year after commission, for all misdemeanors and petty offenses
    B. two years after commission, for all misdemeanors and petty offenses
    C. 5 years after commission, for all felonies
    D. 5 years after commission, for some felonies

15.____

16. A private person in making an arrest is limited as follows:

    A. For an offense, at any hour of day or night
    B. For a crime only, at any hour of any day or night
    C. For a felony only, at any hour of any day or night
    D. All of the above

16.____

17. An appearance ticket directs a specific person to appear in a criminal court in connection with the alleged commission of a designated offense.
This appearance ticket may be issued only by a

    A. local criminal court judge
    B. local criminal court judge or police officer
    C. police officer or authorized public servant
    D. police officer, authorized public servant, or local criminal court judge

17.____

18. An arrest by a private person without a warrant can PROPERLY be made in which one of the following situations?

    A. There is reasonable cause to believe that the person being arrested committed a felony.
    B. The person arrested for a felony has in fact committed the felony.
    C. The person arrested for a misdemeanor has in fact committed the misdemeanor.
    D. The person arrested for any offense has in fact committed the offense.

18.____

19. A peace officer, outside the geographical area of his employment, has reasonable cause   19.____
to believe that a felony was committed in his presence.
In the circumstances,

    A. he may make an arrest, without restriction
    B. he may make an arrest only on the same authority as that of a private person
    C. he may make an arrest during the commission of the felony, immediately thereafter
        or during immediate flight
    D. none of the above

20. After making an arrest, a police officer must perform all required recording, fingerprinting,   20.____
and other related duties.
He MUST do so

    A. immediately
    B. without unnecessary delay
    C. within 24 hours
    D. within 8 hours

21. A police officer, acting without a warrant, may arrest a person   21.____

    A. only in the geographical area of his employment
    B. outside the geographical area of his employment only for a felony
    C. without restriction, for a petty offense committed anywhere in the state
    D. for a crime committed anywhere in the state

22. Summons is a process whose SOLE function is to   22.____

    A. commence a criminal action
    B. substitute for a warrant of arrest, where a warrant may not be issued
    C. produce defendant for arraignment upon a filed accusatory instrument
    D. inform defendant as to nature of the offenses charged

23. A summons may be served by   23.____

    A. any person without restriction
    B. any person at least 18 years old
    C. a police officer, without restriction
    D. a peace officer, without restriction

24. An arrest warrant is addressed to and can be executed   24.____
by

    A. any adult person
    B. a police officer or classification of police officers
    C. a peace officer or classification of peace officers
    D. any person over the age of 18, not a party to the action

25. Which of the following would invalidate an acknowledgment?   25.____

    A. Failure to say deponent is known to notary
    B. Seal is missing
    C. Acts done on Sunday
    D. Affiant misspells his name

35

KEY (CORRECT ANSWERS)

1.	A		11.	A
2.	A		12.	D
3.	C		13.	A
4.	A		14.	A
5.	B		15.	D
6.	B		16.	A
7.	A		17.	C
8.	C		18.	B
9.	D		19.	C
10.	D		20.	B

21.	D
22.	C
23.	C
24.	B
25.	A

———

TEST 3

DIRECTIONS: Each question or incomplete statement is followed by several suggested answers or completions. Select the one that BEST answers the question or completes the statement. *PRINT THE LETTER OF THE CORRECT ANSWER IN THE SPACE AT THE RIGHT.*

1. A warrant of arrest may be executed anywhere in the state   1.____

    A. without restriction, if it is issued by a city court
    B. in all cases, without restriction
    C. in all cases, provided it is appropriately endorsed by a local criminal court of the county where the arrest is to be made
    D. when issued by the city criminal court

2. A warrant of arrest may be executed on any day   2.____

    A. of the week, at any hour
    B. except Sunday, at any hour of the day; but on Sunday only between 9:00 A.M. and 6:00 P.M.
    C. including Sunday, provided it is so endorsed by the issuing court
    D. except Sunday

3. A police officer or court officer of a criminal court may stop a person, under specified circumstances, when he reasonably suspects that the person is committing, has committed, or is about to commit any felony   3.____

    A. or a Class A misdemeanor defined in the Penal Law
    B. or misdemeanor defined in the Penal Law
    C. or any misdemeanor only
    D. only

4. At a hearing on a felony complaint, defendant   4.____

    A. may testify in his own behalf within the discretion of the court, but he has a right to call witnesses
    B. has a right to testify in his own behalf, but he may call witnesses only within the discretion of the court
    C. has a right to testify in his own behalf and to call witnesses
    D. may testify in his own behalf, within the discretion of the court, and call witnesses in his behalf, within the discretion of the court

5. A grand jury, to be legally constituted, MUST consist of _____ members.   5.____

    A. not less than 16 and not more than 23
    B. not less than 12 and not more than 16
    C. not less than 12 and not more than 23
    D. at least 12

6. At a preliminary hearing on a felony complaint,   6.____
    I. the defendant must be present
    II. the defendant has a right to be present, but he may waive this right
    III. the defendant has a right to call witnesses in his behalf
    IV. all witnesses called may be cross-examined

The CORRECT answer is:

   A. I, II   B. II, III   C. I, IV   D. II, IV

7. The number and term of grand juries empanelled for a court are determined generally by   7._____

   A. Supreme Court in the county, on application of the District Attorney showing the estimated need
   B. Rules of the court for which the grand jury is drawn
   C. Judicial Conference regulations
   D. Appellate Division rules

8. The quantum of proof required for a court to hold a defendant for grand jury action on a felony complaint is proof   8._____

   A. affording the court reasonable cause to believe
   B. sufficient for a reasonable man
   C. by a fair preponderance of the evidence
   D. beyond a reasonable doubt

9. The acting foreman of a grand jury is   9._____

   A. chosen by lot
   B. chosen by the court
   C. the second grand juror to be empanelled
   D. chosen by the grand jurors

10. When a grand jury requires legal advice, they may receive it   10._____

   A. only from the court, District Attorney, or an attorney designated by either
   B. either from the court or District Attorney, only
   C. only from the District Attorney
   D. only from the court

11. In all cases, when a motion is made for a change of venue, a(n)   11._____

   A. application for a stay, denied by a Supreme Court justice, may not thereafter be granted by a justice of the Appellate Division
   B. application for a stay, denied by a Supreme Court justice, may be reviewed and granted by a justice of the Appellate Division
   C. stay may be granted only by any Supreme Court justice in the judicial district
   D. stay may be granted by any superior court judge in the judicial district

12. Evidence of mental disease or defect as a trial defense excluding criminal responsibility is admissible   12._____

   A. only as to a defendant who has previously been examined under court order by two qualified psychiatrists
   B. provided the defendant has served and filed timely written notice of intention to rely thereon
   C. provided the People have served a demand on the defendant to give notice of this defense
   D. in all cases without restriction

13. On a defense of alibi,   13.____

    A. the People in all cases are entitled on trial to an adjournment not in excess of 3 days

    B. a court may receive testimony as in D below but on application must grant an adjournment of not less than 7 days

    C. a court may not receive testimony as in D below

    D. a court may receive testimony, in its discretion, from a witness who was not included in defendant's notice of alibi

14. Which of the following statements are CORRECT?   14.____

    I. The People, having the burden of proof, address the jury before defendant at all stages.

    II. A closing address to the jury by the prosecution is required.

    III. A closing address to the jury by both sides is discretionary.

    IV. An opening address to the jury by both sides is discretionary.

    V. The People in all cases must make an opening address to the jury.

The CORRECT answer is:

    A. I, II, III   B. II, III, IV

    C. I, II, IV   D. I, II, V

15. In selecting a jury, the MAXIMUM total number of challenges to alternate jurors that may be exercised by BOTH parties is   15.____

    A. 16   B. 8   C. 4   D. 2

16. A grand jury witness may be called only on request of the   16.____

    A. court, District Attorney, or grand jury

    B. court

    C. District Attorney or the grand jury

    D. grand jury

17. A prospective defendant in a grand jury proceeding who wishes the grand jury to hear a witness in his behalf is limited by the fact that   17.____

    A. the grand jury, in its discretion, may hear the witness if the defendant makes an oral or written request

    B. the grand jury must hear the witness if the defendant makes an oral or written request

    C. the grand jury must hear the witness only if the defendant makes a written request

    D. there may be no legal basis for such a request

18. When a charge has been dismissed by a grand jury following its consideration of the matter, which of the following is CORRECT?   18.____

    A. It may be resubmitted to successive grand juries by court order, without limitation.

    B. It may be resubmitted to a grand jury if a court so authorizes, but no further submission thereafter is permissible.

    C. Without court order, it may be considered by another grand jury, but not by the same grand jury.

    D. It may again be considered by the same grand jury, without court order.

19. An indictment MUST contain
    I.   endorsement, *A True Bill,* signed by the district attorney
    II.   applicable section number of the statute allegedly violated
    III.   date or period when alleged conduct occurred
    IV.   statement in each court that the grand jury accuses the defendant of a designated offense
The CORRECT answer is:

  A. I, II, IV   B. III, IV
  C. II, III, IV   D. I, II, III, IV

19.____

20. With respect to an offense raised to higher grade by reason solely of a previous conviction, which of the following statements is CORRECT?

  A. Under no circumstances is a jury permitted to know of the previous conviction.
  B. The order of trial is in this instance substantially the same as in other cases, except for arraignment on a special information.
  C. Before any proceeding to establish defendant's identity and previous conviction, he must be advised of the privilege against self-incrimination.
  D. The defendant's conviction of the predicate case may be established at any time before the case goes to the jury.

20.____

21. The term *petty offense* includes

  A. no misdemeanors, some violations, all traffic infractions
  B. no misdemeanors, but all violations and traffic infractions
  C. some misdemeanors, all violations and traffic infractions
  D. all misdemeanors, violations, and traffic infractions

21.____

22. Conviction, as defined in CPL, means

  A. entry of guilty plea, or guilty verdict
  B. serving of sentence
  C. entry of final judgment
  D. imposition and entry of sentence

22.____

23. With regard to a non-jury trial, which of the following is CORRECT?

  A. Trial commences when both parties appear, are ready, and the court announces that the case is on trial. The court's determination as to guilt or innocence is properly termed a verdict.
  B. If there is no opening address, trial commences when the first witness is sworn, and the court's determination as to guilt or innocence is properly termed a verdict.
  C. An opening address, if made, commences the trial, and the court's determination of guilt or innocence is properly termed a decision.
  D. There must be an opening address to the court; this commences the trial; and the court's determination of guilt or innocence is properly termed a decision.

23.____

24. In relation to double jeopardy, a person may not be twice prosecuted for the same offense.
Assuming the same offense, which of the following does NOT relate to double jeopardy under CPL?

24.____

A. Defendant is found not guilty after trial in one jurisdiction
B. An accusatory instrument is filed in a court of another country
C. An accusatory instrument is filed in a Federal court
D. An accusatory instrument is filed in a state other than New York

25. Which of the following is NOT applicable to a warrant of arrest?　　　　25.____

A. Its function is to produce defendant for arraignment.
B. It commences a criminal action.
C. It is issued only by a local criminal court.
D. It is addressed to a police officer.

KEY (CORRECT ANSWERS)

1.	D		11.	A
2.	A		12.	B
3.	A		13.	D
4.	B		14.	D
5.	A		15.	A
6.	D		16.	C
7.	D		17.	A
8.	A		18.	B
9.	B		19.	B
10.	B		20.	B

21.	B
22.	A
23.	B
24.	B
25.	B

EXAMINATION SECTION
TEST 1

DIRECTIONS: Each question or incomplete statement is followed by several suggested answers or completions. Select the one that BEST answers the question or completes the statement. *PRINT THE LETTER OF THE CORRECT ANSWER IN THE SPACE AT THE RIGHT.*

1. Peter Poe has been arrested on a charge of petit larceny. A search of police files indicates prior convictions for possessing a dangerous weapon and for illegally using the same. According to Criminal Procedure Law, it would be correct to state, with respect to the release of Poe on bail when arraigned in the court indicated, that he   1.____

   A. can be released on bail by a judge of the district court because such judges can admit to bail perpetrators of any crime
   B. can be released on bail by a judge of the criminal court of the City of New York because petit larceny is a misdemeanor
   C. cannot be released on bail by a judge of the criminal court of the City of New York because Poe has had two prior convictions
   D. cannot be released on bail by a judge of the district court because such judges can only admit to bail defendants charged with an offense

2. John Doe has been arrested in New York County charged therein with murder, first degree. According to Criminal Procedure Law, it would be correct to state, with respect to the release of Doe on bail, that he   2.____

   A. can be released on bail by a justice of the Supreme Court of New York State
   B. can be released on bail by a justice of the Court of Special Sessions of the City of New York
   C. cannot be released on bail by anyone if he had ever before attempted to commit a felony
   D. cannot be released on bail under any circumstances, except by a judge of the district court

3. John Doe has been arrested by an officer on patrol at night and brought to the station house for booking on a charge of disorderly conduct under Section 722 of the Penal Law. According to Criminal Procedure Law, the desk officer must release Doe on bail for appearance before a magistrate the next morning if Doe was charged with   3.____

   A. interfering with a person by placing his hand near such person's pocketbook or pocket
   B. soliciting men for lewd purposes in a public place
   C. engaging in an illegal occupation
   D. causing a disturbance in a bus or acting in a manner disturbing or offensive to others

4. John Doe has been arrested on a charge of disorderly conduct under Section 722 of the Penal Law. The one of the following offenses covered by this section for which Criminal Procedure Law requires the court's approval prior to admitting him to bail is   4.____

   A. jostling against or unnecessarily crowding a person in a public place
   B. acting in such a manner as to interfere with others

C. congregating on a public street and refusing to move on when ordered by the police
D. shouting outside a building at night to the annoyance of a considerable number of persons

5. The hours during which a police officer of superior rank must take bail for a misdemeanor are limited by Criminal Procedure Law to the hours between   5.____

A. 11 A.M. and 8 A.M. the next morning
B. 2 P.M. and 8 A.M. the next morning
C. 11 A.M. and 2 P.M. the same day
D. 2 P.M. and 11 A.M. the next morning

6. Billy Doe, a 13-year-old boy, is the only witness to a crime committed by his 22-year-old uncle with whom he has been staying while on a visit to New York City. According to Criminal Procedure Law, with respect to the production of the child in court, it would be correct to state that a   6.____

A. personal recognizance in writing shall be accepted from Billy's parent or guardian only
B. separate personal recognizance must be taken by the court for each production of the child pending the final termination of the proceedings
C. personal recognizance shall not be accepted in this case from any person
D. personal recognizance shall be vacated on failure to produce Billy in court as ordered and Billy himself taken into custody thereafter

7. The one of the following prerequisites for a permit to possess or dispose of firearms any-where in this state, according to Penal Law is that the applicant must   7.____

A. file a separate new application for each weapon if he wishes at any time to amend his license to include one or more weapons, if he is licensed either to possess weapons as an individual or as a dealer
B. be a resident of the county in which the weapon is to be used, if he is applying for a license to possess and carry a weapon as a merchant or employee of a financial institution
C. not have been convicted of either a misdemeanor or a felony, if he is applying for a permit to possess and carry concealable firearms
D. be a citizen of the United States and over 21 years of age, if he wishes to be either a gunsmith or a dealer in firearms

8. John Doe, a barber, who has been posing as a surgeon specializing in abortions, is on trial. He is charged with having performed an illegal abortion which resulted in the death of Jane X. Before she died, Jane X made a dying declaration naming Doe as the person who had performed the illegal operation. According to Criminal Procedure Law, it would be correct to state that in this prosecution of Doe for abortion Jane X's dying declaration shall   8.____

A. be admitted in evidence without any restrictions
B. be admitted in evidence subject to the same restrictions as in cases of homicide
C. not be admitted in evidence
D. not be admitted in evidence if Jane X voluntarily submitted to the operation fully aware of its possible consequences

9. John Doe, the defendant on a robbery charge, has been released on bail in Manhattan. He goes to the farm home of his parents in Ulster County and fails to appear in court as ordered. As a result, his bail is forfeited and a bench warrant is issued in New York County for his arrest. Criminal Procedure Law provides, with respect to the service of such a bench warrant, that it may

    9._____

    A.   not be served outside New York County, the county of issue
    B.   be served in Ulster County, but only after being endorsed by a magistrate of that county
    C.   be served in Ulster County without being endorsed by a magistrate of that county
    D.   be served in any county, in the same manner as a warrant of arrest, without any exceptions

10. John Smith, an accountant for the Alden Corporation, is dismissed after 20 years with the organization. Angry and disgruntled with the treatment accorded to him by the company, Smith tells Bill Jones, a neighbor, about all he had done to build up the company. He tells Jones how *cheap* the company is and how easy it would be to rob it on any pay day because of the lack of protective devices. He says he hopes someone will do it some day, and goes into great detail about how it could be done successfully. About six months later, without any knowledge on Smith's part, Jones and his brothers, Jim and Bob, successfully rob the Alden Corporation treasurer as he is about to pay off the staff. The holdup nets $40,000.
Four years later, Bob Jones is apprehended. He involves his brothers. Bill Jones, on questioning, describes how Smith had given him the idea for the crime.
According to the Penal Law, it would be most correct to state that Smith

    10._____

    A.   cannot be charged with having any connection with the crime because it took place entirely without his knowledge
    B.   can no longer be arrested or charged with any crime because the statute of limitations for robbery is four years
    C.   can be arrested and charged only with being an accessory because he took no part in the actual commission of the crime
    D.   can be arrested and charged with being a principal to the robbery

11. Charging his pretty wife with infidelity, Joe Doakes has slashed at her face with a razor, causing severe mutilation around her eyes, mouth, and cheeks. This action results in permanent ugly scars. He is taken into custody and held for trial on a charge of maiming. In order to sustain this charge, it is necessary that intent be shown. According to the Penal Law, in connection with intent, with respect to this crime, it is most correct to state that the

    11._____

    A.   disfigurement need not even have been inflicted with felonious intent
    B.   injury must seriously diminish the victim's physical vigor
    C.   disfigurement must be incapable of being repaired by plastic surgery
    D.   mere infliction of the injury is presumptive evidence of the intent

12. Arthur Mason has been released on $50,000 bail as the alleged armed-robber of a supermarket. He fails to appear in court as ordered. According to the Penal Law, it would be most correct for the police to charge Mason, in addition to the original charge, with a

    12._____

    A.   felony for jumping bail, if he fails to surrender himself within 30 days
    B.   misdemeanor for jumping bail, if he fails to surrender himself within 30 days

C.   felony for jumping bail, if he fails to surrender himself within 15 days

D.   misdemeanor for jumping bail, plus the loss of the $50,000 if he fails to surrender himself within 15 days

13.   Bill Walters, who has been subpoenaed as a witness to a holdup murder, is approached by two men, who offer him $10,000 to testify falsely as to what he had seen. When he refuses, they threaten his life. He then agrees, but notifies the police as soon as the two men leave.
According to the Penal Law, the two men can be charged with

    A.   subornation of perjury
    B.   perjury
    C.   suppressing evidence
    D.   dissuading witness from testifying

13.____

14.   According to the Penal Law with regard to the use of force or fear in the crime of robbery, it would be most correct to state that, to constitute robbery,

    A.   force may have been used to obtain possession of the property, but, if this did not occur, force must have been used to escape
    B.   the mere snatching of the property from the hand of the victim without his resistance and without force or violence by the offender is sufficient
    C.   fear is a necessary ingredient regardless of the value of the property taken
    D.   when there is nothing to inspire fear, superior force must have been used, and the property relinquished upon a struggle and upon compulsion

14.____

15.   The State Legislature amended the section of the Penal Law dealing with the making of malicious telephone calls. The amendment added a provision which made it a misdemeanor for a person to maliciously use the telephone

    A.   to threaten to commit a crime against the person called
    B.   to threaten to commit a crime against the teenage daughter of the person called
    C.   for the purpose of using obscene language to any person of the female sex
    D.   for the purpose of using obscene language to a male child under the age of 16 years

15.____

16.   Jane Doe, a model, posed in the nude for several lewd photographs. Joe Hoe did the actual photographing and developed 100 prints of each pose. John Coe, the distributor, was apprehended with all the prints in his possession except for the 10 copies of one pose which he had just sold to Peter Poe. Poe was apprehended at the same time with the purchased pictures in his hand. Under Section 1141 of the Penal Law (obscene prints and articles), it would be most proper to charge a violation thereof to

    A.   J. Doe and J. Hoe only
    B.   J. Coe and P. Poe only
    C.   all four persons
    D.   J. Doe, J. Hoe, and J. Coe only

16.____

17. According to the Penal Law, the one of the following who could be charged with the mis-   17.____
    demeanor of violating the provisions governing immoral shows and exhibitions is

    A. an actor participating in the performance
    B. the manager of the theater or place who permits the immoral show though without
        knowledge of the type of performance involved
    C. the advertising manager of the show
    D. the owner of the premises who rented the theater to the producers of the show
        though without any knowledge of the type of performance involved

18. Two officers on radio motor patrol notice four men acting suspiciously in a parked auto-   18.____
    mobile near a large jewelry store. Upon questioning, the officers learn that the car and its
    driver had been hired for the night by the other three men. Dissatisfied with the evasive-
    ness of the three men with respect to their answers to some of the questions, the officers
    frisk all four. An unlicensed .45 automatic is found on one of the passengers who states it
    does not belong to him. The other passengers know nothing of the presence of the gun.
    According to the Penal Law, the presence of the gun is presumptive evidence of its
    possession by

    A. all the occupants of the automobile
    B. the individual possessing it only
    C. all the occupants except the driver
    D. the individual possessing it and also the real owner

19. John Doe, who has just been convicted of a felony, is being transferred from the city   19.____
    prison to the state prison at Dannemora. While he is waiting under guard at Grand Cen-
    tral Station, his brothers, James and William, try to overpower the guards in order to help
    John escape. They succeed but all three are apprehended in the western part of the
    state two weeks later. According to the Penal Law, James and William

    A. can be charged with a misdemeanor, which is next lesser in degree than the felony
        for which John was convicted
    B. can be charged with a felony because John was convicted of a felony
    C. cannot be charged with a felony, because no weapons were used and the guards
        were not injured
    D. can be charged with either a misdemeanor or a felony, depending on who origi-
        nated the conspiracy

20. Roy Brown enters a drugstore and forces the proprietor into the back room at knife point.   20.____
    He takes all the money he finds in the cash register and in the pharmacist's pocket. He
    ties the pharmacist's hands behind his back with adhesive tape and puts tape across his
    mouth. He sees the pharmacist's 15-year-old daughter in the back room, tapes her
    hands and mouth, and carnally abuses the girl with the intention of eventually raping her.
    Before he can rape her, he is surprised by an officer who comes into the store to check
    whether anyone had come in for treatment of a stab wound. The would-be rapist is
    apprehended while in the act of carnally abusing the girl.
    According to the Penal Law, Brown, if convicted,

    A. cannot be considered within the province of the law dealing with sexual abuse
        unless he administered or forced the girl to take a poison or narcotic intended to
        weaken her resistance
    B. may be sentenced for each crime separately, but the sentences must run consecu-
        tively

C. must be given a definite sentence for armed robbery and also an indeterminate sentence for the sex offense
D. may, in place of the penalty for armed robbery, receive an indefinite sentence of one day to life for the sexual abuse

---

KEY (CORRECT ANSWERS)

1.	B		11.	D
2.	A		12.	A
3.	D		13.	C
4.	A		14.	D
5.	B		15.	D
6.	C		16.	C
7.	D		17.	C
8.	B		18.	B
9.	C		19.	B
10.	A		20.	D

EXAMINATION SECTION

TEST 1

DIRECTIONS: Each question or incomplete statement is followed by several suggested answers or completions. Select the one that BEST answers the question or completes the statement. *PRINT THE LETTER OF THE CORRECT ANSWER IN THE SPACE AT THE RIGHT.*

1. Which class of felonies are divided into subclasses?
   A. Class A B. Class B C. Class C D. Class D

   1._____

2. Can a traffic infraction be classified as a misdemeanor?
   A. Yes, if the punishment is less than one year of imprisonment
   B. Yes, if the punishment is less than fifteen months of imprisonment
   C. No, unless specified in the judgment
   D. No

   2._____

3. Bryan smuggles cocaine out of Mexico in his infant daughter's diaper. He and his daughter are caught de-boarding from a plane at John F. Kennedy Airport.
   At arraignment, Bryan will MOST likely be charged with a
   A. misdemeanor   B. traffic infraction
   C. traffic violation   D. drug trafficking felony

   3._____

4. A "juvenile offender" is defined as a person _____ years old who is criminally responsible for an act constituting murder in the second degree or such conduct as a sexually motivated felony.
   A. twelve   B. thirteen   C. fourteen   D. fifteen

   4._____

5. The New York Penal Law defines "child day care provider" by the definition used in what other law?
   A. Child Welfare Act   B. Social Services Law
   C. Family Court Act   D. Surrogates Court Clerk Law

   5._____

6. Pursuant to the New York Penal Law, a felony without specification of the classification is deemed a Class _____ felony.
   A. A   B. B   C. D   D. E

   6._____

7. The MAXIMUM penalty for a Class B felony is _____ thousand dollars.
   A. ten   B. twenty   C. thirty   D. fifty

   7._____

8. Tony was convicted of stealing a car, which carries a felony designation. Tony maintains that he simply wanted to go for a joyride, but the victim alleges that $4,000 was in the car when it was stolen. The car was eventually returned to the victim; however, the cash was never recovered.
   Can the court legally demand that Tony replay the cash that was never recovered?

   8._____

A. Yes, because that is the amount gained from the commission of the crime
B. No, because one cannot prove he stole the cash
C. No, because Tony simply wanted a joyride
D. No, because the cash was not insured by the vehicle's owner

9. A sentence to pay a fine for a Class A misdemeanor shall not exceed _____ dollars or an amount equivalent to double the value of the property unlawfully disposed of in the commission of the crime.
   A. five hundred
   C. one thousand
   B. eight hundred
   D. two thousand

9.____

10. Marcel posted an advertisement on social media selling a new guitar. A buyer forwarded Marcel $500 and Marcel never delivered the product as he never had a guitar to sell. Marcel was later convicted of the misdemeanor of false advertising. The court imposes an alternative sentence for the crime.
    What is the MOST likely fine Marcel will need to pay?
    A. $250, half the amount he received from the crime
    B. $750, a 50% increase in the amount of money he received from the crime
    C. $1,000, double the amount of money he received from the crime
    D. Marcel will not have to pay any money as he was convicted of a misdemeanor

10.____

11. Which of the following are classified as Class A misdemeanors?
    A. Escape in the third degree
    C. Identify theft in the third degree
    B. Perjury in the third degree
    D. All of the above

11.____

12. Which of the following is a Class B misdemeanor?
    A. Reckless endangerment of property
    B. Coercion in the second degree
    C. Making graffiti
    D. Arson in the fifth degree

12.___

13. Tim is convicted of two misdemeanors, one which is classified as Class A and the other is classified as Class B. For the Class A misdemeanor, the court imposes a term of eight months imprisonment.
    Can the court impose a fine of $500 for the Class B misdemeanor?
    A. Yes, the court can impose a fine in addition to the term of imprisonment
    B. No, the court cannot impose a fine in excess of $250 as this is deemed excessive punishment and not available for appeal
    C. No, the court cannot impose a fine in excess of $400 as this is deemed excessive punishment and not available for appeal
    D. No, the court cannot impose a fine in addition to the term of imprisonment if the offenses were committed through a single act and one offense is a material element of the other

13.____

14. If ABC Corporation is convicted of a felony, what is the maximum amount the company will have to pay?

    A. Five thousand dollars

    B. Ten thousand dollars

    C. Fifteen thousand dollars

    D. An amount not to exceed double the amount of shareholders the company has on record as of the date of the commission of the crime

14.____

15. Soliciting or providing support for an act of terrorism in the second degree is classified as a

    A. misdemeanor

    B. violation

    C. Class D felony

    D. felony of an unspecified degree

15.____

16. Richie is convicted of making a terrorist threat. What is this offense classified as?

    A. Class D felony

    B. Unclassified felony

    C. Unclassified misdemeanor

    D. Civil offense

16.____

17. A firearm that is actually shared, made available, sold, exchanged, given or disposed of among or between two or more persons, at least one of whom is not authorized pursuant to law possess such firearm is defined as a

    A. roundabout gun

    B. community gun

    C. shared gunner

    D. civil weapon

17.____

18. Judge O'Neill is currently presiding over a murder trial, where the defendant ran over a young child with his car. The defense alleges the crime was an accident and that the defendant should be found guilty, if at all, of a lesser offense. The prosecution argues that the defendant intended to kill the victim. In chambers, Judge O'Neill explains to his law clerk that in order to find the defendant guilty of the more serious crime charged, he must have the culpable mental state during the commission of the crime.

A culpable mental state means

    A. intentionally, knowingly or recklessly or with criminal negligence

    B. knowingly but not intentionally

    C. negligent intent but not knowingly or recklessly

    D. none of the above

18.____

19. Derek wants to kill Al who works at the local gym. Al's twin brother exits the gym at 11:45 P.M. and Derek shoots him. Derek alleges that because he meant to kill Al and not Al's twin brother, he should not be found guilty of murder.

What is the likely verdict?

    A. Not guilty, because of a mistake of fact

    B. Not guilty, because Derek has confessed to his crimes

    C. Guilty, because of a mistake of fact

    D. Guilty, because the crime of murder still occurred

19.____

20. Any article or thing which a person confined in a detention facility is prohibited from obtaining or possessing by statute, rule, regulation or order is known as
    A. illicit materials
    B. contraband
    C. magazines
    D. weaponry
20.____

21. Which of the following offenses relating to custody is classified as a misdemeanor?
    A. Escape in the third degree
    B. Absconding from temporary release in the second degree
    C. Resisting arrest
    D. All of the above
21.____

Questions 22-25.

DIRECTIONS: Questions 22 through 25 are to be answered on the basis of the following fact pattern.

Ralph was kidnapped at gunpoint outside of Syracuse. He was taken to an abandoned warehouse by his captors and kept for nearly three days without food or water. Ralph never saw the gun or any other weapons while he was in captivity, but was told he would be killed if he did not go to the bank and empty his bank accounts. After his captors dropped him off at a local bank, Ralph went inside and closed all of his accounts and left the cash outside of the bank in an envelope and ran. Later, Ralph was able to identify all of his captors and at trial alleged that he emptied his bank accounts in duress.

22. Under these circumstances, can Ralph allege that he was under duress?
    A. Yes, he can assert duress as an affirmative defense
    B. No, because Ralph never saw a weapon after the initial kidnapping
    C. No, because Ralph emptied his account on his own free will
    D. No, because Ralph does not know for sure if the captors ever received the cash
22.____

23. When is duress NOT available as a defense?
    A. When a person intentionally or recklessly places himself in a situation in which it is probable that he will be subjected to duress
    B. Duress is always available as a defense
    C. Duress is a rarely used defense and is not available for adults who are capable of acting of their own free will
    D. Duress is not available as a defense if the defense of intentional negligence is also used
23.____

24. If Ralph's captors are convicted of a Class B violent felony, what is the MOST likely outcome of the sentencing in terms of imprisonment?
    A. 1-3 years   B. 5-10 years   C. 5-25 years   D. 25 years to life
24.____

25. Which of the following is MOST likely to be considered in the sentencing of   25.____
    Ralph's captors?
    A. Familial relationship to Ralph, if any
    B. The location Ralph was abducted and how far that location is from
       Ralph's primary residence or domiciliary
    C. Prior criminal history of each offender
    D. Ralph's age

KEY (CORRECT ANSWERS)

1.	A		11.	D
2.	D		12.	A
3.	D		13.	D
4.	B		14.	B
5.	B		15.	C
6.	D		16.	A
7.	C		17.	B
8.	A		18.	A
9.	C		19.	D
10.	C		20.	B

21.	D
22.	A
23.	A
24.	C
25.	C

TEST 2

DIRECTIONS: Each question or incomplete statement is followed by several suggested answers or completions. Select the one that BEST answers the question or completes the statement. *PRINT THE LETTER OF THE CORRECT ANSWER IN THE SPACE AT THE RIGHT.*

1. Prosecutors must prove that Abe and Luke's conspiracy derived from an intentional scheme to defraud investors.
   Which of the following is the MOST appropriate definition of scheme?
   A. A plan between two people to do an agreed upon activity
   B. Any plan, pattern device, contrivance, or course of action intended to deceive others
   C. A plan between three or more people to do something one of them is intent on finishing
   D. A topic of conversation shared between two or more people

   1.____

2. Corrupting the government in the fourth degree is classified as a Class ____ felony and requires that the individual committing the crime either be, or act in concert with a _____.
   A. E; public servant   B. D; person of interest
   C. E; person of interest   D. D; public servant

   2.____

3. A person commits the crime of _____ when being a public servant he or she commits a specified offense through the use of his or her public office.
   A. private coercion   B. public corruption
   C. sentencing   D. acting in dangerous concert

   3.____

4. Arson in the first degree and aggravated enterprise corruption are examples of
   A. A-1 felonies   B. Class C felonies
   C. misdemeanors   D. traffic violations

   4.____

5. If a felon sentence does not carry a term of imprisonment, which of the following will MOST likely be required of the defendant in lieu of jail?
   A. Parole   B. Probation
   C. Active custody   D. Recognizance

   5.____

6. Which of the following is a violation?
   A. Loitering
   B. Criminal solicitation in the second degree
   C. Welfare fraud in the third degree
   D. Bribing a labor official

   6.____

7. Maurice is found guilty of intentionally, and for no legitimate purpose, engaging in a course of conduct directed at his former co-worker, Michelle, that he knows is likely to cause reasonable fear of material harm. Maurice is convicted of which crime?
   A. Battery   B. Negligence   C. Stalking   D. Trespass

   7.____

8. Which of the following carries the LOWEST sanction and is not defined as a crime?   8.____
  A. Felony   B. Misdemeanor
  C. Class A felony   D. Violation

9. Which felony class is the MOST serious?   9.____
  A. Class B   B. Class A   C. Class E   D. Class D

10. An "act" is considered the opposite of a(n) ____. As an example, during 10.____
an interrogation into the disappearance of Andrew's cousin, Andrew fails to
mention that he was the last person to see his cousin alive.
  A. response   B. omission   C. redaction   D. impactful

11. A person acts ____ when his conscious objective is to cause such result 11.____
or to engage in such conduct, whereas a person acts ____ when he is aware
that his conduct is of such nature or that such circumstance exists.
  A. knowingly; recklessly   B. knowingly; negligently
  C. knowingly; criminally   D. intentionally; knowingly

12. Kristin was driving under the influence of alcohol when she crashed her 12.____
brand new car into the front yard of Joe's house, killing his outdoor cat and
knocking over his mailbox. Kristin argues that she is not liable for her actions
because she was intoxicated at the time of the accident. Joe argues that
Kristin intentionally crashed into his house.
What is the effect of intoxication on liability?
Evidence of intoxication
  A. may be offered whenever it is relevant to negate an element of the crime
    charged
  B. is always relevant in disputes involving a vehicle
  C. is only relevant if raised in the initial complaint or otherwise raised prior to
    opening arguments at trial
  D. never has any material effect on the defendant's liability

13. Any contest, game, gaming scheme or gaming device in which the outcome 13.____
depends in a material degree upon an element of change is known as
  A. gambling   B. illicit arson
  C. restriction to chance   D. contest of chance

14. If the court imposes a fine for a felony, the court must also make a finding 14.____
as to the ____ the crime.
  A. amount of the defendant's gain from
  B. defendant's age at the time of
  C. defendant's height at the time of
  D. financial liabilities of the defendant at the time of

15. Jeremy is convicted of a felony and required to pay $15,000 in fines, or double the amount of money he gained in the commission of his crime. The state comptroller is responsible for collecting moneys in excess of _____ received or collected in payment of a fine and depositing the same into the rehabilitative alcohol and substance treatment fund established by the state finance law.
In other words, the total sum of _____ will be deposited into the treatment fund.
    A. $5,000; $10,000   B. $2,000; $13,000
    C. $14,000; $1,000   D. $1,000; $14,000

15.____

16. Which of the following is MOST likely a condition of probation?
    A. Answer all reasonable inquiries by the probation officer
    B. Notify the probation officer prior to any change in address
    C. Notify the probation officer prior to any change in employment
    D. All of the above

16.____

17. When can a sentence requiring the defendant to submit to the use of an electronic monitoring device be imposed?
    A. Only where the court determines that such condition will advance public safety, probationer control or probationer surveillance
    B. Whenever the court pleases and for every type of offense involving a minor
    C. Electronic monitoring devices were deemed unlawful in the State of New York in 2005
    D. Only where the court determines that the defendant's family or alleged victim is in imminent danger

17.____

18. A condition of probation for a convicted sex offender, when the victim of the crime was under the age of eighteen, will always include a prohibition against which of the following?
Knowingly entering into
    A. or upon school grounds
    B. a movie theater
    C. or upon a library
    D. or upon a grocery store or other marketplace

18.____

19. Amara's trial begins on April 1, 2017 and lasts for three months. Amara is found guilty of the crime charged on June 1, 2017 but is not sentenced until September 15th. Amara is sentenced to probation on September 15, 2017 for a period of twelve months.
When does Amara's probation end?
    A. April 1, 2018   B. June 1, 2018
    C. September 15, 2018   D. August 1, 2018

19.____

20. A revocable sentence of imprisonment to be served on days or during certain periods of days, or both, specified by the court as part of the sentence is deemed a(n)
    A. conditional release   B. unconditional sentence
    C. intermittent imprisonment   D. restless release

20.____

21. A conviction of a violation shall be punishable by a fine not to exceed   21.____
     A. $250   B. $500   C. $1,000   D. $5,000

Questions 22-25.

DIRECTIONS: Questions 22 through 25 are to be answered on the basis of the following fact
                pattern.

     Tom and Hank are hanging out after school when Tom dares Hank to steal graffiti on the
side of an apartment building. Tom and Hank are both eighteen and graduating from high
school in the spring. Tom and Hank are both apprehended during the commission of the crime.

22. A person is guilty of _____ when, with intent that another person engage in   22.____
conduct constituting a crime, he solicits, requests, commands, importunes, or
otherwise attempts to cause such other person to engage in such conduct.
This crime is a violation of
    A. criminal solicitation in the fifth degree
    B. criminal trespass
    C. criminal restitution in the first degree
    D. burglary with an accessory

23. Hank alleges that he did not know that making graffiti is a crime, because   23.____
he sees graffiti in New York City all the time.
Has Hank proffered an affirmative defense to the crime of making graffiti?
    A. Yes, he can commit a crime if he did not know what he was doing was
       criminal
    B. Yes, because he offered his defense prior to the start of the trial and in all
       honesty
    C. No, because he was caught in the commission of the crime with another
       person
    D. No, because now knowing he was committing a crime does not absolve
       him of liability

24. Tom insists that he also did know that making graffiti is a crime. Tom is also   24.____
being charged with possession of graffiti instruments. Making graffiti is a Class
_____ misdemeanor whereas possession of graffiti instruments is a Class
_____ misdemeanor.
    A. B; C   B. C; D   C. A; B   D. E; D

25. Given that the crimes Tom is being charged with are misdemeanors, what is   25.____
the MAXIMUM term of imprisonment Tom is facing (in months)?
    A. Six   B. Twelve   C. Eighteen   D. Twenty-four

KEY (CORRECT ANSWERS)

1.	B		11.	D
2.	A		12.	A
3.	B		13.	D
4.	A		14.	A
5.	B		15.	A
6.	A		16.	D
7.	C		17.	A
8.	D		18.	A
9.	B		19.	D
10.	B		20.	C

21.	C
22.	A
23.	D
24.	C
25.	B

EXAMINATION SECTION
TEST 1

DIRECTIONS: Each question or incomplete statement is followed by several suggested answers or completions. Select the one that BEST answers the question or completes the statement. *PRINT THE LETTER OF THE CORRECT ANSWER IN THE SPACE AT THE RIGHT.*

1. Which one of the following statements is LEAST accurate according to Article 8 of the F.C.A.?

    1.____

    A. The proceedings under this article are civil proceedings.
    B. The Family Court does NOT have exclusive jurisdiction over all family offense proceedings.
    C. The phrase "criminal complaint" includes an "information."
    D. If the family offense proceeding begins in the Family Court, it must be terminated there as a civil matter.

2. The one of the following offenses which is NOT considered to be a "family offense" is

    2.____

    A. disorderly conduct
    B. attempted assault
    C. menacing or reckless endangerment
    D. incest

3. A criminal complaint alleging a true family offense which starts in the criminal court and is not withdrawn or dismissed for legal insufficiency may still be transferred to the Family Court within _____ hours.

    3.____

    A. 12   B. 24   C. 48   D. 72

4. According to Article 10 of the F.C.A., an "abused child" is a child whose parents, etc. permit certain conditions harmful to the child to take place, and the child is less than

    4.____

    A. 14   B. 15   C. 16   D. 18

5. According to the F.C.A., a "neglected child" is a child less than _____ years of age whose physical, mental, or emotional condition has been impaired in a certain way.

    5.____

    A. 14   B. 15   C. 16   D. 18

6. Which one of the following statements is LEAST correct according to the Family Court Act in Article 10?

    6.____

    A. A child's "custodian" may include any person continually or at regular intervals found in the same household as the child when the conduct of such person causes or contributes to the abuse or neglect of the child.
    B. A police officer, when the circumstances are proper, may make an emergency removal of a child, without court order and without consent of parents.
    C. If a police officer as in B above acts in good faith in the removal of a child, he shall have immunity from any liability, civil or criminal.
    D. The authority for emergency removal as in B above is limited to police officers.

7. People who may originate a proceeding to determine abuse or neglect are 7.____
      I.   any person at the court's direction
      II. a child protective agency
      III. a police officer
The CORRECT answer is:

  A. I, II
  C. I, III
  B. I, II, III
  D. II, III

8. When a police officer takes a child under the age of 16 into custody, the thing he must do 8.____
immediately according to the F.C.A. is to

  A. notify the parent or other person legally responsible for his care or the person with whom he is domiciled that he has been taken into custody
  B. release the child to the custody of his parent or other person legally responsible for his care upon the written promise, without security, of the person to whose custody the child is released that he will produce the child before the Family Court
  C. forthwith, and without a police station stopover, bring the child before the Family Court
  D. forthwith deliver the child to a place certified by the State Division for Youth as a juvenile detention facility for the reception of children

9. The one of the following which is NOT required to be alleged in a petition to have some- 9.____
one declared a "juvenile delinquent" is that the

  A. respondent did an act, which if done by an adult, would constitute a crime and specifying the act and the time and place of its commission
  B. respondent was a person under 16 years of age at the time of the alleged act
  C. respondent requires supervision, treatment, or confinement
  D. offense involved either physical injury to the victim or the use of a dangerous weapon

10. The required quantum of evidence in a fact finding hearing concerning juvenile delin- 10.____
quency proceedings shall be

  A. a preponderance of the evidence
  B. beyond a reasonable doubt
  C. probable cause
  D. reasonable cause to believe

11. An "adjournment in contemplation of dismissal" may NOT be granted when a J.D. is 11.____
found to have committed a

  A. Class A felony
  B. "designated felony act"
  C. felony involving physical force
  D. robbery where a senior citizen is the victim

12. Where a child has been found to have committed a "designated Class A felony act" and 12.____
the court determines that "restrictive placement" is necessary, the respondent shall be
"placed" with the Division for Youth for an initial period of _____(s).

  A. 10
  B. 5
  C. 3
  D. 2

13. When the order for restrictive placement is made in connection with a youth found to have committed a "designated felony act" other than a "designated Class A felony act," the respondent shall be "placed" with the Division for Youth for an initial period of _____ (s).

    A. 10   B. 5   C. 3   D. 2

13.____

14. A 15-year-old boy has been arrested and charged with J.D. He is currently living with his 20-year-old sister. His parents reside in a city 500 miles away. You have tried to notify them but have been unsuccessful.
Your NEXT step should be to

    A. continue trying to notify parents
    B. take him to a secure facility and question him further
    C. release him on recognizance to his 20-year-old sister
    D. advise him of his rights and question him to get the facts

14.____

15. According to the F.C.A., a private person may take a person under 16 into custody in cases in which he may arrest for a crime under 140.30 of the C.P.L. The private person may then
       I. take the child to the child's home
      II. take the child to a Family Court
     III. deliver the child to a police officer or a peace officer
The CORRECT answer is:

    A. I, II, III   B. I, III
    C. II, III   D. III *only*

15.____

16. Under the provisions of the Family Court Act, in which of the following arrests of a juvenile delinquent must fingerprints be taken?

    A. John, age 11, commits robbery 1st degree
    B. Linda, age 12, commits robbery 2nd degree
    C. Robert, age 13, commits robbery 3rd degree
    D. Jane, age 14, commits burglary 3rd degree

16.____

17. If a juvenile delinquent is taken into custody and is charged with a crime which is NOT a "designated felony," and is to be issued a Family Court Appearance Ticket, the return date of such Appearance Ticket shall be no later than _____ after its issuance.

    A. 72 hours   B. 5 days   C. 10 days   D. 14 days

17.____

18. According to the provisions of the Family Court Act in Article 8, which of the following offenses is NOT a "family offense" even if it occurs between members of the same family or household?

    A. harassment   B. menacing
    C. assault 1st degree   D. assault 2nd degree
    E. disorderly conduct

18.____

19. According to Section 822 of the Family Court Act, only certain persons are authorized to originate family offense proceedings. With respect to who may so originate, which of the following statements is INCORRECT?   19.____

    A. Any person in the relation to the respondent of spouse, parent, child, or member of the same family or household
    B. A duly authorized agency, association, society, or institution
    C. Any peace officer or police officer
    D. A person on the court's own motion

20. Under the provisions of the Family Court Act in Section 158, if a person is taken into protective custody as a material witness, the total period of protective custody may NOT exceed _____ days.   20.____

    A. 7   B. 14   C. 21   D. 35   E. 42

KEY (CORRECT ANSWERS)

1.	D	11.	B
2.	D	12.	B
3.	D	13.	C
4.	D	14.	A
5.	D	15.	A
6.	D	16.	A
7.	A	17.	D
8.	A	18.	C
9.	D	19.	C
10.	B	20.	E

TEST 2

DIRECTIONS: Each question consists of a statement. You are to indicate whether the statement is TRUE (T) or FALSE (F). *PRINT THE LETTER OF THE CORRECT ANSWER IN THE SPACE AT THE RIGHT.*

1. An adjudication as a J.D. does NOT operate as a forfeiture of any right or privilege to hold public office EXCEPT where it involves a "designated felony act" involving serious physical injury to a senior citizen.   1.____

2. Family offense proceedings are civil proceedings whose objective is to provide practical help to family members.   2.____

3. The Family Court and the Criminal Courts have concurrent jurisdiction over most "family offenses." (HAD-ARM)   3.____

4. An arrest is NOT a requirement for bringing a HAD-ARM offense before the Family Court, but it is in order to bring the offense before the Criminal Court.   4.____

5. The **general** rule is that when a choice of either the Criminal Court or Family Court is made, and 72 hours go by, the choice of court becomes a final choice.   5.____

6. A police officer may originate a family offense proceeding under Article 8.   6.____

7. A "certificate of warrant" issued by the clerk of the Family Court expires 90 days from the date of issue, but can be renewed from time to time by the clerk of the court.   7.____

8. The presentation of a valid certificate of warrant to a police officer authorizes him to arrest the respondent named therein.   8.____

9. At a fact-finding hearing under Article 8, only evidence which is competent, material, and relevant may be admitted.   9.____

10. Findings at an Article 8 fact-finding hearing must be based on proof beyond a reasonable doubt.   10.____

11. Evidence at a "dispositional" hearing under Article 8 must be relevant and material.   11.____

12. The age of an "abused" child under Article 10 is less than 18.   12.____

13. The age of a "neglected" child under Article 10 is less than 16.   13.____

14. An "abandoned" child under Article 10 is within the definition of a "neglected" child.   14.____

15. Notwithstanding the fact that a Criminal Court may be exercising jurisdiction over the facts giving rise to "abuse" or "neglect," the Family Court has jurisdiction over proceedings brought under Article 10 for the protection of the child.   15.____

16. If the Family Court concludes that the processes of the Family Court are *inappropriate*, the matter may be transferred to the Criminal Court.   16.____

17. A police officer may make an emergency removal of an abused or neglected child when there is reason to believe the child is in imminent danger to life or health.   17.____

18. The above emergency removal may be made over the objections of parents and without court order.   18.____

19. A police officer may originate proceedings under Article 10.   19.____

20. In an Article 10 fact-finding hearing, any adjudication that the child is abused or neglected must be based on a preponderance of the evidence.   20.____

KEY (CORRECT ANSWERS)

1.	F		11.	T
2.	T		12.	T
3.	T		13.	F
4.	F		14.	T
5.	T		15.	T
6.	T		16.	T
7.	T		17.	T
8.	T		18.	T
9.	T		19.	F
10.	F		20.	T

EXAMINATION SECTION
TEST 1

DIRECTIONS: Each question or incomplete statement is followed by several suggested answers or completions. Select the one that BEST answers the question or completes the statement. *PRINT THE LETTER OF THE CORRECT ANSWER IN THE SPACE AT THE RIGHT.*

1.   A _____ person is chargeable with the support of his or her spouse and, if possessed of sufficient means or able to earn such means, may be required to pay for his or her support a fair and reasonable sum, as the court may determine, having due regard to the circumstances of the respective parties.   1._____
     A. reasonable   B. married   C. sufficient   D. supportive

Questions 2-5.

DIRECTIONS: Questions 2 through 5 are to be answered on the basis of the following fact pattern.

     Perry and Susan are married for five years. Their only child, Linda, is enrolled in a private elementary school when Perry and Susan divorce. Linda's school tuition is $12,000 per year. Perry currently earns $50,000 per year. As a real estate agent, Susan's salary fluctuates but on average she earns around $40,000 per year.

2.   What is the combined parental income if Susan has full legal custody of Linda after the divorce?   2._____
     A. $50,000
     B. $40,000
     C. $90,000
     D. The sum cannot be determined if Susan's salary fluctuates

3.   Perry recently lost his job and wants to have his child support modified. Can Perry request the support collection unit review the child support order for cost of living adjustment purposes?   3._____
     A. No, because Perry's job loss is not a result of a cost of living change
     B. Yes, because Perry lost his job
     C. Yes, but only if Perry can prove he has no income
     D. Yes, but only if Susan approves of the review

4.   In the case of Perry, Susan, and Linda, the child support percentage is _____% of the combined parental income for one child.   4._____
     A. 17   B. 25   C. 29   D. 31

5. Perry earns extra money delivering newspapers on the weekends. He is paid by check by the distributor and earns cash tips around the holidays. Is this income he earns from his weekend job considered income for child support purposes?
    A. Only payment from the distributor is considered income.
    B. Only cash tips are considered income.
    C. Both checks and cash tips are considered income.
    D. Neither payment is considered income.

5.____

6. Where may proceedings to establish paternity be originated?
    A. In the county where the mother of the child lives
    B. In the county where the child resides or is found
    C. In the county where the putative father resides
    D. All of the above

6.____

7. Laila is eight months old and lives in Massachusetts with her mother. When Laila was two months old, Laila's mother decided to move out of New York State to flee from Laila's abusive father. Laila's mother would like to file a child support order.
Where is Laila's home state?
    A. Massachusetts
    B. New York
    C. The state where the putative father resides
    D. The state of the most convenient venue

7.____

8. The term "issuing state" is defined as the state in which a tribunal issues a support order or renders a judgment determining
    A. parentage   B. jurisdiction   C. venue   D. domicile

8.____

9. James does not live in New York, but was staying in Albany with his mother when he was personally served with a summons and petition to enforce a child support order. James's son, Dex, lives in Brooklyn with James's ex-girlfriend.
Can the New York Family Court exercise jurisdiction over James?
    A. No, because James does not live in New York
    B. No, because James does not live with Dex's mother
    C. Yes, because he was personally served within the state
    D. Yes, but only if James consents to jurisdiction

9.____

10. Which of the following parties are eligible to commence a family offense proceeding?
    A. The spouse of the respondent
    B. A duly authorized agency, association, or institution
    C. Any person on the court's motion
    D. All of the above

10.____

11. After the filing of a petition by the petitioner in a family offense proceeding, the court will

    A. issue a summons or issue a warrant
    B. advise all parties of the right to retain legal representation
    C. direct that the respondent post bail for the amount set by the court
    D. issue a commitment order directing the respondent be remanded to the custody of the county sheriff

11.____

12. A temporary order of protection is

    A. an admission of guilt
    B. proof of a crime
    C. not a finding of wrongdoing
    D. reason for probable issuance

12.____

Questions 12-15.

DIRECTIONS: Questions 12 through 15 are to be answered on the basis of the following fact pattern.

Bryan and his sister, Amanda, were involved in a physical altercation outside of their home in Buffalo, New York. Bryan is 25 and Amanda is 16. While it is unclear how the altercation began, the district attorney would like to investigate the incident further. After the hearing in Family Court, the district attorney requests a copy of the family offense proceeding.

13. May the Family Court provide a copy of the transcript to the district attorney?

    A. No, because the incident is not criminal in nature
    B. No, because family offense proceedings are sealed
    C. No, because family offense proceedings are not recorded or otherwise transcribed
    D. Yes

13.____

14. Where will the Family Court proceedings take place?

    A. In the county where the incident occurred
    B. In the county that Bryan chooses
    C. In the county that Amanda chooses
    D. In the county the district attorney chooses

14.____

15. Amanda has requested the court issue a TRO for her protection against her brother, Bryan. A TRO is also known as a

    A. temporary restitution order
    B. temporal restraining order
    C. temporary restraining order
    D. transitional restitution order

15.____

16. What information is contained in a permanency hearing report?

    A. The health and well-being of a child
    B. Reasonable efforts that have been made since the last hearing to promote permanency
    C. The recommended permanency plan for the child
    D. All of the above

16.____

17. Decisions and final orders of the Family Court are appealed to which judicial body? 17.____
    A. The appellate division of the Supreme Court of the Judicial Department in which the Family Court order was issued
    B. The surrogate's division of the Supreme Court of the Judicial Department in which the Family Court order was issued
    C. The Third Circuit Court
    D. The final appeals unit of the New York Supreme Court

18. An appeal as of right shall be taken by filing the _____ notice of appeal with the clerk of the Family Court in which the order was made and from which the appeal is taken. The appellant shall file _____ copies of such notice, together with the proof of service, with the clerk of the Family Court who shall forthwith transmit one copy of such notice to the clerk of the appropriate appellate division. 18.____
    A. first; three   B. original; two   C. first; three   D. original; four

19. Which court has exclusive original jurisdiction in proceedings to establish paternity? 19.____
    A. The Appellate Court   B. The Supreme Court
    C. The Family Court   D. Surrogates Court

20. Can Jeremy, who is 25, file a petition to return to foster care after being discharged from foster care? 20.____
    A. Yes, as he was previously in the foster care system
    B. Yes, as he is consenting to return to foster care of his own free will
    C. No, because he cannot return to foster care without the consent of his adoptive parents
    D. No, because he is 25

21. Judge O'Connor would like to visit the local elementary school to check in on two different students who were recently placed into foster care. May Judge O'Connor do so? 21.____
    A. Yes; the judge may do so in an official capacity
    B. Yes, but only if she does not identify herself as a judge
    C. Yes, but only if she does not identify herself as a public servant
    D. Yes, but only if she garners the consent of the foster care agency

22. What days may a warrant of arrest be executed? 22.____
    A. Monday through Friday   B. Weekends only
    C. Monday through Saturday   D. Any day of the week

23. At what time may a warrant of arrest be executed? 23.____
    A. Only between the hours of 9:00 A.M. and Midnight
    B. Only before 9:00 A.M.
    C. Only after sunset
    D. Any hour of the day or night

24. Shephard lives in Essex County, but sometimes stays with his mother who lives in Nassau County. Because of the distance between the two residences, Shephard has been spending increasingly more time with his mother and les time at his own residence in Essex County. While staying with his mother, Shephard is personally served with court papers relating to his paternity suit in Essex County.
Can the court exercise jurisdiction over Shephard in Nassau County?
    A. No, because Shephard is not a resident of Nassau County
    B. No, because Shephard did not waive his rights to be served in Nassau County
    C. Yes, because Shephard availed himself of the benefits of statewide travel
    D. Yes, because the Family Court may send proceeds in any matter in which it has jurisdiction into any county of the state for service or execution

24.____

25. Marie's son, Tom, is being accused of willful nonpayment of child support. Marie is furious with Tom's ex-wife and during the proceeding continues to berate and scream at Tom's attorney and the judge.
Can Marie be found guilty of contempt of court in Family Court?
    A. No, because contempt is reserved for criminal courts only
    B. No, because contempt is reserved for civil courts only
    C. Yes, because Marie is a danger to the parties' legal representation
    D. Yes

25.____

KEY (CORRECT ANSWERS)

1.	B	11.	A
2.	C	12.	C
3.	A	13.	D
4.	A	14.	A
5.	C	15.	D
6.	D	16.	D
7.	A	17.	A
8.	A	18.	B
9.	C	19.	C
10.	D	20.	D

21.	A
22.	D
23.	D
24.	D
25.	D

TEST 2

Questions 1-2.

DIRECTIONS: Questions 1 and 2 are to be answered on the basis of the following fact pattern.

Jim was recently made aware that his estranged wife, Marissa, has requested an order of protection from him.

1. What is the purpose of an order of protection?
   An order of protection is issued to
   A. compel the payment of child support
   B. stop violence within a family, or within an intimate relationship
   C. compel the payment of alimony or other support obligation
   D. warn the respondent that a restraining order will follow after the order of protection is stamped and filed

   1.____

2. After Marissa requests the order of protection, what may Jim file in response?
   A. Jim is ineligible to file a response.
   B. Jim may file an answer to the petition and a counter-claim.
   C. Jim must file a summons to compel Marissa to provide evidence of abuse.
   D. Jim may file a demand for further discovery.

   2.____

3. Teresa has commenced a proceeding in Family Court to prove the paternity of her daughter, Sara. Teresa has named Lewis as the respondent in her petition as she alleges he is Sara's father. After filing the paternity proceeding petition, the court may issue a summons which will require Lewis to do which of the following?
   A. Show cause why the declaration of paternity should not be made
   B. Respond to written discovery demands forwarded by Teresa and/or Teresa's legal counsel
   C. Appear in the Family Court in the county where Teresa currently resides to answer for the action
   D. Personally appear at a preliminary conference in the judge's chambers to respond to the petition

   3.____

4. Which of the following is MOST likely to be linked to the issuance of a warrant by the Family Court?
   A. Proceeding to compel support by the mother
   B. Proceeding to compel support by the father
   C. A proceeding to challenge the testing directive
   D. All of the above

   4.____

5. Which of the following are court rules that govern attorneys for children?   5.____
   A. Prescribed workload, including maximum number of children that can be represented at any given time
   B. The times that attorneys for children may enter and exit the courtroom for hearings
   C. The dates at which hearings can be scheduled, including which days of the week attorneys may appear for the hearings
   D. A requirement that all attorneys for children be a minimum age before engaging as counsel

6. Tina was placed on probation shortly after her proceeding to compel support   6.____
   for her daughter. As a condition of Tina's probation, she is ordered to abstain from drugs and alcohol. Tina has missed her last three appointments with her probation officer.
   According to the New York Family Court Act, if at any time during the period of probation the court has reasonable cause to believe that the respondent has violated a condition of the probation order, it may issue a _____ order.
   A. support   B. research   C. disciplinary   D. search

7. An order of sequestration may be issued for what purpose?   7.____
   Sequestration is the act of
   A. removing the respondent from the jurisdiction of the underlying hearing
   B. removing, separating, or seizing the possessions of the owner for the benefit of creditors
   C. holding possessions of the owner in trust for the benefit of the trust's beneficiaries
   D. compelling payment from a respondent who has absconded from custody

8. Upon a finding that a respondent has failed to comply with any lawful order of   8.____
   support, the court may do which of the following?
   A. Order the respondent to pay a money judgment
   B. Suspend the respondent's driving privileges
   C. The court may impose an order of sequestration upon the respondent
   D. All of the above

9. In New York City, which body represents the social services commissioner?   9.____
   A. Corporation Counsel of the City of New York
   B. The District Attorney's office
   C. Counsel of the Supreme Court of New York
   D. Counsel of the Appellate Division of the Supreme Court of New York

10. Stephanie and Danielle, each 10 years old, are half-sisters and live with their   10.____
    father. Stephanie was removed by Social Services and placed into foster care approximately one year ago. Danielle is being removed by Social Services. Where will Danielle MOST likely be placed?
    A. With Stephanie, as placement with half-siblings is presumptively in the best interests of the child
    B. With Stephanie, but only if Danielle so chooses

    C. To foster care that is separate from Stephanie, so as to not confuse or
alienate the child

    D. To the Department of Social Services and Probation

11. A child under the age of eighteen who is in a state of want or suffering to a
lack of sufficient food, clothing, shelter, or medical or surgical care is referred to
as a(n)

    A. abandoned child   B. child in need of supervision

    C. destitute child   D. desperate child

11.____

12. The term "arrears" generally refers to

    A. past money owed or due

    B. the percentage of alimony in dispute

    C. the amount of child support in dispute

    D. a fixed amount of money due to the court (i.e, escrow)

12.____

13. A destitute child proceeding may be originated by which person or party?

    A. The Commissioner of Social Services only

    B. An authorized child services agency

    C. The parents of the child

    D. Any caretaker of the child

13.____

14. A minor who is the subject of a _____ or a person in need of supervision
proceedings is presumed to lack the requisite knowledge and maturity to waive
the appointment of an attorney.

    A. child support proceeding   B. family offense proceeding

    C. juvenile delinquency   D. child placement hearing

14.____

15. The costs for attorneys for children shall be payable by the

    A. Commissioner of Social Services

    B. Family Court in which the attorney serves

    C. State of New York

    D. City of New York

15.____

16. A proceeding to determine capacity is MOST likely to occur in which of the
following scenarios?

    A. Gabriel, 16, committed a misdemeanor while playing a game of "truth or
dare" with his three closest friends

    B. Anne, 15, a mentally distributed teenager who sexually assaulted her
younger brother

    C. Rachel, 21, who has a violent streak and often yells and hits her parents

    D. Jamal, 20, who recently stole a bike from a neighbor's backyard

16.____

17. The court shall not consent to the entry of an admission unless it has advised
the respondent of his or her right to a

    A. fact-finding hearing   B. trial by jury

    C. trial by the bench   D. pre-trial conference

17.____

18. Jamie's attorney would like to file a motion to seal after a finding of delinquency on Jamie's behalf. The notice of such motion shall be served upon the presentment agency not less than _____ days prior to the return date of the motion. Answering affidavits shall be served at least _____ days before such time.

    A. 10; 5   B. 8; 2   C. 11; 6   D. 15; 9

18.____

19. Daniel is an attorney for a large law firm in Manhattan. Daniel and his wife are in the midst of a divorce and related child support hearing. The court has asked Daniel's employer to provide full information with respect to Daniel's earnings.

Must Daniel's employer comply?

    A. No, because the information is not necessary in the child support hearing

    B. No, unless Daniel consents to the release of such information

    C. No, because the court is not authorized to retrieve such information

    D. Yes

19.____

20. Does an indigent adult have the right to be represented by counsel and/or to confer with counsel?

An indigent

    A. adult may only confer with counsel, but must pay for the legal representation

    B. adult may be represented by counsel upon the consent of the court

    C. adult may be represented by counsel but cannot choose his or her counsel

    D. person has the right to be represented by counsel of his or her choosing

20.____

21. The parents of Matilda would like to stop her placement into foster care. Matilda's parents terminated their parental rights nearly three years, but heard that Matilda would be placed into foster care by her adoptive parents.

Which party is the MOST appropriate person(s) to file a motion to terminate Matilda's placement into foster care?

    A. Matilda   B. Matilda's birth parents

    C. Matilda's adoptive parents   D. Matilda's attorney

21.____

22. Which of the following qualifies as an initial appearance?

    A. The preliminary conference between the parties' legal representation

    B. The date the respondent first appears before the court after the petition is filed

    C. The first day of a trial in which the respondent and petitioner will see one another

    D. The judge's first order

22.____

23. Nontestimonial evidence from the respondent, which may be ordered by the court upon motion made by the petitioner, is also known as

    A. a subpoena-related inquiry   B. discovery

    C. interrogation   D. a demand by investigation

23.____

24. If a motion under the motion to terminate placement is denied, it may not be renewed for a period of _____ days after the denial, unless the order of denial permits renewal at an earlier time.

    A. 30   B. 60   C. 90   D. 120

24.____

25. A motion that is renewed and filed after the required period of time is also referred to as a(n) _____ motion.

    A. recurring   B. successive   C. unrestricted   D. untimed

25.____

KEY (CORRECT ANSWERS)

1.	B		11.	C
2.	B		12.	A
3.	A		13.	A
4.	D		14.	C
5.	A		15.	C
6.	D		16.	B
7.	B		17.	A
8.	D		18.	B
9.	A		19.	D
10.	A		20.	D

21.	C
22.	B
23.	B
24.	C
25.	B

EXAMINATION SECTION

TEST 1

DIRECTIONS: Each question or incomplete statement is followed by several suggested answers or completions. Select the one that BEST answers the question or completes the statement. *PRINT THE LETTER OF THE CORRECT ANSWER IN THE SPACE AT THE RIGHT.*

1. Which of the following parties is authorized to administer oaths?
   A. All court clerks
   B. Court bailiffs
   C. Judges only
   D. Judge's clerks only

1.____

2. Janelle has been retained as Stephanie's defense attorney. Stephanie is charged with felony burglary in the first degree.
   When must Janelle file a notice of appearance with the court?
   A. Before opening argument
   B. Before her first appearance in court or 10 days after her appointment, whichever is sooner
   C. 10 days after her appointment as Stephanie's attorney
   D. No later than Stephanie's first scheduled arraignment

2.____

3. Tony is a new associate at the law offices of Deck & Decker, LLP. He needs to file a motion to dismiss for his managing attorney's client and is unsure of where to deliver the papers for the court's consideration.
   Unless directed to do directly by the court, papers for consideration of the court should be delivered to
   A. the presiding judge
   B. the clerk's office of the trial court in the appropriate courtroom
   C. any of the judges in the appropriate courtroom
   D. the bailiff or court officer on duty

3.____

4. How many terms of court are in one year?
   A. 12   B. 13   C. 26   D. 52

4.____

5. Upon otherwise excluded from a courtroom by the judge, the Family Court is open to the
   A. families having business in the court only
   B. extended families having business in the court only
   C. public
   D. judge's law clerks and court officers only

5.____

6. Which of the following is a factor the judge may consider in excluding someone from the courtroom during a Family Court proceeding?
   The person is
   A. causing or likely to cause a disruption in the proceedings
   B. related to a member of the family in the court
   C. related to the judge or other clerk
   D. an alternate court officer

6.____

7. Which of the following are appropriate considerations for a pre-trial conference?
    A. Completion of discovery
    B. Admissions of fact
    C. Possibilities for settlement
    D. All of the above

7.____

8. In any proceeding to determine temporary or permanent custody or visitation, once a hearing or trial is commenced, it shall proceed to conclusion within _____ days.
    A. 30
    B. 60
    C. 90
    D. 120

8.____

Questions 9-12.

DIRECTIONS: Questions 9 through 12 are to be answered on the basis of the following fact pattern.

Tim and Kat have two children together. After their divorce, Tim was ordered to pay child support in the amount of $480 per month. Soon after divorcing, Tim lost his job as a paralegal with a local law firm but quickly found another job that paid more than double his paralegal salary. Tim has not paid child support in over six months. Kat recently learned that Tim has been earning more than enough money to pay the monthly support obligation as well as the amount Tim owes in arrears.

9. What must Kat file in order to schedule a hearing to determine nonpayment of child support?
    A. A petition that alleges willful violation of an order of support
    B. A subpoena that requires Tim to hand over his bank statements
    C. A summons that requires Tim to hand over his bank statements
    D. A notice of deposition to inform Tim that a complaint will follow

9.____

10. After the judge or support magistrate commences a hearing to determine whether Tim is purposefully evading paying child support, how many adjournments can each side request?
    A. Unlimited
    B. Up to two adjournments each
    C. Only one adjournment can be permitted, and only to secure counsel
    D. No adjournments are permitted

10.____

11. The hearing must conclude within how many days of commencement?
    A. 30
    B. 60
    C. 90
    D. 120

11.____

12. Assume that testimony must be taken in the hearing between Tim and Kat. The testimony will be given by Tim's former employer, Bob, who has recently moved to Idaho.
    Can Bob provide testimony by telephone or other electronic means?
    A. Yes, with court approval and if the request is completed using an official form
    B. Yes, if Kat and Tim both consent to the method of testimony delivery

12.____

C. Yes, if Kat and Tim both consent in writing at least fifteen days prior to the scheduled hearing date
D. No

13. Which of the following must be submitted with a petition to terminate the birth mother's rights?
    A. Sworn written statement by the mother naming the father
    B. A blood sample of the child's maternal grandmother
    C. A blood or other DNA sample of the child's paternal grandmother
    D. A sworn written statement by any individual familiar with both the mother and father who can attest to the identity of both parties

13._____

14. When a child is placed in foster care, he or she comes under the jurisdiction of the _____ Court.
    A. Surrogates   B. Civil   C. Criminal   D. Family

14._____

15. Judge Slater presided over the hearing regarding Baby Jay's foster care placement. In a subsequent proceeding, Baby Jay's mother has decided to voluntarily terminate her parental rights.
    Will Judge Slater be assigned to the parental rights hearing?
    A. No
    B. Yes, if practicable
    C. Yes, if specifically requested by Baby Jay's current guardian
    D. Yes, if specifically requested by the parent requesting her rights be terminated

15._____

16. If a child in a custody proceeding is Native American, that child is subject to which of the following?
    A. Social Services Law   B. Indian Child Welfare Act
    C. Child Welfare Act of Natives   D. Division of American Children

16._____

17. Which of the following papers is required in an adoption proceeding?
    A. Certified copy of the birth certificate of the adoptive child
    B. Certified marriage certificate, where the adoptive parents are married
    C. A proposed order of adoption
    D. All of the above

17._____

18. The court may determine the best interests of the child in an adoption proceeding factoring in which of the following?
    A. The sexual orientation of the adoptive parents
    B. The race or ethnicity of the adoptive parents
    C. The age of the adoptive child
    D. None of the above

18._____

19. At any scheduled call of a calendar or at any conference, if all parties do not appear, the court may note the _____ on the record.
    A. dismissal   B. acquittal
    C. acquiescence   D. default

19._____

20. In any discontinued action, the attorney for the defendant shall file a stipulation or statement of discontinuance with the county clerk within _____ day(s) of such continuance.

    A. one   B. ten   C. fifteen   D. twenty

20.____

21. Unless the court otherwise provides, where the attorney of record for any party arranges for another attorney to conduct the trial, the trial counsel must be identified in writing to the court and all parties no later than 15 days after the pretrial conference or, if there is not a pretrial conference, at least _____ days before trial.

    A. 10   B. 5   C. 15   D. 30

21.____

22. A preliminary examination of a witness or juror by a judge or counsel prior to trial is known as the process of

    A. de jure   B. benchmarking
    C. voir dire   D. stare decisis

22.____

23. Which two pieces of information are attorneys prohibited from sharing in the process identified in Question 22?
Counsel may not
    A. read from any pleadings or information potential jurors of the amount of money at issue
    B. identify their client or provide any background to the dispute at issue
    C. reveal their true identities or provide any detail as to where the dispute at issue took place
    D. provide any details about the case but may provide details on the identity of their client

23.____

24. A bifurcated trial is MOST appropriate in which of the following circumstances?
    A. A bar owner serves alcohol to a minor and may be both criminally liable and civilly liable for the damages to the minor
    B. A disgruntled neighbor who yells at his neighbor and kicks over his garden gnomes is sued
    C. A civil dispute between Amy and her former employer has come to the surface after Amy accuses her employer of sexual harassment
    D. A dispute between friends that is settled outside of court

24.____

25. Each attorney appearing in a proceeding shall file a
    A. written notice of appearance   B. written order of appearance
    C. oral notice of appearance   D. written issue of notice

25.____

KEY (CORRECT ANSWERS)

1.	A	11.	B
2.	B	12.	A
3.	B	13.	A
4.	B	14.	D
5.	C	15.	B
6.	A	16.	B
7.	D	17.	D
8.	C	18.	D
9.	A	19.	D
10.	C	20.	D

21.	A
22.	C
23.	A
24.	A
25.	A

TEST 2

DIRECTIONS: Each question or incomplete statement is followed by several suggested answers or completions. Select the one that BEST answers the question or completes the statement. *PRINT THE LETTER OF THE CORRECT ANSWER IN THE SPACE AT THE RIGHT.*

1.   Mark wants to postpone determination of his visitation rights to see his daughter, Maddie. He believes he has a better chance of getting to see Maddie more if he lives within an hour of Maddie's mother and Mark is not moving until the end of next month.
     Generally, what is the time limitation on custody and/or visitation determination once a hearing is commenced?
     A. 30 days   B. 60 days   C. 90 days   D. 120 days

1.____

2.   Which party assigns criminal actions to judges?
     A. Chief Justice of the New York Supreme Court
     B. Nassau County Supreme Court
     C. The Presiding Judge in the district of jurisdiction
     D. The Chief Administrator of the Courts

2.____

3.   A _____ of court is a designated unit of the court in which specified business of the court is to be conducted by a judge or quasi-judicial officer.
     A. unit   B. division   C. part   D. sequence

3.____

4.   Tim has escaped from the Child Center in Albany. When a child absconds from a facility to which he or she was duly remanded, what action must an authorized representative of the facility take?
     Written notice must be given to the clerk of the court from which the remand was made within _____ hours.
     A. 24   B. 36   C. 48   D. 72

4.____

5.   Which of the following individuals is qualified to serve as a Support Magistrate?
     A. Margaret, a senior paralegal with the Utica Family Court
     B. Jamal, a former court bailiff who has been an acting family law attorney for the last six years
     C. Sharon, a Colorado criminal court chief justice
     D. Amy, a New York City police officer who is family with child custody issues

5.____

6.   Support magistrates shall be appointed as nonjudicial employees of the Unified Court System on a full-time basis for a term of _____ years and, in the discretion of the Chief Administrator, may be reappointed for a subsequent _____-year terms.
     A. 1; 2   B. 3; 5   C. 3; 3   D. 3; 6

6.____

7. Ed and Elizabeth were married for eight years and four children together.
    Ed filed for divorce, alleging that Elizabeth had an affair with one of Ed's
    coworkers, Tom. Ed is seeking full custody of all four children and wants the
    court to deny Elizabeth alimony and child support.
    Which of the following statements is a finding of fact?
    A. Elizabeth is most likely having an affair with Tom.
    B. Elizabeth is more than likely an adulterous spouse.
    C. Ed and Elizabeth were married for eight years.
    D. Elizabeth's request for child support is frivolous.

    7.____

8. A certified copy of the birth certificate of the child must accompany which of
    the following hearings?
    A. An adoption proceeding
    B. Petition to terminate a birth mother's rights
    C. Extra-judicial surrender of a child
    D. All of the above

    8.____

9. Which of the following qualify as a "special application" which must be made
    in writing and accompanied by affidavits setting forth the reason(s) for the
    application?
    A. Dispense with the statutorily required personal appearance
    B. Period of residence of a child
    C. Period of waiting after filing of the adoption petition
    D. All of the above

    9.____

10. Rachel, a probation officer, has been asked to conduct an investigation into
    the guardianship of McKenzie, a recently orphaned four-year-old girl, in foster
    care. The court would like to appoint a guardian but needs a disinterested
    person to interview McKenzie's next of kin before rendering a decision.
    Is Rachel authorized to conduct such an investigation?
    A. No, because Rachel is not an attorney
    B. No, because Rachel is not a certified private investigator
    C. Yes, because Rachel is presumably over the age of 18
    D. Yes, because an investigation by a disinterested person is authorized if
        requested by the court

    10.____

11. When a petition for temporary guardianship has been filed by an adoptive
    parent, the clerk of the court in which the petition has been filed shall distribute
    a written notice to the adoptive parents and lawyers who have appeared, and
    to the Commissioner of _____ or the Director of the _____, as appropriate.
    A. Mental Health; Family Court
    B. Court Services; Child Welfare Services
    C. Social Services; Probation Service
    D. Social Services; Family Court Services

    11.____

12. Bella would like to terminate her parental rights and surrender her daughter to foster care. Bella, however, is unsure of how to proceed and is nervous to speak with any of the court officers or court clerks. Bella currently lives in Utica County, New York.
    Which of the following individuals is designated to speak with Bella about bringing a proceeding under the Family Court Act before the proceeding is commenced?
    A. Commanding officer of any law enforcement agency providing police service in Utica County
    B. Utica County district attorney
    C. The clerk of the Family Court and the clerk of the criminal court of Utica County
    D. All of the above

12._____

Questions 13-15.

DIRECTIONS: Questions 13 through 15 are to be answered on the basis of the following fact pattern.

James is sixteen and does not attend school. He continuously disobeys his parents and has been caught selling drugs from his parent's home on at least one occasion.

13. James MOST likely qualifies as a(n)
    A. incarcerated person
    C. indemnified individual
    B. person in need of supervision
    D. indigent prisoner

13._____

14. May James' parents hire an attorney to represent James?
    A. No, the attorney will represent James and his parents wholly
    B. No, James must be proven guilty before an attorney can be appointed
    C. No, there is no such "Attorney for Child" concept in New York State
    D. Yes

14._____

15. James sold cocaine from his parent's apartment to an acquaintance of his from his old school. The buyer of the drugs, Sam, died of an overdose. Sam's parents have sued James. How is a court case against James commenced?
    A. Sam's parents must file a PINS petition in Family Court.
    B. A subpoena must be served on James' parents.
    C. An indictment must be filed in the county where the commission of the crime occurred or, in this case, in the county where James' parents reside.
    D. Discovery demands should be fulfilled by both sides before an action can be commenced.

15._____

16. Proceedings for adoption from an authorized agency shall be calendared within _____ days of the filing of the petition to review said petition and determine if there is an adequate basis for approving the adoption.
    A. 20   B. 30   C. 45   D. 60

16._____

17. Assume the same facts as in Question 16. The court shall schedule the appearance of the adoptive parent(s) and the child before the court, for approval of the adoption within _____ days of the date of the review.
    A. 20   B. 30   C. 45   D. 60

17.____

18. Is there a time limit for proceedings involving custody or visitation?
    A. Yes, once a hearing or trial is commenced, it must proceed to conclusion within 90 days
    B. Yes, once a hearing or trial is commenced, it must proceed to conclusion within 120 days
    C. No, as each case must be determined by the specific fact pattern presented to the court
    D. No, unless there is a petition from either party to expedite the proceeding

18.____

19. Admissions of fact, fixing a date for fact-finding and dispositional hearings are most appropriately confined to a
    A. pre-trial conference
    B. subpoena conference
    C. disposition hearing
    D. engagement of counsel determination

19.____

20. Which of the following individuals is LEAST likely to be permitted to access the pleadings of a Family Court case?
    A. A child who is a party to a proceeding
    B. Parents who are legally responsible for the care of the child subject to a proceeding
    C. A reporter for the New York Ledger
    D. An authorized representative of the child protective agency involved in the proceeding

20.____

21. The general public or any person may be excluded from a Family Court courtroom only if the judge presiding in the courtroom determines, on a case-by-case basis such exclusion
    A. is warranted in that case
    B. would prejudice the rights of the child
    C. would prejudice the rights of the parents
    D. would bring negative press to either party's attorney

21.____

22. Which of the following two documents are provided by the Family Court to assist in filing an appeal?
    A. Request for Appellate Division Intervention Form; Notice of Appeal
    B. Subpoena Request Form; Notice of Appeal
    C. Request for Appellate Division Intervention Form; Order of Appeal
    D. Order of Appeal; Notice of Appeal

22.____

23. The _____ shall conduct preliminary conferences with any person seeking to have a juvenile delinquency petition filed, concerning the advisability of requesting that a juvenile delinquency petition be filed and in order to gather information needed for a determination of the suitability of the case for adjustment.
    A. Chief Judicial Administrator
    B. Probation Service
    C. Court Clerk
    D. Family Services

23.____

24. Can hearings be recorded?
    A. No
    B. Not unless all parties consent in writing at least 60 days prior to arraignment
    C. Not unless the court's clerk approves
    D. yes

24.____

25. John's hearing to determine whether he is willfully not paying child support is scheduled for Tuesday morning. On Monday night, John becomes extremely ill with food poisoning.
    Will John's hearing be adjourned?
    A. No, under no circumstances will a hearing for willful nonpayment be adjourned
    B. No, unless the court's clerk is able to communicate John's illness to the court within 24 hours of the hearing
    C. Yes, if the court bailiff consents to the adjournment
    D. Yes, the hearing may be adjourned for illness of a party or other good cause

25.____

KEY (CORRECT ANSWERS)

1.	C		11.	C
2.	D		12.	D
3.	C		13.	B
4.	C		14.	D
5.	B		15.	A
6.	B		16.	D
7.	C		17.	B
8.	D		18.	A
9.	D		19.	A
10.	D		20.	C

21.	A
22.	A
23.	B
24.	D
25.	D

———

EXAMINATION SECTION

TEST 1

DIRECTIONS: Each question or incomplete statement is followed by several suggested answers or completions. Select the one that BEST answers the question or completes the statement. *PRINT THE LETTER OF THE CORRECT ANSWER IN THE SPACE AT THE RIGHT.*

1. Gary owns an apartment in downtown Brooklyn. Gary resides in Watkins Glen and rents the apartment in Brooklyn. His tenant moved out of the Brooklyn apartment about two weeks ago. Since then, he has received e-mails from friends in Brooklyn that a transient individual, Sean, has been sleeping in the apartment by breaking in the back window.
   Does a landlord-tenant relationship exist between Gary and Sean?
   A. Yes, because Gary owns the apartment
   B. Yes, because Sean is the rightful tenant of the apartment
   C. No, because Sean has not been in possession of the apartment for thirty consecutive days
   D. No, because Sean has not informed Gary that he wants to be Gary's tenant

1.____

2. If a landlord/tenant relationship exists and the grounds are met for a special proceeding to take place, the landlord must give the tenant _____ day notice of the special proceeding.
   A. ten   B. fifteen   C. twenty   D. twenty-five

2.____

3. A real property proceedings may be brought by which of the following party(ies)?
   A. A landlord
   B. A person forcibly put or kept out
   C. The lessee of the premises, entitled to possession
   D. All of the above

3.____

4. A special proceeding to recover real property can be initiated in which of the following venues?
   A. County court
   B. District court
   C. Justice court
   D. Each of the above, and a court of civil jurisdiction in a city

4.____

5. How does James start a special proceeding to recover real property from his tenant, Marisol?
   A. James should file a complaint in civil court.
   B. James should file a notice of petition and petition to commence the action.
   C. James must arrange for the service of a subpoena upon Marisol.
   D. James should attempt to evict Marisol himself once Marisol stops paying rent.

5.____

Questions 6-8.

DIRECTIONS: Questions 6 through 8 are to be answered on the basis of the following fact pattern.

Jeremy wants to buy property in an up-and-coming neighborhood of Suffolk County. He enlists his friend and former co-worker, Danielle, to help him find a suitable house at a bargain. Danielle is a native of the area in which Jeremy wants to buy. Jeremy buys a home and asks Danielle to act as the landlord.

6.   Danielle advertised the house for rent online. She subsequently rented the home to a man who used the house as the center of an illegal gambling ring. Danielle knows that the home is being used for that purpose, but does not inform Jeremy.
What is Danielle obligated to do given her knowledge of the activities happening at the house?
    A. Danielle has a duty to vacate the premises.
    B. Danielle, as the landlord, must make an application of removal of the tenant.
    C. Danielle is obligated to evict the tenants using brute force.
    D. Danielle is obligated to inform the local court of the activities taking place at the home.

6._____

7.   Is Jeremy responsible for knowing how the rented property is being used?
    A. No, because Jeremy is not the landlord
    B. No, because Jeremy does not live near the property and has no way of knowing that the property is being used for illegal purposes
    C. Yes, because Jeremy can visit or drive by the property and clearly see it is used for illegal gambling purposes
    D. Yes, because Jeremy is the owner of the property

7._____

8.   If Danielle does not bring an action to remove the tenants from the property, who is eligible to do so as if he/she is the owner of the property?
    A. Local law enforcement agency   B. Danielle's neighbors
    C. Jeremy's neighbors   D. The State of New York

8._____

9.   After a final judgment for the landlord, the court shall issue a(n) _____ direct to the sheriff of the county or marshal of the city in which the property is situated, describing the property and commanding the officer to remove all persons.
    A. indictment   B. subpoena   C. warrant   D. summons

9._____

10.   Court marshals appear at Bethany's apartment to execute the warrant for her eviction.
How much notice must the marshals provide Bethany?
_____ hours, excluding weekends and holidays.
    A. 24   B. 36   C. 72   D. 86

10._____

11. What effect does the warrant for an eviction have on the relationship between
the landlord and tenant according to the New York Real Property Actions and
Proceedings Law?
The warrant _____ the landlord-tenant relationship.
   A. solidifies   B. redeems   C. rescinds   D. cancels

11.____

12. Jason was served with a notice of petition for removal from his landlord,
Eric. Jason has never been late on his rent, but has not paid Eric since his
lease expired two months ago.
May Jason respond to Eric's petition and, if so, how?
   A. No, Jason must vacate the premises immediately.
   B. Jason can respond, but only after he has vacated the premises.
   C. Jason can respond directly to Eric and record the conversation so that it
       can be preserved and presented to the court at a later date.
   D. Yes, Jason can prepare and file an answer to Eric's petition.

12.____

13. Assume the same facts as in Question 12. After Eric filed a notice of petition,
the court decided it needs more information before moving on in the
proceedings. In lieu of a notice of petition, the court may require which of the
following?
   A. Order to show cause
   B. Specific description of the noise complaints or other grounds for eviction
   C. Payment receipts
   D. Formal complaint and deposition testimony

13.____

Questions 14-17.

DIRECTIONS: Questions 14 through 17 are to be answered on the basis of the following facts.

Dawn did not keep a copy of the lease her tenant, Mike, signed. Mike does not have a
copy of the lease either. Mike maintains that the lease term has not expired, while Dawn says
the lease ended a month ago.

14. At trial, the lease term is considered a
   A. fact in dispute   B. triable issue of fact
   C. respondent's contention   D. contentious fact

14.____

15. The apartment that Mike rents in Manhattan is in a building with eight other
rental units. The court that hears the dispute between Dawn and Mike must
first and foremost have
   A. contacts with Mike and Dawn   B. jurisdiction
   C. res ipsa   D. pro se litigant allowance

15.____

16. During the summary proceeding, the court's preliminary asks if there is any undisputed amount of rent owed. Assuming that Mike agrees that he is already behind one month of rent and Dawn agrees, who will the court direct Mike to deliver that rent payment to?

    A. The court for safekeeping
    B. An escrow account established by Mike, but put in Dawn's name
    C. An escrow account which names the County Clerk as the legal owner
    D. Directly to Dawn

16.____

17. The amount in dispute between Mike and Dawn is $5,000. Mike wants to countersue Dawn for $3,000; however, Mike refuses to deposit the disputed amount of money to the court. Mike has not paid any portion of the $5,000. Upon application, what actions can Dawn ask the court to take?

    A. Dismiss without prejudice Mike's counterclaims and defenses and grant judgment for Dawn
    B. Imprison Mike for non-payment of rent
    C. Garnish Mike's paychecks for the back payment of rent, and other arrears
    D. Restrict Mike's counterclaims as to only those relating to monetary damages

17.____

18. The term "constructive eviction" is defined as a(n)

    A. circumstance where the landlord does something or provides or, in the adverse, does not do something or fails to provide, that renders the property uninhabitable
    B. circumstance where the tenant deems the property uninhabitable and informs the landlord of the condition
    C. eviction notice that was served upon a tenant with a material defect
    D. illegitimate eviction, such as evicting the wrong occupant or eviction executed prior to proper service upon the tenant

18.____

19. If a stipulation is made between the parties in a special proceeding, other than a stipulation solely to adjourn or stay the proceeding, and either the petitioner or the respondent is not represented by counsel, the court shall

    A. fully describe the terms of the stipulation to that party
    B. accept the stipulation and record the stipulation in a deposition hearing
    C. reject the stipulation unless expressly consented to by both parties in writing
    D. continue with the hearing

19.____

20. An "undertenant" is also considered a(n)

    A. subtenant   B. overtenant   C. lessor   D. assignor

20.____

21. Upon proper proof of the existence of a condition that constructively evict the tenant from a portion of the premises that is likely to become dangerous to life, health or safety, the court before which the case is pending may _____ proceedings to dispossess the tenant for non-payment of rent.

    A. adjourn   B. joinder   C. stay   D. rectify

21.____'

22. If service is mailed to the respondent for the notice of petition, service is deemed complete after which of the following events?
    A. Filing of the notice
    B. Filing the proof of service
    C. Commencement of the action
    D. Start of trial

22.____

Questions 23-25.

DIRECTIONS: Questions 23 through 25 are to be answered on the basis of the following passage.

In a proceeding to recover the possession of premises in the City of New York occupied for dwelling purposes upon the ground that the occupant is holding over and continuing in possession of the premises after the expiration of his term and without permission of the landlord may stay the issuance of a warrant and also stay an execution to collect the costs of proceeding for a period of not more than __1__ months, if it appears that the premises are used __2__ purposes; that the application is made in good faith; that the applicant cannot within the neighborhood secure suitable premises similar to those occupied by him and that he made __3__ efforts to secure such other premises, or that by reason of other facts it would occasion extreme hardship to him or his family if the stay were not granted.

23. Please fill in the number of months for Blank #1.
    A. one   B. two   C. six   D. eight

23.____

24. Please fill in the correct word for Blank #2.
    A. illegal   B. dwelling   C. illicit   D. residential

24.____

25. Please fill in the correct phrase for Blank #3.
    A. due and reasonable
    B. fair and reasonable
    C. reasonable and due
    D. reasonable and fair

25.____

KEY (CORRECT ANSWERS)

1.	C
2.	A
3.	D
4.	D
5.	B

6.	B
7.	D
8.	A
9.	C
10.	C

11.	D
12.	D
13.	A
14.	B
15.	B

16.	D
17.	A
18.	A
19.	A
20.	A

21.	C
22.	B
23.	C
24.	B
25.	A

EXAMINATION SECTION

TEST 1

DIRECTIONS: Each question or incomplete statement is followed by several suggested
answers or completions. Select the one that BEST answers the question or
completes the statement. *PRINT THE LETTER OF THE CORRECT ANSWER
IN THE SPACE AT THE RIGHT.*

1.   A "person acting as a parent" is defined as a person who has physical custody   1.____
or has had physical custody for a period of _____ months, including any
temporary absence, within one year immediately before the commencement of
a child custody proceeding and has been awarded legal custody by a court or
claims a right to legal custody under the law of this state.
    A. four concurrent   B. six consecutive
    C. eight consecutive   D. ten concurrent

2.   Samantha and her son, Gary, spend the summer months with her parents   2.____
in North Dakota. During the school year, however, Samantha returns to New
York. Samantha's child custody case with Gary's father has been ongoing in
New York for over eight months.
Should the custody case be heard in North Dakota or New York?
    A. North Dakota, since Gary spends a significant amount of time there
        during the year
    B. North Dakota, unless Gary's father objects for reasonable cause
    C. North Dakota, but only if Samantha petitions the court in New York and
        obtains the required permissions
    D. New York

3.   If a court declines to exercise jurisdiction over a child custody hearing because   3.____
it determines that a court of a different state is a more appropriate forum, the
court is said to have raised the issue of a(n)
    A. indeterminate venue   B. inconvenient venue
    C. inconvenient forum   D. indeterminate jurisdiction

4.   A warrant to take physical custody of a child may be executed in which of   4.____
the following scenarios?
    A. Imminent risk of suffering serious physical harm
    B. Removal from the state
    C. Imminent risk of death
    D. All of the above

5.   Even though the Family Court does not have jurisdiction to modify a child   5.____
custody determination, it may issue a temporary order to enforce which of the
following?
    A. Visitation schedule made by another state
    B. Permanent child custody order finalized in another state
    C. Alimony payment schedule finalized in another state
    D. Child support payment arrangement schedule finalized in another state

6. According to the New York Domestic Relations Law, a law enforcement   6.____
officer may take any lawful action _____ necessary to locate a child.
    A. legally   B. reasonably   C. absolutely   D. willfully

Questions 7-10.

DIRECTIONS: Questions 7 through 10 are to be answered on the basis of the following facts.

Mike is planning on moving to New York with his two children, Emma and Courtney. Mike wants to ensure that the child custody determination that was finalized in Virginia between he and his ex-wife, Jill, is recognized in New York.

7. What can Mike do to ensure the courts in New York are notified of the final   7.____
order?
    A. Stop by his local courthouse and speak to a clerk
    B. Send a certified letter to the local police station to notify them that the order is in place
    C. Request to register the child custody determination in New York State
    D. E-mail the Manhattan Family Court division requesting a personal meeting to outline the order

8. Assume that Mike has properly informed the New York courts of the child   8.____
custody determination in Virginia. Jill is informed of Mike's actions by notice, but disagrees that the child custody agreement is final.
Can Jill contest the filing?
    A. Yes, but only if she receives Mike's consent to contest
    B. Yes, but only if their children, Emma and Courtney, live with Jill at least full-time
    C. Yes, she may contest and request a hearing to contest the validity of the determination within twenty days of service of notice
    D. No

9. Under what grounds can Jill contest the validity of Mike's filing?   9.____
    A. The court in Virginia that presided over the hearing did not have jurisdiction over the child custody determination.
    B. The order Mike filed was vacated, stayed or modified by a court with proper jurisdiction.
    C. Jill was not properly served.
    D. Any of the above

10. If Jill disagrees that the child custody agreement is final, but ignores the   10.____
service of notice, what are the consequences?
    A. Jill's rights to Emma and Courtney are deemed waived.
    B. Mike's filing is confirmed as a matter of law and Jill will be notified of this confirmation by service.
    C. Jill will need to make her late request in person in New York.
    D. Mike can formally request the court to waive Jill's parental rights.

11. Suppose that Amy had legal and physical custody over her niece, Rebecca, for the first three years of Rebecca's life. Amy is moving to Wyoming for work and consequently can no longer maintain physical custody of Rebecca. Can the courts depose, or take, Amy's testimony for the custody hearings over the phone?

11.____

    A. Yes, if Amy lives in another state and the record is preserved appropriately

    B. No, because Amy is not otherwise incapacitated and is capable of making herself available to a New York court

    C. No, unless the court receives permission from the successor legal guardian

    D. No

12. Unless the court enters a temporary emergency order, the enforcing court may not stay an order enforcing a child custody determination pending

12.____

    A. requests otherwise   B. adjudication

    C. appeal   D. abdication

13. In a lengthy and contentious child custody case, John and Liz have accumulated enormous legal bills and other debts. Liz is ultimately the prevailing party in the case.
What costs can the court impose upon John?

13.____

    A. None, as Liz cannot be reimbursed for legal fees in a child custody case

    B. Liz's legal fees only

    C. Necessary and reasonable expenses incurred including attorney's fees and travel expenses

    D. All of Liz's expenses incurred during the hearings and trial, including her meals

14. A child custody determination was finalized between Amal and Jack in Lebanon. Jack petitions the court to vacate the order as it is invalid in New York. Jack ultimately would like to come to a new agreement between he and Amal regarding visitation.
The court will treat the order from the Lebanese court as

14.____

    A. not binding, since neither Jack nor Amal live in Lebanon anymore

    B. binding, or otherwise as if the Lebanese court was a part of the United States

    C. binding, for a period of 90 days

    D. binding, for a period of up to one year or until both parents establish New York residency, whichever is longer

15. Jamal is having difficulty getting along with his son's mother, Tanya. Jamal tells his friend, Chris, who happens to be an assistant district attorney, that Tanya prevents Jamal from seeing his son. Can Chris represent Jamal in a child custody modification hearing against Tanya?

15.____'

    A. No

    B. Not unless Tanya consents

    C. Not unless the court consents

    D. Yes, but only in a non-binding arbitration forum

16. The New York Domestic Relations Law does not apply to which two situations involving a child?   16.____
    A. Emergency medical care and surrogacy
    B. Adoption and guardianship
    C. College education expenses and surrogacy
    D. Emergency medical care and adoption

17. Baby Jane was abandoned on Interstate 95 on the New York side of the New Jersey border. After being discovered, the Manhattan Family Court ordered the baby to the custody of the New York Department of Child Services. Baby Jane's father, a New Jersey resident, discovered the baby had been abducted and demanded the baby be returned to his care, arguing the Manhattan Court did not have jurisdiction over the matter.   17.____
Did the Manhattan Court have jurisdiction?
    A. No, because Baby Jane's closest kin is an out-of-state resident
    B. No, because Baby Jane could have been left on the New Jersey side of the border
    C. Yes, because Baby Jane was found on the New York side of the border
    D. Yes, because Baby Jane was abandoned in the state

18. What issue, according to the New York Domestic Relations Law, must be handled expeditiously and given priority on the court's calendar in child custody cases if raised?   18.____
    A. Alimony   B. Jurisdiction
    C. Registration of final orders   D. Guardianship

19. A child custody proceeding that pertains to an Indian child is not subject to Article 5-A of the New York Domestic Relations Law to the extent that is governed by the   19.____
    A. Indian Sovereignty provisions
    B. Twentieth Amendment
    C. Indian Child Welfare Act
    D. Child Welfare and Indian Commitments Act

20. Before a child custody determination can be made, which two processes must be completed?   20.____
Service of notice and
    A. an opportunity to be heard   B. establishment of jurisdiction
    C. filing of a complaint   D. filing of a subpoena

21. Cynthia has physical custody over her daughter with her ex-wife, Mary. For child custody hearings, is Cynthia required to appear to the hearings with her daughter?   21.____
    A. The court may require Cynthia to appear in person with the child.
    B. Cynthia is always required to appear in person with the child.
    C. Cynthia is only allowed to appear with the child if Mary is given proper notice of the child's appearance
    D. Cynthia is not required under any circumstances to appear, even if the court requests so.

Questions 22-23.

DIRECTIONS: Questions 22 and 23 are to be answered on the basis of the following facts.

Sean and Erica want to modify their child custody determination. Sean and Erica lived in Florida for eight years before moving to New York. Their daughter, Brenda, was conceived in Florida and is now five years old, living with Erica full time.

22. The FIRST step in modifying a child custody determination is to   22.____
   A. serve Sean and Erica with proper notice and demand Erica appear in court with Brenda
   B. evaluate the current order to determine whether custody is split equally between both parents
   C. determine whether a proceeding to enforce a child custody determination has begun in another state
   D. allow Sean and Erica to make a formal request for modification by entering motion

23. If a proceeding to enforce a child custody determination has begun in another   23.____
   state, the court in New York may do which of the following?
   A. Continue with the modification hearing under conditions the court deems appropriate
   B. Ignore the other state's determination regardless of the outcome
   C. Request that both parties return to Florida to finish the proceeding
   D. Require that the child appear in court and ask the child which court's decision will be in her best interest

24. In the first pleading to the court, a party must know which of the following   24.____
   information?
   A. Child's present address
   B. Places where the child has lived in the last five years
   C. The names and addresses of the individuals that lived with the child in the last five years
   D. All of the above

25. In a child custody determination, each party has an affirmative duty to   25.____
   A. inform the court of any proceeding that will affect the current proceeding
   B. notify the court of a change in the child's mental or physical condition
   C. inform the court of a potential change in address for either party
   D. notify the court of a change in the party's legal representation

KEY (CORRECT ANSWERS)

1.	B		11.	A
2.	D		12.	C
3.	C		13.	C
4.	D		14.	B
5.	A		15.	A
6.	B		16.	D
7.	C		17.	D
8.	D		18.	B
9.	D		19.	C
10.	B		20.	A

21.	A
22.	C
23.	A
24.	D
25.	A

———

EXAMINATION SECTION

TEST 1

DIRECTIONS: Each question or incomplete statement is followed by several suggested answers or completions. Select the one that BEST answers the question or completes the statement. *PRINT THE LETTER OF THE CORRECT ANSWER IN THE SPACE AT THE RIGHT.*

1. A putative father is generally defined as
   A. a man who claims or is alleged to be the father of a child whom is not married to the child's mother at the time of birth
   B. a man who is the father of the child but does not sign the birth certificate
   C. a man who is the alleged father of the child based on the fact that he is married to the child's mother at the time of the child's birth
   D. the child's presumptive father at law

   1.____

2. Which of the following people are entitled to notice to proceedings?
   A. Person identified as the father in a sworn written statement by the mother
   B. Any person recorded on the birth certificate as the child's father
   C. Any person adjudicated by the court as the child's father
   D. All of the above

   2.____

3. James is listed as the father on Bella's birth certificate, but has been twice convicted of rape in the second degree. Bella is the result of rape.
   Is James entitled to receive notice of Bella's guardianship hearing?
   A. Yes, because he is the legal father
   B. Yes, because he signed the birth certificate as the father
   C. Yes, unless Bella's mother objects to James receiving notice
   D. No

   3.____

4. A surrender for adoption executed by a parent, parents or guardian who is in foster care shall be executed only before a judge of the _____ court.
   A. surrogates   B. family   C. civil   D. probate

   4.____

5. Bill and Joel are both possible fathers to Diana's newborn baby. Diana only invited Bill to the hospital and he subsequently signed the birth certificate. After the birth, however, Bill lost contact with Diana. Joel has taken care of the baby since the child's birth.
   Who is the presumed father of Diana's baby?
   A. Bill
   B. Joel
   C. Whomever Diana designates as the father
   D. Whichever man Diana names in a sworn written statement as the father

   5.____

6. Which of the following is NOT listed as finding of legislative intent?   6._____
    A. Is it desirable for children to grow up with a normal family life in a permanent home
    B. It is generally desirable for the child to remain with or be returned to the birth parent because the child's need for a normal family life will usually best be met in the home of its birth parent, and that parents are entitled to bring up their own children unless the best interests of the child would be thereby endangered
    C. It is desirable for the child to live in one residence until the age of majority with both parents
    D. The state's first obligation is to help the family with services to prevent its break-up or to reunite if the child has already left home

7. The term "child" shall mean a person under the age of _____ years.   7._____
    A. sixteen   B. eighteen   C. twenty-one   D. twenty-five

Questions 8-9.

DIRECTIONS: Questions 8 and 9 are to be answered on the basis of the following passage from the New York Social Services Law.

    "Permanently neglected child" shall mean a child who is in the care of an authorized agency and whose parent or custodian has failed for a period of either at least _____ or fifteen out of the most recent twenty-two months following the date such child came into the care of an authorized agency substantially and continuously or repeatedly to maintain contact with or plan for the future of the child, although physically and financially able to do so, notwithstanding the agency's diligent efforts to encourage and strengthen the parental relationship when such efforts will not be detrimental to the best interests of the child."

8. Please fill in the blank.   8._____
    A. one year   B. two years   C. three years   D. four years

9. The New York City agency tasked with ensuring the welfare of children and their families is called   9._____
    A. State of Children's Welfare Agency
    B. Administration for Children's Services
    C. Department of Child Welfare
    D. Agency of Family Services and Children's Needs

10. Rachel was placed in the home of her adoptive parents last July. What date is used to record the placement?   10._____
    A. The date of the adoption agreement will be recorded in a bound volume maintained by the agency along with the names of the adoptive parents
    B. The date the child moves into the home of the adoptive parents
    C. The date the child agrees to move into the home of the adoptive parents
    D. The date the adoptive parents agree to adopt a child

11. Surrenders must be written and can be either _____.
    A. jurisdictional or extra-territorial   B. judicial or extra-judicial
    C. judicial or ex-parte   B. jurisdictional or extra-judicial

11.____

12. In cases where a surrender is not executed and acknowledged before a judge, the authorized agency to which the child was surrendered shall file an application for approval in which court?
    A. The court in which the adoption proceeding is expected to be filed or, if not known, the family or surrogates court in the county in which the agency has its principal office
    B. The family or surrogates court in the county where the child was born
    C. The family or surrogates court in the county where the child was raised for the first eighteen months of life
    D. The court in which the adoption proceeding was already filed

12.____

13. Which of the following is NOT required to be stated in the affidavit accompanying the surrender?
    A. Date, time, and place where the surrender was executed and acknowledged
    B. A written statement that the parent was provided with ha copy of the surrender
    C. A statement that the parent executed and acknowledged the surrender
    D. A statement that the child executed and acknowledged the surrender

13.____

14. Katie is fifteen years old. Before Katie can be committed to the guardianship and custody of foster care, which of the following is MOST likely to occur at a court proceeding?
    A. The child care agency will likely provide proof of the likelihood the child will be adopted.
    B. The court may, in its discretion, consider Katie's wishes in determining who would be promoted by the commitment or guardianship
    C. The child's parents' wishes will be a strong consideration and the court will author a separate opinion on the matter
    D. The potential adoptive parents will be deposed so that a sworn, written statement can accompany Katie's permanent file with the court

14.____

Questions 15-16.

DIRECTIONS: Questions 15 and 16 are to be answered on the basis of the following passage.

    The date of the child's entry into foster care is the earlier of __1__ days after the date on which the child was removed from the home or the date the child was found by a court to be an abused or neglected child pursuant to Article 10 of the __2__ Act.

15. Fill in the number of days for Blank #1.
    A. 20   B. 30   C. 60   D. 80

15.____

16. Fill in the name of the act for Blank #2.
    A. Family Court   B. Child Welfare
    C. Emancipated Child   D. Surrogates

16.____

17. Carol and Tom want to sign the surrender to terminate their parental rights of their child, but cannot afford an attorney.
May they request the court to appoint a lawyer on their behalf free of charge?
    A. No, because Carol and Tom must pay for their own attorney
    B. No, because Carol and Tom are initiating the proceeding
    C. No, because Carol and Tom do not need an attorney to execute a surrender
    D. Yes

17.____

18. What rights does a parent forfeit in a surrender, unless different terms are specifically agreed to?
    A. The right to visit the child
    B. The right to write to or otherwise learn about the child
    C. The right to speak to the child
    D. All of the above

18.____

19. Where will the surrender be recorded?
In the office of the county clerk where the
    A. surrender is executed   B. child was born
    C. biological parents reside   D. adoptive parents reside

19.____

20. Can the executed surrender which places a child in the custody of an authorized agency also be used to commit the same child to the custody of the child's maternal grandparents?
    A. Yes, because they are in the same bloodline
    B. Yes, because a surrender operates to place the child anywhere the child is safe
    C. No, because the surrender is deemed to only apply to the commitment to the authorized agency; any other document is not deemed a surrender
    D. No, because the surrender cannot be re-executed or re-signed after the authorized agency signs the document

20.____

21. May the court disapprove a surrender?
    A. No, once executed the court cannot nullify the document
    B. No, because the court does not have the authority to disapprove a surrender
    C. Yes, and if the court does so the surrender is deemed resigned
    D. Yes, and if the court does so the surrender is deemed nullified

21.____

22. The _____ is a state level legal option for unmarried males to document through a notary public any female they engage in intercourse, for the purpose of retaining parental rights for any child they may father.
    A. pool of potential fathers   B. putative father registry
    C. unmarried father registry   D. putative biological dad registry

22.____

23. What is the purpose of a permanency hearing?　　　　　　　　　　　　　23.____
    A. To determine in which county a child should reside
    B. To determine the best interests of the child and develop a permanent plan for the placement of the child
    C. To develop a plan to determine the best interests of the child in three-year increments
    D. To schedule parties to testify on behalf of the child

24. When must the first permanency hearing be scheduled relative to when the　　24.____
    place in the custody of the authorized agency, and thereafter how often must they continue thereafter?
    _____ months after the child is placed and every _____ thereafter.
    A. 8; 6 months　　　B. 6; month　　　C. 9; 5 months　　D. 10; 2 months

25. Which of the following are possible options for disposition of the child after　　25.____
    the fact-finding hearing?
    A. Releasing the child to the parents or guardian with supervision from the child protective agency
    B. Placing the child in foster care for a period of time
    C. Suspended judgment
    D. All of the above

KEY (CORRECT ANSWERS)

1.	A		11.	B
2.	D		12.	A
3.	D		13.	D
4.	B		14.	B
5.	A		15.	C
6.	C		16.	A
7.	B		17.	D
8.	A		18.	D
9.	B		19.	A
10.	A		20.	C

21.	D
22.	B
23.	B
24.	A
25.	D

EXAMINATION SECTION

TEST 1

DIRECTIONS: Each question or incomplete statement is followed by several suggested answers or completions. Select the one that BEST answers the question or completes the statement. *PRINT THE LETTER OF THE CORRECT ANSWER IN THE SPACE AT THE RIGHT.*

1. Leandra's Law, codified at 1192-2(b) is BEST defined as prohibiting driving
   A. while intoxicated
   B. while intoxicated with another person in the car
   C. while intoxicated with a child under the age of 15 in the car
   D. with a child under the age of 15 in the car

   1.____

2. A DWAI violation is the abbreviation for driving
   A. while ability impaired   B. while ability impugned
   C. with aggravated impairment   D. while aggravated impairment

   2.____

3. What is the blood alcohol level that, once reached or exceeded, definitely determines a violation of intoxication?
   A. .06   B. .07   C. .08   D. .09

   3.____

Questions 4-6.

DIRECTIONS: Questions 4 through 6 are to be answered on the basis of the following fact pattern.

   Three years ago, Jamal was convicted of driving while intoxicated and paid a fine of $350. After celebrating his co-worker's retirement at a local bar, Jamal is pulled over during a routine traffic stop and found, once again, to be operating a vehicle under the influence of alcohol.

4. What is the MAXIMUM fine Jamal may be ordered to pay?
   A. $300   B. $350   C. $500   D. $750

   4.____

5. What is the MAXIMUM term of imprisonment Jamal may face and in what facility?
   A. 15 days, penitentiary or county jail
   B. 30 days, penitentiary or county jail
   C. 45 days, penitentiary or county jail
   D. 60 days, penitentiary or county jail

   5.____

6. Assume that Jamal is convicted a third time of driving under the influence of alcohol. He will be found guilty of a
   A. violation   B. misdemeanor
   C. felony   D. aggravated assault

   6.____

7. Which of the following may the court require as a condition for a sentence in violation of the Vehicle and Traffic Law?   7._____
   A. Attend a single session of the Victim Impact Program
   B. Recreate the scene of the crime
   C. Pay restitution directly to the victim's family, if one exists
   D. Permanent incarceration

8. Samantha is worried that her license may be suspended because she has driven without car insurance for over a year.   8._____
   Which of the following parties has the authority to revoke or suspend her license?
   A. County judge
   B. Superintendent of state police
   C. Commissioner of Motor Vehicles
   D. Any of the above

9. Katie was given an appearance ticket after she was caught driving over 120 miles per hour outside of Syracuse. Police Officer Lee believed he stumbled on a drag racing ring. Katie, however, never appeared in court.   9._____
   What is the likely punishment?
   A. Imprisonment for no less than three years
   B. Imprisonment for no less than five years
   C. Mandatory alcohol rehabilitation program
   D. Suspension for failure to answer an appearance ticket

Questions 10-11.

DIRECTIONS: Questions 10-11 are to be answered on the basis of the following fact pattern.

Daniel owed taxes for the 2014 tax year. He set up a payment plan with the New York Department of Taxation and Finance, but failed to make a single payment.

10. Pursuant to NYVTL, which of the following is the Commissioner of Taxation and Finance (or his or her agent) empowered to do?   10._____
   A. Suspend Daniel's license
   B. Place a metered tracker on Daniel's motor vehicle which will only allow Daniel to drive a mile or so in any direction before automatically powering down
   C. Revoke Daniel's car registration
   D. Ban anyone in Daniel's household from operating his car for personal or business use until the taxes are paid in full

11. After being contacted about his punishment for failure to pay taxes, Daniel sues the Commissioner of Taxation and Finance. Daniel alleges that because he is unable to drive his vehicle he cannot get to work and will lose his job.   11._____
   Is Daniel likely to prevail in a lawsuit against the Commissioner?

Daniel will
- A. be successful since he needs a car for work
- B. not be successful if he cannot prove his car is his only mode of transportation
- C. not be successful because he was put on notice he owed back taxes
- D. not be successful because the NYVTL specifically provides that no person shall right the right to commence a court action against the Commissioner for this purpose

Questions 12-14.

DIRECTIONS: Questions 12 through 14 are to be answered on the basis of the following fact pattern.

Ed knows that his friend Tom has had his license suspended at least ten times. Tom has failed to appear or pay for multiple tickets and each suspended license violation occurred on a different day. Tom asks to borrow Ed's car to drive from Buffalo to Brooklyn to visit his girlfriend, and Ed agreed.

12. What crime is Ed guilty of?   12._____
    Facilitating unlicensed operation of a
    A. motorcycle   B. motor vehicle
    C. motor vehicle as a misdemeanor   D. motor vehicle in the first degree

13. The LEAST Ed will pay in a fine is _____ in addition to a possible sentence   13._____
    of _____ and a term of imprisonment.
    A. $1,000; probation   B. $2,000; probation
    C. $3,000; probation   D. $5,000; restitution

14. The crime Ed is guilty of is classified as a   14._____
    A. minor infraction   B. major infraction
    C. Class A felony   D. Class E felony

15. Amy's brother, Bob, was visiting her in Hudson. He parked his SUV in a   15._____
    no standing zone and his car was towed. Amy attempted to get the car
    released, but she did not have the proper documentation to do so.
    An impounded vehicle shall not be released unless the person who redeems it
    furnishes satisfactory evidence of _____ and financial security.
    A. license   B. rehabilitation
    C. registration   D. insurance

16. Police officers saw Travis selling drugs out of his car. After Travis was   16._____
    arrested, his car was impounded. Travis's car was initially held as evidence,
    but the assistant district attorney no longer needs the car as evidence. Travis
    wants to claim his car, but the car cannot be released until he presents a(n)
    A. affidavit from the arresting officers
    B. release from the assistant district attorney
    C. sworn testimony from the alleged drug buyers
    D. bail bond

17. Aggravated failure to answer appearance tickets or pay fines will be imposed on a person who has at least _____ separate suspensions, imposed on at least _____ separate dates.   17.____
    A. 10; 20   B. 20; 20   C. 15; 15   D. 15; 20

18. Assume that Natalie is convicted of aggravated failure to answer appearance tickets or pay fines.   18.____
What is her MAXIMUM possible punishment?
    A. Fine of $500, imprisonment of 180 days, or both
    B. Fine of $100, imprisonment of one year, or both
    C. Fine of $500 only
    D. Fine of imprisonment of 180 days only

Questions 19-20.

DIRECTIONS: Questions 19 and 20 are to be answered on the basis of the following fact pattern.

Robert has let his daughter, Veronica, borrow his car, even though he knew Veronica's license was suspended. She was only driving a short distance and promised to be home in a half hour. Instead, Veronica was pulled over and arrested for driving with a suspended license.

19. What type of crime has Robert committed?   19.____
    A. Felony   B. Serious traffic infraction
    C. Traffic infraction   D. Misdemeanor

20. Assuming that Robert continues to allow Veronica to borrow his car, even though her license remains suspended, Robert is availing himself of which of the following crimes?   20.____
Facilitating aggravated unlicensed operation of a motor
    A. vehicle   B. vehicle in the second degree
    C. vehicle with felonious intent   D. vehicle with aggravated intent

Questions 21-22.

DIRECTIONS: Questions 21 and 22 are to be answered on the basis of the following fact pattern.

Dave failed to renew his medical certification for his commercial driver's license (CDL).

21. Within sixty days of Dave's certification status being changed to "non-certified," the Commissioner will do which of the following?   21.____
    A. Revoke Dave's CDL completely.
    B. Downgrade Dave's CDL to a learner's permit.
    C. Downgrade Dave's CDL to a non-commercial driver's license.
    D. Suspend Dave's license indefinitely.

22. Suppose that Dave simply forgot to submit the required medical variance documentation at the intervals imposed by law.
What will the consequences be?
   A. Dave's license will still be revoked.
   B. Dave's license will still be suspended indefinitely.
   C. Dave will be able to retain his CDL but on a part-time basis.
   D. The Commissioner will follow the same action as if the certification was not renewed.

22._____

23. Adam is charged with operating a commercial vehicle without a CDL. Adam claims that he has a CDL, but neglected to carry it with him at the time he was arrested.
What must Adam produce evidence that he had a valid CDL in order to be dismissed of the charges?
   A. Before his appearance in court
   B. Before the trial begins
   C. Before an attorney is selected
   D. Before the charges are finalized

23._____

24. Peter was convicted of homicide arising out of operation of a motor vehicle in Georgia.
Can Peter's license in his home state of New York, which was obtained before he moved to Georgia, be revoked?
   A. No, because he is a Georgia resident and his New York license is unaffected
   B. No, because the incident did not occur in New York
   C. Yes, because Peter is a New York native
   D. Yes

24._____

25. Emily approached a busy traffic intersection and discovered that traffic agents were directing traffic because the light was out. Emily became enraged that the traffic agents were not allowing her to make a right turn. Emily exited her vehicle and attacked the traffic enforcement agent. Emily was convicted of assault in the third degree.
Emily's license will be suspended for a period of not less than _____ days or more than _____ days.
   A. 30; 60   B. 45; 60   C. 30; 180   D. 60; 180

25._____

KEY (CORRECT ANSWERS)

1.	C		11.	D
2.	A		12.	D
3.	C		13.	A
4.	D		14.	D
5.	B		15.	C
6.	B		16.	B
7.	A		17.	B
8.	D		18.	A
9.	D		19.	C
10.	A		20.	B

21.	C
22.	D
23.	A
24.	D
25.	C

EXAMINATION SECTION

TEST 1

DIRECTIONS: Each question or incomplete statement is followed by several suggested answers or completions. Select the one that BEST answers the question or completes the statement. *PRINT THE LETTER OF THE CORRECT ANSWER IN THE SPACE AT THE RIGHT.*

1. Forcible touching is classified as a   1.____
   A. Class A Misdemeanor   B. Class B Misdemeanor
   C. Class C Misdemeanor   D. Felony

2. Inciting to riot is classified as a   2.____
   A. Class B Misdemeanor   B. Grand Felony
   C. Class A Misdemeanor   D. Felony

3. A misdemeanor is defined as an offense, other than a traffic infraction,   3.____
   for which a sentence to a term of imprisonment in excess of _____ day(s) may
   be imposed, but for which a sentence to a term of imprisonment in excess of
   _____ year(s) cannot be imposed.
   A. six; one   B. five; one   C. fifteen; two   D. fifteen; one

4. Fortune telling, falser personation and creating a hazard are all classified as   4.____
   A. felonies   B. misdemeanors
   C. violations   d. minor infractions

5. A motorist, Jan, ran a traffic light at the intersection of Buffalo Avenue and   5.____
   Rochester Way. Jan is afraid that she has committed a misdemeanor because
   she was applying lipstick as she was driving and nearly hit a fire hydrant after
   she realized she blew the light.
   What is Jan guilty of committing?
   A. A traffic infraction, which is not a misdemeanor
   B. A traffic infraction, also known as a misdemeanor
   C. A Class A Misdemeanor
   D. A Class B Misdemeanor

6. If James is sentenced to a period of probation, which of the following is MOST   6.____
   likely to accompany the sentence?
   A. The conditions of the sentence, including not leaving the state or
      abstaining from alcohol
   B. The address of James's probation officer and how to get there from
      James's home address
   C. The address of the judge presiding over James's probation hearing
   D. The jury instructions which were given to the jury in James's trial

2 (#1)

7. For a Class A Misdemeanor, other than sexual assault, what is the MAXIMUM period of probation?
    A. Two years   B. Three years C. Four years   D. Five years

7.____

8. For a Class A Misdemeanor sexual assault, the period of probation is _____ years.
    A. four   B. five   C. six   D. seven

8.____

9. The conditions of probation or conditional discharge shall be determined by the
    A. jury
    C. court
    B. parole officer
    D. prosecuting attorney

9.____

10. When imposing a sentence of probation or conditional discharge, the court may consider restitution and require which of the following?
    A. The defendant avoid injurious habits
    B. Work in a respectable retail environment
    C. Study to become a nurse or other healthcare professional
    D. Participate in an alcohol or substance abuse program of the defendant's family's choosing

10.____

11. If Bill has been convicted of a traffic violation which caused the serious physical injury or death of another person, which of the following may the court require as a condition of probation?
    A. Anger management course
    B. Motor vehicle accident prevention course
    C. Defense driving course
    D. Motor skills and research methodology course

11.____

12. Unconditional discharge may be imposed for a felony as long as the court sets forth the
    A. actions the defendant has taken not to repeat his or her illicit behavior
    B. reasons for its actions
    C. skills or other licenses of the defendant
    D. other crimes the defendant is alleged to have committed

12.____

13. Pursuant to Article 65 of the New York Penal Law, as a condition of probation for sex offenders, the court may impose which of the following additional conditions?
    Reasonable limitation on
    A. food obtained from local grocery stores
    B. his or her use of the internet
    C. the amount of money expended on gaming devices
    D. extracurricular activities

13.____

14. Pursuant to Article 70 of the New York Penal Law, the court must inquire that parents of a minor committed to the Department of Corrections grant the minor the capacity to consent to
    A. routine dental treatment
    B. mental health treatment, but only if needed
    C. routine medical treatment, but only if required
    D. routine medical, dental, and mental health services and treatment

14.____

15. If a defendant is given a sentence of life imprisonment without parole, where will the defendant be committed?
    A. Custody of the City Department of Corrections
    B. Custody of the State Department of Corrections
    C. Custody of the State Department of Corrections and community supervisions for the remainder of the life of the defendant
    D. Rikers Island

15.____

16. A court sentence may run
    A. concurrently or consecutively
    B. concurrently or contemporaneously
    C. consecutively or respectively
    D. concurrently or coincidentally

16.____

17. Rich has been convicted of a felony murder of his cousin, Eric. While released on $5,000,000 bail, he is alleged to have murdered a shopkeeper in Albany. Rich is convicted of 25 years for the murder of Eric and 30 years for the murder of the shopkeeper. The sentences will run _____ for a total of _____ years incarceration.
    A. consecutively; 30   B. consecutively; 55
    C. concurrently; 55   D. contemporaneously; 30

17.____

Questions 18-19.

DIRECTIONS: Questions 18 and 19 are to be answered on the basis of the following information.

Paul and Amy have filed for divorce. Amy has been granted $450 per month in alimony, but Paul has not paid in over seven months. Amy has been living with her sister, Meredith, for over a year and because Paul has not paid Amy alimony, Amy has not been able to pay Meredith rent.

18. May Meredith petition the court to enforce the judgment against Paul?
    A. Yes, because Meredith is materially affected by Paul's nonpayment.
    B. Yes, because Meredith is Amy's sibling and thereby part of her nuclear family.
    C. No, because Amy has only been living with Meredith for a part of Paul's period of noncompliance with the court order.
    D. No.

18.____

19. A petition to enforce the judgment against Paul would need to be brought   19.____
    in which court?
    A. State of New York
    B. Supreme Court or a Court of Competent Jurisdiction
    C. Manhattan Family Court
    D. Criminal Court

20. During a support proceeding in family court, which of the following will   20.____
    MOST likely be accompanied to a sworn statement of net worth?
    A. Pay stubs from the year the individual earned the most, and the least,
       amount of money
    B. Tax return without any accompanying documentation
    C. W-2 tax and wage statements
    D. Current paycheck stub, most recently filed income tax returns, and the
       W-2 wage and income statements

Questions 21-22.

DIRECTIONS: Questions 21 and 22 are to be answered on the basis of the following
information.

Candace filed for divorce from Jason last January. Jason and Candace have agreed to a
support arrangement between themselves. Jason will pay Candace $300 per month, except
during the summer months of June, July, and August, when Jason is temporarily out of work
due to his occupation as a teaching paraprofessional.

21. What must Candace produce to the Court for approval?   21.____
    A. The agreement itself which must be reduced to writing
    B. Jason's bank statements, proving he can afford to pay $300 per month
    C. Jason's pay stubs, proving he is customarily out of work during the
       summer months
    D. The agreement is automatically approved given that the parties arranged
       the details themselves.

22. Who will approve the document Candace produces to the Court?   22.____
    A. The jury
    B. The attorney(s) representing Jason
    C. The court only
    D. The court or support magistrate

23. A summons was served on Jamal requiring him to appear for a family   23.____
    court proceeding involving his sister and father. Jamal failed to appear. The
    court may issue a(n) _____ directing that Jamal be arrested and brought before
    the court.
    A. indictment   B. subpoena   C. issue   D. warrant

24. With respect to the finding of the court and according to the New York Family Court Act, the effect of the issuance of a temporary order of protection is
    A. essentially a finding of guilt
    B. admission by the parties that the defendant will harm his or herself and others
    C. not a finding of wrongdoing
    D. a precursor to a felony conviction

    24.____

25. Assume that a warrant is issued for Daniel in Richmond County. Where will Daniel be taken if he is taken into custody in Suffolk County?
    A. A family judge in Suffolk County
    B. A family judge in Richmond County
    C. A family judge in New York City
    D. The Supreme Court

    25.____

KEY (CORRECT ANSWERS)

1.	A		11.	B
2.	C		12.	B
3.	D		13.	B
4.	B		14.	D
5.	A		15.	C
6.	A		16.	A
7.	B		17.	B
8.	C		18.	D
9.	C		19.	B
10.	A		20.	D

21.	A
22.	D
23.	D
24.	C
25.	A

TEST 2

DIRECTIONS: Each question or incomplete statement is followed by several suggested answers or completions. Select the one that BEST answers the question or completes the statement. *PRINT THE LETTER OF THE CORRECT ANSWER IN THE SPACE AT THE RIGHT.*

1.   Which of the following is a defendant the LEAST likely to hear when being brought before the court pursuant to a warrant?
He or she will be
    A. informed of the contents of the petition
    B. given the opportunity to present witnesses
    C. advised of their right to counsel
    D. given the option of having the public hear the case

1.____

2.   If the initial return of a summons or warrant is before a judge of the court, when support is an issue, the judge must make a(n) _____ order, either temporary or permanent with regard to support.
    A. reasonable   B. timely   C. immediate   D. seasoned

2.____

3.   Kevin has petitioned the court for temporary child support for his daughter, Maddie, from his ex-wife Katie. Katie objects to any determination of child support even though Maddie lives with Kevin full time. Katie argues that Kevin makes more money than her and there is no outstanding emergency or other issue that warrants the need for child support.
May the court make an order for temporary child support?
    A. No, because Kevin earns more than Katie.
    B. No, because there is no impending emergency or issue warranting support.
    C. Yes, because Maddie lives with Kevin.
    D. Yes, because the court may make an order for temporary support sufficient to meet the needs of the child without a showing of immediate need.

3.____

4.   Dante is deemed an "eligible offender" because of his prior conviction of armed robbery. An eligible offender is an individual
    A. with a prior conviction
    B. with a prior conviction of a felony with a deadly weapon
    C. who has a prior conviction of an offense, but has not been convicted of more than once of a felony
    D. with at least one prior felony conviction

4.____

5.   How many votes are required from the State Board of Parole to issue a certificate of good conduct for an eligible offender?
_____ unanimous votes
    A. Two   B. Three   C. Five   D. Four

5.____

6. Jim is interested in obtaining a certificate of good conduct from the New York State Board of Parole after serving time for a Class C Felony.
What is the MINIMUM amount of time that must pass before the Parole Board can grant Jim a certificate of good conduct, assuming he satisfies all other requirements of the Board?
   A. One year
   B. Eighteen months
   C. Two years
   D. Three years

6.____

7. Leandra's Law specifies that no person shall operate a motor vehicle while impaired or otherwise intoxicated with a child aged _____ years or less as a passenger.
   A. twelve
   B. thirteen
   C. fifteen
   D. eighteen

7.____

8. Liam was convicted of driving under the influence of alcohol when he was nineteen in California, his home state. In an attempt to escape his license suspension of one year, he moved to New York to live with his aunt.
Is Liam's license still suspended?
   A. Yes, his license is suspended in California only
   B. Yes, his license is suspended in New York and California
   C. Yes, his license is suspended in all states
   D. No

8.____

9. An adult driving under the combination of drugs and alcohol for the first time will MOST likely be convicted of a
   A. traffic infraction
   B. sanction offense
   C. misdemeanor
   D. felony

9.____

10. James has been hired as a marketing assistant for a local pharmaceutical company. After he received his offer letter from the Human Resources Department with his starting salary and start date, he received a call from Sylvia, the HR Coordinator. She informed James that a mistake had been made and the company did not realize James had a criminal record. She rescinded the employment offer and apologized to James for the inconvenience.
Did the company violate any law?
   A. No, the company is permitted to rescind the offer since James is a felon
   B. No, the company informed James of the situation before he started his employment
   C. Yes, the company should have completed his background search prior to sending his offer of employment
   D. Yes

10.____

11. Before Daniel started law school, he became a licensed HVAC technician working for his father's air conditioning repair business. After law school, he became a licensed attorney. Daniel also owns a handgun for which he has a permit. Which of the following are considered "licenses" under the New York Corrections Law Article 23-a?
   A. HVAC license only
   B. HVAC and Bar licenses only
   C. HVAC and Firearm licenses only
   D. HVAC, Bar and Firearm licenses

11.____

12. When Marissa was 19, she began working for a local accountant, Bill. After one year as an intern, she began to steal cash and other gifts Bill received from his clients. Bill reported her to authorities and she was convicted of larceny. Seven years later, Marissa is denied employment as an accountant with a local CPA firm.
Why is this permitted under the New York Corrections Law?
    A. There is a direct relationship between the offense she committed and the employment she is seeking.
    B. Denial of employment is only permitted after ten years has passed since the conviction, not seven years.
    C. Marissa was not a minor when she committed the crime.
    D. The CPA firm is not permitted to deny Marissa employment in this situation.

13. Once a child custody determination has been decided, it is conclusive unless and until the
    A. parents move out of state
    B. child moves out of state with one of the parents
    C. order is modified or changed
    D. judge nullifies the order due to noncompliance

14. When Bob and Sharon were dating, they lived in Connecticut and moved to Westchester County after they got married. They had their son, Jayden, soon after and when Jayden turned six years old, Bob and Sharon divorced. Bob moved back to Connecticut and has petitioned the court for full legal and physical custody of Jayden. The child custody determination hearings have started in New York and Bob would like his sister, Michelle, to testify on his behalf at the hearing. Michelle lives in Connecticut.
May Bob's sister testify?
    A. No
    B. No, because she lives in Connecticut
    C. Yes, even though she lives in Connecticut
    D. Yes, because she is a material witness to Bob and Sharon's marriage

15. A private placement adoption is MOST accurately defined as any adoption
    A. of a minor other than that placed by an authorized agency
    B. organized by three or more parties
    C. of a minor organized directly by the parties of the adoptee child
    D. of a minor other than that placed by a government agency

16. James wants to adopt his stepdaughter, Stephanie, so that he can include her in his will. James is still married to Stephanie's mother, Diane.
May James adopt Stephanie?
    A. It cannot be determined because it is not known if Stephanie is a minor.
    B. Yes, because James has a legitimate reason for adopting Stephanie.
    C. No, because James requires Diane's signature or consent to adopt Stephanie.
    D. No, because James cannot adopt Stephanie for the purpose of inheritance or support rights.

12.____ 13.____ 14.____ 15.____ 16.____

17. Which of the following individuals will be entitled to notice of adoption pursuant to the New York Domestic Relations Law?
    A. A person determined by a court to be the father of the child
    B. The great-aunt of the child
    C. The doctor, midwife, or other person who delivered the child
    D. The maternal grandfather of the child

17._____

18. Grounds for divorce in New York include all of the following EXCEPT`
    A. Cruel and inhuman treatment of the plaintiff by the defendant
    B. Abandonment of the plaintiff for a period of one or more years
    C. Confinement of the defendant in prison for a period of three or more consecutive years after the marriage of the plaintiff and defendant
    D. The dissolution of the common law marriage between the plaintiff and defendant

18._____

Questions 19-20.

DIRECTIONS: Questions 19 and 20 are to be answered on the basis of the following information.

Amanda wants to file for divorce from Todd on the grounds of adultery. Todd carried on an affair with Amanda's co-worker, Rebecca, nearly six years ago. When Amanda discovered the affair six years ago, she immediately moved out.

19. Will Amanda's petition for divorce be granted?
    A. Yes, because adultery is a ground for divorce in the State of New York.
    B. No, because the affair was forgiven.
    C. No, because Amanda allowed Todd to have an affair and implicitly forgave him by living with him at the time the affair began.
    D. No, because Amanda's petition for divorce was not commenced within five years after the discovery of the affair.

19._____

20. Does Amanda have the right to a trial by jury on the issues concerning the grounds for granting her divorce from Todd?
    A. No, because the adulterous affair is settled as fact
    B. No, because the affair is presumed to have ended and/or become immaterial once the divorce petition is filed
    C. No, because there is no right to a trial by jury for divorce cases
    D. Yes, because there is a right to trial by jury of the issues of the grounds for divorce.

20._____

21. According to the New York Criminal Procedure Law, the prosecution of a petty offense must be commenced within _____ year(s).
    A. one   B. two   C. three   D. four

21._____

22. According to the New York Criminal Procedure Law, the prosecution for a misdemeanor must be commenced within _____ year(s).
    A. one   B. two   C. three   D. four

22._____

23. Joel, the treasurer for ABC Limited, Inc., has been stealing from the company for approximately three years. The CEO of ABC Limited, Billy, discovered the larceny nearly two years ago. Billy fired Joel but never brought charges for the theft.
Will Billy be able to prosecute Joel for larceny?
   A. Yes, because prosecution for larceny committed by a person in violation of a fiduciary duty may be commenced within three years
   B. Yes, because prosecution for larceny committed by a person in violation of a fiduciary duty may be commenced within two years
   C. No, because prosecution for larceny committed by a person in violation of a fiduciary duty must commence within one year
   D. No.

23.____

24. After a criminal action is commenced, the defendant is entitled to a _____ trial.
   A. deliberate   B. quick   C. thorough   D. speedy

24.____

25. Must the court furnish a defendant with a copy of the felony complaint during arraignment?
   A. No, because a court may furnish this information but is not required to
   B. No, because a court must furnish the complaint before trial but not at arraignment
   C. No, because the court must determine whether the defendant is to be held for grand jury
   E. Yes

25.____

KEY (CORRECT ANSWERS)

1.	D		11.	B
2.	C		12.	A
3.	D		13.	C
4.	C		14.	C
5.	B		15.	A
6.	D		16.	D
7.	C		17.	A
8.	A		18.	D
9.	C		19.	D
10.	D		20.	D

21.	A
22.	B
23.	D
24.	D
25.	D

TEST 3

DIRECTIONS: Each question or incomplete statement is followed by several suggested answers or completions. Select the one that BEST answers the question or completes the statement. *PRINT THE LETTER OF THE CORRECT ANSWER IN THE SPACE AT THE RIGHT.*

1. Aggravated criminal contempt, aggravated family offense, and absconding from a community treatment facility are classified as
   A. E Felonies
   B. Violent Felonies
   C. Misdemeanors
   D. Felonies

   1.____

2. Aggravated harassment in the second degree and arson in the fifth degree are examples of
   A. Felonies
   B. Misdemeanors
   C. A Misdemeanors
   D. Violent Felonies

   2.____

3. Murder in the first degree will always be classified as a(n)
   A. Misdemeanor
   B. E Felony
   C. Felony
   D. Minor Felony

   3.____

4. A "child born out of wedlock" is
   A. any child of marriage unless dissolved
   B. any children born after the parents are married
   C. a child born after the marriage license is obtained, but before the parents are legally married
   D. any children born between two consenting adults

   4.____

5. The social welfare law maintains that in the case of neglect or inability of the parents to provide for the support and education of the child, the child is supported by the
   A. next closest kin to the mother
   B. next closest kin to the father
   C. child welfare agency of the state
   D. county, city, or town chargeable under the provision of the social welfare law

   5.____

6. The district attorney who conducts a hearing upon a felony complaint represents, or hears, the case on behalf of the
   A. county   B. city   C. people   D. government

   6.____

7. If after a hearing on a felony complaint there is a reasonable cause to believe that a defendant committed an offense that was not a felony, the court may
   A. reduce the charge but keep the felony charge on record
   B. keep the felony charge on record until the defendant is proven innocent of the lesser crime
   C. reduce the charge to one for such non-felony offense
   D. release the defendant on his or her own recognizance

   7.____

8. May a court order the removal of an action that begins in criminal court to family court?   8.____
   A. Yes, but only if the court states on record the factors upon which the determination is based
   B. Yes, but only if there are two related parties at issue
   C. Yes, but only if the complaining party consents to such a removal
   D. Yes, but only justice is better served if the case were removed to family court

9. Proceedings to establish paternity may be originated in which court?   9.____
   The court in the
   A. county where the mother or child resides or in the county where the putative father resides or is found
   B. city where the birth father lives
   C. county where the mother lives
   D. county where the mother birthed the child

10. If a juvenile offender defendant waives a hearing upon a felony complaint, the court must order that the defendant be held for   10.____
   A. the action of the grand jury   B. capacity hearings
   C. guardianship determination   D. the results of paternity

11. Bail is defined as   11.____
   A. cash or deposit   B. deposit or bail
   C. cash or bail   D. bail or cash

12. For the purposes recognizance, bail and commitment, an "obliger" is MOST appropriately defined as the   12.____
   A. defendant
   B. person who executes the bail bond on behalf of the defendant, assuming the undertaking
   C. co-defendant
   D. person who signs a contract indicating that they intend to post bail bond in the future

13. An appearance bond is a bail bond in which the only obligor is the   13.____
   A. defendant or principal
   B. property secured therewith
   C. defendant's co-conspirators, if any
   D. contract of appearance of the defendant

Questions 14-15.

DIRECTIONS: Questions 14 and 15 are to be answered on the basis of the following
             information.

Ed's mother has posted bail in the amount of $250,000 for Ed's release after he was
charged with aggravated assault. The court imposed the condition that Ed appear for
subsequent hearings related to the charges. Ed failed to appear for the second hearing before
Judge O'Connor, who then issued a warrant for his arrest. Ed claimed his mother became
gravely ill which is why he did not appear for his hearing.

14. What is the effect of Ed's failure to appear on the bail previously posted?   14._____
     The bail is
     A. unequivocally forfeited.
     B. generally forfeited, unless the court finds Ed had sufficient excuse for
         missing his appearance.
     C. reduced given the nature of Ed's mother's health condition.
     D. forfeited unless Ed's mother can produce a doctor's note.

15. Assume that the bail has been forfeited. The local criminal must pay the   15._____
     forfeited bail to the
     A. local village justice
     B. treasurer or other financial officer if it is a city court or the state
         comptroller if it is a town or village court
     C. chief justice directly
     D. treasurer of the junior congressional member of the State of New York

16. What does Leandra's Law prohibit?   16._____
     A. Driving while intoxicated with a person less than 15 years of age as a
         passenger in the vehicle
     B. Driving while under the influence of alcohol with other passengers in the
         vehicle
     C. Driving while under the influence of drugs or alcohol with a passenger
         less than 12 years of age in the vehicle
     D. Driving while intoxicated

17. An elderly gentleman, Dave, was assaulted at his 70th birthday celebration   17._____
     by another elderly man, Frank, who is ten years younger than Dave. Dave
     suffered various minor injuries.
     What is the MOST appropriate charge against Frank?
     A. Assault 3   B. Assault 2
     C. Harassment   D. Violent misdemeanor

18. According to the New York Civil Practice Law and Rules, when a defendant   18._____
     has failed to appear, plead, or proceed to trial of an action, what is the MOST
     appropriate remedy for a plaintiff?
     A. Resume judgment   B. Dismissal action
     C. Default judgment   D. Increase in charge

19. The party responsible for adopting rules of the courts including the preparation
and publication of court calendars of the unified court system is the
    A. chief justice of the Civil Courts   B. chief administrator of the courts
    C. comptroller of the currency   D. bailiff of the unified court system

19.____

20. Katie sues Terry for breach of contract after Terry failed to appear for
Katie's baby shower and deliver food as the contracted caterer. Terry filed a
cross-claim against Samuel, whom she hired to drive her to the venue of
Katie's shower. Terry alleges that because Samuel never picked her up as
agreed upon, she failed to perform the catering contract for Katie.
The action to join the claims is also known as
    A. correction of claims   B. severance of claims
    C. joinder of claims   D. class action

20.____

21. Generally, when actions involving a common question of law or fact are
pending before the court, the court may order the actions be _____ to avoid
unnecessary costs or delay.
    A. combined   B. categorized   C. classified   D. consolidated

21.____

22. Justice O'Connor has ordered that certain claims in an action before the
court be heard separately, or severed, from one another.
Who is now responsible for determining the order of when each of the newly
severed claims are heard?
    A. The chief justice, if not Justice O'Connor
    B. The constable
    C. The court
    D. The attorneys of record

22.____

23. Which of the following is a prerequisite to the filing of a class action?
    A. The class is so numerous that joinder of all members is impracticable.
    B. The attorneys for each class member approves the joinder of the class.
    C. Less than 500 persons embody the entire class.
    D. The class acts as a whole and accept the settlement paid as a lump sum.

23.____

24. The order permitting a class action shall do which of the following?
    A. Describe the class   B. Set out the demand for the class
    C. Name the attorneys of record   D. Detail the action generally

24.____

25. A class action cannot be dismissed, discontinued, or compromised without
the
    A. consent of the attorneys of record
    B. approval of the court
    C. approval of the class
    D. approval of the court after a full hearing on the merits of the defense

25.____

KEY (CORRECT ANSWERS)

1.	D		11.	C
2.	B		12.	B
3.	C		13.	A
4.	B		14.	B
5.	D		15.	B
6.	C		16.	A
7.	C		17.	B
8.	A		18.	C
9.	A		19.	B
10.	A		20.	C

21.	D
22.	C
23.	A
24.	A
25.	B

TEST 4

DIRECTIONS: Each question or incomplete statement is followed by several suggested answers or completions. Select the one that BEST answers the question or completes the statement. *PRINT THE LETTER OF THE CORRECT ANSWER IN THE SPACE AT THE RIGHT.*

1. During a criminal trial, where an error or other legal defect in the proceedings occurs that prejudices the defendant, the court must declare a _____ upon motion of the defendant.
   A. hung jury
   B. recantation
   C. mistrial
   D. error of motion

   1.____

2. Which party can file a motion for mistrial if it is physically impossible to proceed with the trial in conformity with the law?
   A. Defendant
   B. Plaintiff
   C. The court
   D. All of the above

   2.____

3. After issuing a trial order of dismissal which has the effect of dismissing the entire indictment, the court does which of the following immediately?
   A. Discharge the defendant from custody or exonerate the bail.
   B. Notify the defendant's next of kin
   C. Notify the complaining witness and/or victim of the dismissal
   D. Arrange for a possible appeal from the plaintiff and/or the people

   3.____

4. Generally, when the court has imposed a sentence of imprisonment, when is the last time the sentence can be changed, suspended, or interrupted?
   A. Before the sentence has commenced
   B. After the sentence has been served
   C. After the arraignment, but before the conclusion of the trial
   D. After the instructions on the charge(s) are read to the jury

   4.____

5. Judge Smith rendered a verdict in a criminal case in Essex County. However, the court did not have jurisdiction over the case. The PROPER remedy is
   A. dismissal
   B. hung jury
   C. mistrial
   D. vacate judgment

   5.____

6. The court may vacate a judgment, upon motion of the defendant, for which of the following grounds?
   A. The judgment was procured by duress.
   B. The material evidence at trial was true, but presented in a way that painted the defendant in a negative light.
   C. Material evidence was obtained for trial via search warrant or other lawful device.
   D. All of the above

   6.____

7. Rachel, a licensed eighth grade teacher, was recently convicted of felony   7.____
   larceny. Who must be notified of Rachel's felony conviction?
   A. Rachel's next of kin
   B. The New York Comptroller, who must garnish Rachel's pay
   C. The Department of Education
   D. The Parole Board of New York

8. Jamal knowingly filed a false financing statement for his contractor business,   8.____
   indicating that he owes more money than he actually does to his bank lender.
   Jamal was convicted of intentionally filing a false financing statement under the
   Uniform Commercial Code (UCC).
   Who must be notified of Jamal's conviction?
   A. The Office of the UCC
   B. The New York Secretary of State
   C. The Chief Justice
   D. The Parole Board of New York

9. During jury selection, Dawn's lawyer did not object to any potential jurors.   9.____
   Once the trial began, Dawn's attorney raised the objection that juror number 3,
   Richard, may be biased against Dawn.
   What is the MOST appropriate response to Dawn's attorney's objection?
   A. A challenge to the jury panel must be made before the selection of the
      jury commences, therefore overruled
   B. A challenge to the jury panel must be made before the selection of the
      jury ends, therefore overruled
   C. A challenge to the jury panel must be made before the selection of the
      jury commences, therefore accepted
   D. Sustained

10. A criminal trial jury consists of not less than _____ members.   10.____
    A. fourteen   B. nine   C. six   D. twelve

11. Pursuant to Article 270 of the New York Criminal Procedure Law, either   11.____
    party may examine prospective jurors regarding their qualifications to serve as
    jurors. However, the court cannot allow the questioning to
    A. become repetitious, irrelevant, or involve questioning of a juror's
       knowledge of the rules of law
    B. reduce to questioning of the individual's family history or other
       background
    C. involve asking the prospective juror about his prior service on a jury
    D. contain questions that are relevant to the case, but asked in a rude or
       belittling manner

12. How many peremptory challenges may either side exercise during jury   12.____
    selection?
    A. One   B. Two
    C. Three   D. Dependent on the type of case

13. A challenge for cause of a prospective juror which is not made before he is   13.____
sworn as a trial juror shall be deemed to be
    A. accepted   B. rebuked   C. waived   D. refuted

14. According to Section 270.16 of the New York Criminal Procedure Law,   14.____
the examination of prospective jurors by either party is permitted to take place
outside the presence of other prospective jurors for which type of case?
    A. Matrimonial cases, involving the adoption of a stepchild or adopted child
    B. Surrogates cases, involving complicated estates
    C. Capital cases, in which the crime charged may be punishable by death
    D. All such cases as long as the defense moves first

15. A peremptory challenge is defined as a(n)   15.____
    A. objection to a prospective juror for which no reason need be assigned
    B. objection to a prospective juror for which there must be a reason
       assigned
    C. objection to a prospective juror for justified cause
    D. trial objection

16. At what point in a trial is the jury provided with general instructions concerning   16.____
its basic functions, duties, and conduct?
After the jury has been sworn _____ opening address.
    A. but before the people's   B. and after the people's
    C. but before the defense's   D. and after the defense's

17. Pursuant to Section 270.45 of the New York Criminal Procedure Law, the   17.____
court may in its discretion either permit a jury to _____ during recesses and/or
adjournments or direct that they be continuously kept together during such
periods under the supervision of an appropriate public servant.
    A. not communicate with one another
    B. not make eye contact with one another
    C. refrain from using their mobile phones
    D. separate

18. If a defendant pleads not responsible by reason of mental disease or defect,   18.____
the court will ask him or her which of the following?
    A. About the offense or offenses charged in the indictment
    B. Family background
    C. Feelings or mental state at the time of the hearing
    D. Additional information not previously asked by counsel

19. Assuming the same facts as Question 18, by answering the questions posed   19.____
by the court, the defendant has effectively
    A. lost his right to appeal by waiver
    B. waived his or her right to not be compelled to incriminate him or herself
    C. harmed him or herself
    D. waived his or her rights under the Second Amendment

20. Before accepting a plea of not responsible by reason of mental disease or defect, the court must find and state which of the following on record in detail?
    A. That the affirmative defense of lack of criminal responsibility by reason of mental disease or defect would be proven by the defendant at trial by a preponderance of the evidence
    B. That the defendant entered the plea under duress
    C. That the court is satisfied the defendant has been diagnosed with a generally accepted mental disease
    D. That the defendant can speak for himself

20.____

21. Intermittent imprisonment is defined as
    A. revocable sentence of imprisonment to be served on days or during certain periods of days, or both, specified by the court
    B. irrevocable sentence of imprisonment to be served part time
    C. revocable sentence of imprisonment to be served on weekends only
    D. another form of irrevocable release based on one's own recognizance

21.____

22. If John is currently serving an intermittent sentence of imprisonment and is then sentenced to a definite sentence of three years, when will he begin his definite sentence?
    A. After the conclusion of his intermittent sentence
    B. After a hearing of the court to determine which sentence takes priority
    C. After thirty days
    D. Immediately

22.____

23. Burglary in the first, second, and third degree is classified as a
    A. misdemeanor
    B. minor infraction
    C. felony
    D. subordinate crime

23.____

24. The crime of conspiracy is
    A. always classified as a felony
    B. always classified as a misdemeanor
    C. sometimes classified as a felony, but in other instances classified as a misdemeanor
    D. not a crime

24.____

25. The criminal sale of a firearm is
    A. always classified as a felony
    B. always classified as a violent felony
    C. sometimes classified as a felony, but in other instances classified as a misdemeanor
    D. not a crime if there is no buyer

25.____

―――――――

KEY (CORRECT ANSWERS)

1.	C		11.	A
2.	D		12.	D
3.	A		13.	C
4.	A		14.	C
5.	D		15.	A
6.	A		16.	A
7.	C		17.	D
8.	B		18.	A
9.	A		19.	B
10.	D		20.	A

21.	A
22.	D
23.	C
24.	C
25.	D

EXAMINATION SECTION

TEST 1

DIRECTIONS: Each question or incomplete statement is followed by several suggested answers or completions. Select the one that BEST answers the question or completes the statement. *PRINT THE LETTER OF THE CORRECT ANSWER IN THE SPACE AT THE RIGHT.*

Questions 1-3.

DIRECTIONS: Questions 1 through 3 are to be answered on the basis of the following passage.

Bryan accused his uncle, Jeremy, of petty larceny after he discovered $300 in cash was missing from his car's glove compartment. As a defense, Jeremy testified that he left the car windows rolled down while he ran errands and, therefore, it was possible that someone else stole the money. Bryan initiated the lawsuit against Jeremy after Jeremy refused to give Bryan $300.

1. The dispute is BEST deemed a(n)
   A. congenial dispute
   B. adversarial proceeding
   C. stipulated matter
   D. raised issue

1.____

2. Bryan and Jeremy would have recounted their respective statement of the facts in which of the following documents?
   A. Affidavit   B. Notice   C. Subpoena   D. Warrant

2.____

3. Assume that Jeremy wants to change his accounting of the events that led to the theft from Bryan's car. Jeremy would need to _____ his statement of facts.
   A. relieve   B. amend   C. recount   D. rename

3.____

4. Jared's mother is accused of child abuse. At her arraignment, Jared begins yelling obscenities at the judge. Jared is held in
   A. grievance
   B. collateral estoppel
   C. contempt of court
   D. recognizance

4.____

5. Attorneys in a libel and defamation lawsuit are not prepared for their pretrial conference. The attorneys, jointly, petition the court for a _____, which would allow for a postponement of the hearing and provide each side with more time to gather information for trial.
   A. hearing adjustment
   B. continuance
   C. leverage
   D. codicil

5.____

6. Given that Lindsay has been found guilty of mail fraud, a federal crime and felony, she is now considered a _____ felon.
   A. convicted   B. contrived   C. imperiled   D. contracted

6.____

Questions 7-9.

DIRECTIONS: Questions 7 through 9 are to be answered on the basis of the following
              passage.

Tim and Lisa are in the midst of a contentious legal battle. Tim has accused Lisa, his former employer, of paying him less than minimum wage. Lisa, an owner of a local restaurant, maintains that Tim was paid in accordance with the laws of New York State. As part of ___(7)___, Tim was asked by Lisa's attorney to turn copies of all paystubs during his employment at the restaurant. Tim never complied; instead he stopped responding to all requests from Lisa's attorney and the judge. Additionally, he stopped ___(8)___ at court hearings. Consequently, the judge issued a ___(9)___ in Lisa's favor.

7.   The CORRECT word to fill in space number 7 is   7.____
      A. discovery   B. investigation
      C. interrogatories   D. motions

8.   The CORRECT word to fill in space number 8 is   8.____
      A. recounting   B. revisiting   C. defending   D. appearing

9.   The CORRECT word to fill in space number 9 is   9.____
      A. default judgment   B. support judgment
      C. cause of action   D. in rem motion

10.   A subordinate employee to the clerk who is empowered to act in the place of   10.____
      the clerk in the official business of the court is also known as the
      A. regular clerk   B. municipal judge
      C. supervisory magistrate   D. deputy clerk

11.   A divorce decree is equivalent to a(n)   11.____
      A. order of the court   B. void certificate
      C. effective disclaimer   D. dismissal order

Questions 12-13.

DIRECTIONS: Questions 12 and 13 are to be answered on the basis of the following passage.

Robert was ordered to pay child support three years ago. Since then, Robert has not missed any payments, as they are deducted automatically from his paycheck, but he has recently lost his job. Robert would like to petition the court for a downward ___(12)___ of the child support law.

12.   The CORRECT word to fill in space number 12 is   12.____
      A. modification   B. recipient   C. treatment   D. restitution

13.   Robert is subject to   13.____
      A. garnishee   B. indictment   C. incarceration D. garnishment

Questions 14-15.

DIRECTIONS: Questions 14 and 15 are to be answered on the basis of the following passage.

The judge in the Bronx County Criminal Court has asked her clerk to take notes during the trial of The People vs. Joe Smith. More specifically, the judge requested that the clerk record any factor that may reduce the severity of the crime raised by the defense. Mr. Smith is accused of armed robbery and attempted arson. The prosecutor asked Mr. Smith if he was of sound mind during the incident, whether he was at the scene of the crime during the night in question, and whether he was with anyone while the crime was being committed. Mr. Smith denied knowing anything about the robbery or the arson.

14.   The judge has asked the clerk to identify   14.____
        A. mitigating factors   B. letters testamentary
        C. litigant application(s)   D. raison d'etre

15.   Which of the following has Mr. Smith NOT provided in his testimony?   15.____
        A. Jurisdiction   B. Alibi
        C. Plea bargain   D. Indemnification

Questions 16-19.

DIRECTIONS: Questions 16 through 19 are to be answered on the basis of the following
                      passage.

Lily and Dan Johnson are suing the landscaping company that used to mow their lawn. The landscaping company is owned by Richard. The Johnsons did not sign a contract for Richard's company to mow their lawn, but two of Richard's workers continued to mow the Johnson's lawn for the entire summer of 2016. Lily received a bill for $2,000 in May of 2016 and disputes the bill. Richard countersued, claiming the Johnson's did not honor the contract that was rightfully in place for mowing services. The Court estopped Richard's company from performing all landscaping activities for the Johnsons and their respective parties.

16.   What is the cause of action for Richard's claim?   16.____
        A. Fraud   B. Breach of contract
        C. Libel   D. Negligence

17.   Who are the cross-claimants in this case?   17.____
        A. Richard's company
        B. Lily and Dan
        C. Richard and Richard's contractors
        D. There are no cross-claimants in this matter

18.   Which parties are consanguineous, or related by blood?   18.____
        A. Lily and Dan   B. Lily and Richard
        C. Dan and Richard   D. None of the parties

19. What did the court order Richard's company to do?   19._____
    A. Stop landscaping activities
    B. Stop mailing bills to the Johnsons
    C. Stop engaging the Johnsons in conversations about landscaping
    D. Continue landscaping activities

Questions 20-22.

DIRECTIONS: Questions 20 through 22 are to be answered on the basis of the following
              passage.

The Southern District Court of New York is a court of __(20)__ jurisdiction, meaning that
the court only has jurisdiction over actions authorized by law. In a class action suit, heard at the
District Court, there are more than one hundred plaintiffs that are suing a New York-based
manufacturer of a particular drug. Some plaintiffs claim that the drug causes death while others
claim the drug is illegally manufactured. All claims have been __(21)__ in the class action suit.
One requirement in a class action suit is that the class be represented by the same __(22)__.

20. The CORRECT word to fill in space number 20 is   20._____
    A. limited   B. unlimited   C. timely   D. wholly

21. The CORRECT word to fill in space number 21 is   21._____
    A. consolidated   B. remarkable   C. accepted   D. stipulated

22. The CORRECT word to fill in space number 22 is   22._____
    A. litigants   B. judge   C. jury   D. counsel

Questions 23-25.

DIRECTIONS: Questions 23 through 25 are to be answered on the basis of the following
              passage.

During cross-examination by Jackson, Katie stated that she witnessed someone leaving
the scene of an accident in a red car. The driver, she said, was a male with blond hair like the
defendant, Adam. During the direct examination by Carl, Katie said the driver had blondish–
reddish hair.

23. Who is Adam's attorney?   23._____
    A. Carl
    B. Jackson
    C. Katie
    D. Adam is not represented by counsel

24. In which court is this trial MOST likely to be held?   24._____
    A. Civil   B. Criminal   C. Surrogates   D. Family

25. Who is Katie's attorney?   25.____
    A. Jackson
    B. Carl
    C. Katie is not represented by counsel
    D. It is unclear if Katie has an attorney

––––––––––

KEY (CORRECT ANSWERS)

1.	B		11.	A
2.	A		12.	A
3.	B		13.	D
4.	C		14.	A
5.	B		15.	B
6.	A		16.	B
7.	A		17.	D
8.	D		18.	D
9.	A		19.	A
10.	D		20.	A

21.	A
22.	D
23.	B
24.	B
25.	D

––––––––––

TEST 2

1. A case that has been decided is declared _____ by the court.   1._____
   A. adjudicated   B. annulled
   C. detrimental   D. acknowledged

Questions 2-4.

DIRECTIONS: Questions 2 through 4 are to be answered on the basis of the following passage.

Three different individuals approach the clerk's desk at different times, each in need of assistance in filing their lawsuit. Amy wants to respond to a notice that she received in the mail that names her as a party in a lawsuit. Bill wants to start a lawsuit and name a party. Carl wants to respond to a lawsuit in which he has been named, and sue the person that sued him. Amy, Bill, and Carl each want to know what they would need to get started.

2. Amy needs to file a(n)   2._____
   A. letter   B. response   C. answer   D. reply

3. Bill needs to file a(n)   3._____
   A. immediate interrogatory   B. complaint
   C. affiant   D. codicil

4. Carl is MOST likely seeking to file a   4._____
   A. counterclaim   B. restitution claim
   C. defamatory issuance   D. interlocutory demand

5. If a jury finds that there is insufficient evidence to convict, the recorded verdict   5._____
   is not guilty and the case results in a(n)
   A. reversal   B. acquittal   C. recusal   D. repository

Questions 6-8.

DIRECTIONS: Questions 6 through 8 are to be answered on the basis of the following passage.

At the close of a bench trial, the defendant, John Ash, was found not guilty. The plaintiff in the case against Mr. Ash, Mr. Steel, wants to appeal the verdict. Mr. Steel's friend, Mr. Smith, wants to file a brief in support of her friend. Mr. Smith is an attorney and her brief would take the form of a memorandum of law.

6. Mr. Steel is which of the following in the appellate case?   6._____
   A. Appellate   B. Appellee   C. Appellant   D. Affirmation

7. If Mr. Ash was found guilty, could Mr. Steel file an appeal?   7.____
    A. Yes, any party can appeal any verdict.
    B. Yes, Mr. Steel has an affirmative right to appeal a verdict he is a party to.
    C. No, Mr. Steel can only appeal in federal court.
    D. No, Mr. Steel would not need to file an appeal if Mr. Ash was found guilty.

8. Mr. Smith is seeking to file a(n)   8.____
    A. amicus brief
    B. dissertation brief
    C. motion in limine
    D. motion of law

9. During arraignment, the defendant may choose to have one of two types of   9.____
trials. A jury trial will consist of 6-12 jurors, with _____ while a _____ trial will
be decided by a single judge.
    A. alternates; brief
    B. alternate jurors; bench
    C. alternative jurors; trustee
    D. alternate jurors; hearing

10. A _____ bankruptcy can occur in two circumstances; the debtor can be a   10.____
business or an individual involved in business and the debts are for business
purposes.
    A. liquidation
    B. reorganization
    C. business
    D. restitution

Questions 11-12.

DIRECTIONS: Questions 11 through 12 are to be answered on the basis of the following passage.

As is standard procedure in many divorce cases, the judge presiding over Brian and Kate's divorce has asked that the parties attempt to settle matters in __(11)__, or the dispute resolution process in which an impartial third party assists the parties to reach a mutually acceptable settlement. Both Brian and Kate request additional time to decide on whether to complete that process, which is granted by the judge.

11. The CORRECT word to fill in space number 11 is   11.____
    A. arbitration
    B. mediation
    C. dispute training
    D. mandamus

12. Which of the following was MOST likely granted by the judge?   12.____
    A. Adjournment
    B. Adjudication
    C. Allegation
    D. Acknowledgment

13. The clerk is responsible for calling the cases scheduled for the day, also   13.____
termed a
    A. calendar call
    B. document review
    C. docketing
    D. case certification

Questions 14-16.

DIRECTIONS: Questions 14 through 16 are to be answered on the basis of the following passage.

In an effort to speed matters along in the courtroom, Judge Johnson would like the clerks to begin summarizing the hearings on the daily docket at the beginning of each day. Judge Johnson asks that pleadings submitted by pro se parties be given special attention. Specifically, the judge wants to know if any of the pleadings are defective on their face. If so, the judge would like the clerk to assist the litigants in correcting the pleadings before the hearing so as not to waste the court's time.

14.   Pro se litigants are those   14._____
      A. who represent themselves in any kind of case
      B. that represent others on a pro bono basis
      C. that represent family members for a small fee or on a volunteer basis
      D. who represent themselves under anonymity

15.   Which of the following are considered pleadings?   15._____
      A. Motion to dismiss   B. Answer
      C. Complaint   D. All of the above

16.   A defective complaint would be one that   16._____
      A. listed the parties' names   B. did not state a cause of action
      C. did not list a location of the action   D. contains a notary public stamp

Questions 17-19.

DIRECTIONS: Questions 17 through 19 are to be answered on the basis of the following passage.

As documents are filed with the Court, they are stamped with a __(17)__ date which usually indicates the date a motion will be heard in court. Jamie is at the clerk's desk and wants to know if this date is picked and asks the clerk for guidance.

17.   The CORRECT word to fill in space number 17 is   17._____
      A. blank   B. expedited   C. return   D. sealant

18.   Which of the following should be considered in the selection of the above   18._____
      date?
      I.   Notice to the other parties.
      II.   Day of the week the proper court hears motions
      III.   Convenience of the clerk
      IV.   Will of the attorneys
      The CORRECT answer is:
      A. None of the above   B. I, II, III
      C. I, IV   D. I and II

19. Motions to the court must include which of the following?
    A. Full address of the courthouse
    B. Relief sought
    C. Part, room, and time the motion will be heard
    D. All of the above

19.____

Questions 20-25.

DIRECTIONS: Questions 20 through 25 are to be answered on the basis of the following passage.

    Harper hired Janelle to write articles for Harper's online magazine. Harper paid Janelle for two articles, then ceased paying Janelle. In Civil Court, Janelle sued Harper for fraud and breach of contract. In a countersuit, Harper sued Janelle for defamation. The clerk is asked to first confer with the parties about a date for __(20)__ or a conference with the judge to discuss discovery and possible settlement. Harper is representing herself at trial as she cannot afford an attorney, while Janelle is represented by Jane. Janelle submits an affidavit to the court, swearing to the events that led up to her filing a suit against Janelle.

20. The CORRECT word to fill in space number 20 is
    A. pretrial
    B. pre-sentence investigation
    C. restraining order hearing
    D. show cause hearing

20.____

21. Harper is _____ and considered a _____ litigant.
    A. incapable; pro se
    B. injunction; pro bono
    C. indigent; pro se
    D. incarcerated; per diem

21.____

22. If Harper were to prevail in her suit, which of the following is she MOST likely to recover?
    A. Janelle's imprisonment
    B. Janelle's probation
    C. Payment of fines
    D. Asset seizure and forfeiture

22.____

23. If Janelle were to prevail in her suit against Harper, which of the following is she LEAST likely to recover?
    A. Back-payment for the articles written
    B. Punitive damages for fraud and breach of contract
    C. Monetary damages for breach of contract
    D. Harper's imprisonment

23.____

24. Which of the following is likely to be entered into evidence?
    A. Employment contract(s)
    B. Paystubs
    C. Articles written and websites where the articles were published
    D. All of the above

24.____

25. Who is the affiant in Janelle's affidavit?
    A. Harper
    B. Harper's attorney
    C. Janelle
    D. Janelle's attorney

25.____

KEY (CORRECT ANSWERS)

1.	A		11.	B
2.	C		12.	A
3.	B		13.	A
4.	A		14.	A
5.	B		15.	D
6.	C		16.	B
7.	D		17.	C
8.	A		18.	D
9.	B		19.	D
10.	C		20.	A

21.	C
22.	C
23.	D
24.	D
25.	C

———

EXAMINATION SECTION

TEST 1

DIRECTIONS: Each question or incomplete statement is followed by several suggested answers or completions. Select the one that BEST answers the question or completes the statement. *PRINT THE LETTER OF THE CORRECT ANSWER IN THE SPACE AT THE RIGHT.*

Questions 1-5.

DIRECTIONS: Questions 1 through 5 are to be answered on the basis of the following passage.

The jury could not decide the verdict in the case of *The People of New York vs. Tim Jones*. One of the main reasons why the jury was deadlocked was because the jury found the presentation of the evidence by the prosecutor and the defense was quite confusing. One of the major focal points in the case was the __(1)__ of __(2)__ against the defendant, Tim Jones. When the jury initially came back to the courtroom and announced they could not come to a decision, the judge asked that the jury return to __(3)__. Three hours later, after still not arriving at a decision, the judge declared the jury to be a hung jury. Because it was a jury trial and not a __(4)__ trial, the court polled the jury.

1. The CORRECT word to fill in space number 1 is   1.____
   A. admissibility   B. entertainment
   C. exclusion   D. branding

2. The CORRECT word to fill in space number 2 is   2.____
   A. documents   B. testimony   C. ex parte   D. voir dire

3. The CORRECT word to fill in space number 3 is   3.____
   A. deliberations   B. group   C. court   D. bench

4. The CORRECT word to fill in space number 4 is   4.____
   A. bench   B. regular   C. heightened   D. closed

5. A _____, unlike a hung jury, is an invalid trial caused by a fundamental error.   5.____
   A. erroneous trial   B. deadlocked jury
   C. bilateral trial   D. mistrial

Questions 6-7.

DIRECTIONS: Questions 6 and 7 are to be answered on the basis of the following passage.

Two former friends are embattled in a legal dispute whereby one friend, James, accuses the other, Robin, of negligence and fraud. In addition to a complaint, James also submitted an __(6)__ accounting the events that led up to the lawsuit. James is not represented by counsel. Robin, however, is represented by an attorney. James is considered a __(7)__ litigant.

6. The CORRECT word to fill in space number 6 is   6._____
    A. motion   B. document   C. affidavit   D. complaint

7. The CORRECT word to fill in space number 7 is   7._____
    A. represented   B. pro se   C. individual   D. per diem

8. Testimony is a type of _____, which is more broadly defined as information   8._____
presented and/or used to persuade the fact finder to decide the case in favor of
one side or the other.
    A. evidence   B. conference
    C. pre-hearing motion   D. deposition

9. Erin is accused of following her former boss home, burglarizing his home and   9._____
assaulting him. The crimes are serious, especially the charge of assault which
is punishable by imprisonment for more than one year. Consequently, Erin will
be charged with at least one _____.
    A. felony   B. misdemeanor
    C. offense   D. civil crime

10. A _____ is a body of 16-23 citizens who listen to evidence of criminal allegations,   10._____
which is presented by the prosecutors, and determine whether there is
probable cause to believe an individual committed an offense.
    A. jury   B. alternate jury
    C. grand jury   D. exculpatory hearing

11. The same body returns an _____ if there is probable cause to believe an   11._____
individual committed an offense.
    A. indictment   B. information   C. conviction   D. acquittal

12. If the same is presented by a government body, the body returns an _____.   12._____
    A. information   B. verdict   C. ex-parte   D. ramification

Questions 13-16.

DIRECTIONS: Questions 13 through 16 are to be answered on the basis of the following
passage.

Stacy appears at the Nassau County Courthouse to support her cousin, Dave, who is on
trial for attempted robbery. While Stacy knows Dave is innocent, the testimony presented by
the prosecutor is convincing. The prosecutor calls four different witnesses who testified they
saw Dave point a gun at an elderly gentleman and demand that he turn over his wallet and
cellphone. The defense ___(13)___ and does not present any evidence. The prosecutor and
defense then both presented their ___(14)___ to the jury, which summarized their cases ___(15)___.

13. The CORRECT word to fill in space number 13 is   13._____
    A. persists   B. re-examines   C. rests   D. repositions

14. The CORRECT word to fill in space number 14 is   14.____
    A. closing argument   B. opening arguments
    C. summaries   D. depositions

15. The CORRECT word to fill in space number 15 is   15.____
    A. in brief   B. in totality
    C. amicus   D. sua sponte

16. Which part of the trial did Stacy miss?   16.____
    A. Closing argument   B. Opening argument
    C. Evidence presentation   D. Direct examination

Questions 17-20.

DIRECTIONS: Questions 17 through 20 are to be answered on the basis of the following passage.

During jury deliberations, two jurors cannot seem to agree. Melissa feels strongly that the defendant is innocent and continues to argue with another juror, Jim, who strongly believes the defendant is guilty of a __(17)__ , which is a crime punishable by death. Melissa argues that much of the evidence presented during the trial was __(18)__ and should not be considered because it creates a __(19)__ against the defendant.

17. The CORRECT word to fill in space number 17 is   17.____
    A. capital offense   B. delinquency
    C. delinquent crime   D. obstructionist offense

18. The CORRECT word to fill in space number 18 is   18.____
    A. admissible   B. triable   C. presentable   D. inadmissible

19. The CORRECT word to fill in space number 19 is   19.____
    A. demands   B. bias   C. recant   D. confusion

20. What is the term used to described the outcome if Melissa, Jim, and the other   20.____
    jurors do not agree on a verdict?
    A. Suspended jury   B. Hung jury
    C. Dreaded jury   D. Misguided jury

Questions 21-25.

DIRECTIONS: Questions 21 through 25 are to be answered on the basis of the following passage.

The pre-trial process, like the actual trial, takes place in multiple __(21)__ . Hearings are scheduled by __(22)__ between the parties and the judge. If the factfinder is not a judge, the __(23)__ is selected in a separate process called voir dire. __(24)__ are argued in court before a trial begins, in which an issue relating to the case is decided. Finally, the trial begins once a __(25)__ has been set. Even then, the case may settle before the start of opening statements.

21. The CORRECT word to fill in space number 21 is

    A. parts   B. pieces   C. units   D. slices

21.____

22. The CORRECT word to fill in space number 22 is

    A. schedules   B. calendars   C. conference   D. telephone

22.____

23. The CORRECT word to fill in space number 23 is

    A. jury   B. panel   C. composition   D. attorneys

23.____

24. The CORRECT word to fill in space number 24 is

    A. Motions   B. Witnesses

    C. Issue statements   D. Stipulations

24.____

25. The CORRECT word to fill in space number 25 is

    A. trial date   B. defendant

    C. judge   D. final conference

25.____

KEY (CORRECT ANSWERS)

#		#	
1.	A	11.	A
2.	B	12.	A
3.	A	13.	C
4.	A	14.	B
5.	D	15.	A
6.	C	16.	B
7.	B	17.	A
8.	A	18.	D
9.	A	19.	B
10.	C	20.	B

#	
21.	A
22.	C
23.	A
24.	A
25.	A

TEST 2

DIRECTIONS: Each question or incomplete statement is followed by several suggested answers or completions. Select the one that BEST answers the question or completes the statement. *PRINT THE LETTER OF THE CORRECT ANSWER IN THE SPACE AT THE RIGHT.*

Questions 1-3.

DIRECTIONS: Questions 1 through 3 are to be answered on the basis of the following passage.

In a divorce proceeding, Alice and Tom have each filed for __(1)__ of their son, Jack. Alice wants Jack to live with her full time, and Tom has asked the court for the same. In their petitions, each party has outlined why living with them would be in the __(2)__ of the child. The family court judge has taken account of all the evidence and is currently deliberating on the final __(3)__.

1. The CORRECT word to fill in space number 1 is   1.____
    A. physical custody   B. alimony
    C. child support   D. restraining order

2. The CORRECT word to fill in space number 2 is   2.____
    A. best interests   B. sustaining interests
    C. limited interests   D. maternal wishes

3. The CORRECT word to fill in space number 3 is   3.____
    A. issue   B. order   C. motion   D. request

4. A _____ is a sworn statement containing facts about a child involved in a   4.____
    case, including the full name of the child, date of birth, current and past
    residences, and other information as may be required by law.
    A. surrogates certificate   B. custody affidavit
    C. remembrance order   D. restraining order

Questions 5-7.

DIRECTIONS: Questions 5 through 7 are to be answered on the basis of the following passage.

Bill is on the witness stand providing details on when he last saw Kevin. Bill and Kevin do not know one another. Bill believes that he saw Kevin in the bank two months ago, just before the bank was robbed. Kevin is accused of writing bad checks. Bill's attorney questions him on the stand, then Kevin's attorney questions Bill on the stand. Kevin does not take the stand in his own defense.

5. Kevin's attorney will _____ Bill.   5.____
    A. examine   B. decipher
    C. impeach   D. cross-examine

6. Bill is providing which of the following? 6._____
    A. Testimony   B. Interrogatory
    C. Illustrative examination   D. Demonstration

7. Kevin is exercising his right against 7._____
    A. self-inducement   B. judgment
    C. self-incrimination   D. perjury

8. In a criminal case, one of the major issues is whether the defendant had a 8._____
guilty mind, or _____. Without it, the charge from second degree murder would
drop to manslaughter, given the lack of premeditation.
    A. anger reduction   B. mens rea
    C. exclusionary rule   D. per diem application

Questions 9-11.

DIRECTIONS: Questions 9 through 11 are to be answered on the basis of the following
                passage.

    Mary brought a wrongful death __(9)__ against a manufacturer of antibiotic ointment after
her husband applied the ointment to an open wound on his knee and became fatally ill. In her
lawsuit, Mary alleges that the manufacturer knew certain shipments of the ointment had been
tainted and did not issue a recall to consumers. After a lengthy trial, the court awarded her
punitive __(10)__. Assume that the manufacturer Mary sued was ABC, Inc. The manufacturer
of the ointment Mary's husband used, however, is Ointment, Inc. The judge __(11)__ the case
__(12)__, allowing Mary to bring the suit again after the correct manufacturer was identified.

9. The CORRECT word to fill in space number 9 is 9._____
    A. action   B. exercise   C. request   D. application

10. The CORRECT word to fill in space number 10 is 10._____
    A. funds   B. null award
    C. compensatory   D. damages

11. The CORRECT word to fill in space number 11 is 11._____
    A. dismissed   B. acquitted   C. relieved   D. excused

12. The CORRECT word to fill in space number 12 is 12._____
    A. without prejudice   B. knowingly
    C. erroneously   D. with prejudice

13. A tort action would most likely be filed and litigated in _____ court, rather than 13._____
criminal court.
    A. Civil   B. Surrogate's   C. Supreme   D. District

14. Newlyweds Richard and Erica are in the process of closing on their new home   14.____
in Bronx County. An examination of public records to determine the state of a
title and confirm that the seller of a property is its legal owner is deemed a
    A. title search   B. seizure
    C. lien in assets   D. forfeiture

15. Ronnie was convicted of assault with a deadly weapon in Orange County   15.____
Supreme Court and sentenced to eleven years imprisonment. The verdict in
Ronnie's case was
    A. nolo contendere   B. moot   C. arraigned   D. guilty

16. Eric's hearing, stemming from an alleged petty larceny, was scheduled for   16.____
Friday at 3 P.M. At noon, Eric's mother informed him that his grandmother had
passed. Eric rushed to the hospital in disbelief, missing his hearing. Eric's
attorney was not informed by Eric that he would not be able to attend the
hearing. Eric's _____ will certainly be detrimental to his case.
    A. failure to appear   B. failed deposition
    C. failed interrogatory   D. failed hearing

17. During a break, one of the jurors in the *Tim James v. Alpha, Inc.* spots one of   17.____
the courthouse judges speaking to a lawyer in the Tim James case. The juror
has witnessed a possible
    A. ex-parte communication   B. domiciled conversation
    C. un-docketed conversation   D. delinquent conversation

Questions 18-20.

DIRECTIONS: Questions 18 through 20 are to be answered on the basis of the following
                passage.

    In a __(18)__, the attorneys for the Estate of Abe Smith and Red Bank, Inc. are
attempting to determine the scope of possible trial. The Estate of Abe Smith is suing the bank
for mismanagement of the estate's funds.

18. The CORRECT word to fill in space number 18 is   18.____
    A. probationary hearing   B. pretrial conference
    C. protective order hearing   D. pleading

19. Red Bank, Inc. is identified as the _____ in the case.   19.____
    A. litigant   B. plaintiff   C. appellant   D. defendant

20. The case will MOST likely be heard in _____ Court.   20.____
    A. Criminal   B. Surrogate's   C. Bankruptcy   D. Family

21. To avoid trial, Benjamin agrees to a _____ which requires that he serve three   21.____
years in jail, followed by five years of probation.
    A. dismissal   B. reduced issue
    C. plea bargain   D. unilateral contract

22. Jamal and Nicole want to legally separate. Jamal and Nicole are both   22._____
represented by attorneys. Jamal's attorney, Sam, went to law school with
Nicole's attorney, Barbara. Who are the litigants in this case?
    A. Jamal only   B. Jamal and Nicole
    C. Nicole only   D. Sam and Barbara

Questions 23-25.

DIRECTIONS: Questions 23 through 25 are to be answered on the basis of the following
                      passage.

    A jury is selected in a criminal trial in Suffolk County Supreme Court. Each __(23)__ as
selected from a larger pool and subjected to __(24)__, or the process of questioning each
prospective juror about their qualifications to serve on a panel. After the trial concludes, the
judge delivers formal instructions, or the __(25)__ on the law before the jury can begin their
official deliberations.

23. The CORRECT word to fill in space number 23 is   23._____
    A. party   B. juror
    C. representative   D. attorney

24. The CORRECT word to fill in space number 24 is   24,_____
    A. voir dire   B. peremptory challenge
    C. exclusionary rule   D. exclusion-based bias

25. The CORRECT word to fill in space number 25 is   25._____
    A. jury charge   B. mandate
    C. directive   D. affirmative response

KEY (CORRECT ANSWERS)

1.	A		11.	A
2.	A		12.	A
3.	B		13.	C
4.	B		14.	A
5.	D		15.	D
6.	A		16.	A
7.	C		17.	A
8.	B		18.	B
9.	A		19.	D
10.	D		20.	B

21.	C
22.	B
23.	B
24.	A
25.	A

EXAMINATION SECTION

TEST 1

DIRECTIONS: Each question or incomplete statement is followed by several suggested answers or completions. Select the one that BEST answers the question or completes the statement. *PRINT THE LETTER OF THE CORRECT ANSWER IN THE SPACE AT THE RIGHT.*

1. While waiting for jury selection, one of the prospective jurors asks you how long a typical trial lasts.
   Which of the following is the MOST appropriate response?
   A. Trials can be lengthy.
   B. The length of trials varies widely, but every aspect of it is important.
   C. Civil trials typically last three to five days, while criminal trials are generally five to ten days.
   D. Decline to respond for fear of appearing biased.

1.____

2. One of the jurors appears faint and starts to wobble while seated in the jury box.
   How should you handle the situation?
   A. Let one of the other jurors come to the ailing juror's aid first.
   B. Alert the court officer of what you see and ask that the trial be held indefinitely.
   C. Politely interject the trial proceedings and ask the juror if he or she is feeling well.
   D. Alert the court officer who may or may not escort the juror out of the courtroom.

2.____

3. During trial, you believe that you see the defendant winking at one of the jurors. No one else seems to notice their interaction, including the judge.
   Which of the following actions would you take?
   A. Alert the judge in chambers
   B. Tell the court officer during a break in trial
   C. Interrupt the trial to make all parties aware of the behavior
   D. Confirm with the juror in question that the defendant is winking at her to determine if the feeling is mutual

3.____

4. During a recess in the trial, the defendant's expert witness is seen chatting with one of the alternate jurors outside the courthouse. While it is unclear what they are talking about, it seems to be a friendly exchange of information.
   What should you do before the court is called back to order?
   A. Tell the juror she must disclose her conversation with the expert witness in open court
   B. Tell the expert witness he must disclose the conversation with the juror in open court
   C. Inform the plaintiff's attorney about the conversation
   D. Inform the judge about the conversation

4.____

Questions 5-8.

DIRECTIONS: Questions 5 through 8 are to be answered on the basis of the following fact
pattern.

After a TRO is issued to the plaintiff, the ex-wife of the defendant, both parties are free to
go. The defendant appeared in court and rigorously opposed his ex-wife's request. His ex-wife
already has sole custody of their three children and he seems incredibly distraught by the
judge's grant of her request.

5.   In a follow-up hearing, where the plaintiff is requesting to extend a TRO, the   5.____
     defendant does not show up. Instead, the defendant's brother appears at the
     hearing on his behalf. Is the defendant's brother permitted to voice his
     concerns about extending the TRO?
     The defendant's brother
        A. is not a party to the action and must wait outside of the courtroom during
            proceedings.
        B. is welcome to testify on his brother's behalf
        C. can testify on his brother's behalf as long as he remains calm while doing
            so
        D. can testify on his brother's behalf so long as the plaintiff's sister can
            testify on her behalf

6.   A TRO is a _____ restraining order, while a QDRO is a qualified _____ order.   6.____
        A. temporary; domicile relations   B. territorial; domicile relations
        C. temporary; domestic revision   D. temporary; domestic relations

7.   How many alternate jurors are typically sworn in for trial?   7.____
        A. Up to 12   B. Up to 14   C. Up to 10   D. Up to 6

Questions 8-10.

DIRECTIONS: Questions 8 through 10 are to be answered on the basis of the following fact
pattern.

While those waiting for the court to open file into the hallway, an argument breaks out
between two women and one man. When you intervene between the parties, you discover the
two women are arguing over custody of a child – who is standing nearby – and the man is one
of their attorneys. Barbara is the biological mother of the child. Tina raised the child from birth.
Tina and her attorney, Bill, came with the child to court today.

8.   Which party should stay with the child?   8.____
        A. The biological mother, Barbara, of the child should stay with the child
            while they await for court to begin.
        B. Tina and Bill should stay with the child since she raised the child from
            birth.

C. The parties should separate and the child should come with you to a sequestered part of the courthouse.

D. Tina and Bill should stay with the child as petitioners of the court, Barbara should wait in a separate area away from all three and refrain from contact.

9. Which of the following are Barbara and her attorney MOST likely to request in court?　　　9.____
   A. An order of protection
   B. Order to expunge
   C. Order to impeach
   D. Deposition

10. Should you tell the judge about the behavior of the parties during the hearing?　　10.____
   A. You can inform the judge if asked, but not during the hearing itself.
   B. You can inform the judge if asked, but should wait until a hearing is not in session.
   C. Before the hearing is set to begin, you should inform the judge of your encounter with the parties and let the judge decide how to best confront the situation between all involved.
   D. No.

Questions 11-14.

DIRECTIONS:　Questions 11 through 14 are to be answered on the basis of the following fact pattern.

At district court, a trial of a group of alleged rapists has drawn a huge crowd of spectators at each day of the hearings. Two of the defendants are locals of Nassau County, while the other is a local of Richmond County. The trial date has been set and moved multiple times.

11. Which of the following will the defendants MOST likely be charged with?　　11.____
   A. An information
   B. A felony
   C. A misdemeanor
   D. An indictment

12. In reading the charge, which of the following is LEAST likely to appear?　　12.____
   A. The name of the attorneys of record
   B. The names of the victims
   C. The number of counts of each crime
   D. The name of the judge hearing the case

13. There are likely to be multiples of which during this trial?　　13.____
   A. Multiple court officers
   B. Multiple attorneys
   C. Multiple charges
   D. All of the above

14. The venue of the trial is MOST likely to be　　14.____
   A. Nassau County
   B. Richmond County
   C. Determined by the jury
   D. Determined by the judge

Questions 15-17.

DIRECTIONS: Questions 15 through 17 are to be answered on the basis of the following fact
pattern.

In the Supreme Court Foreclosure Part, a variety of parties are awaiting for hearings to
begin. Homeowners, attorneys, creditors, and trustees anxiously talk amongst themselves.
Based on your knowledge of foreclosure procedures, answer the following questions.

15.   As you approach the foreclosure part, a woman rushes toward you. She is   15.____
      incredibly upset and begins to cry as soon as she begins speaking. She tells
      you that she cannot wait any longer for her hearing to begin because her
      mother just had an accident and she must rush to the hospital.
      If she misses her court date, what should she be MOST concerned with as it
      relates to her foreclosure case?
         A. Having to reschedule her court date to defend herself
         B. Defaulting and, therefore, her creditor(s) prevailing against her
         C. Answering a motion to show cause from the bank
         D. Answering a complaint from the bank

16.   One of the most frequent questions you are asked is whether a bank can   16.____
      accelerate the mortgage loan against a homeowner/borrower after the
      homeowner has made a few late payments.
      Acceleration is
         A. requiring a borrower to immediately pay off the balance of the loan
         B. the amount of money owed on the mortgage
         C. the document showing the ownership of a mortgage or deed of trust
         D. the basic repayment plan the homeowner/borrower initially agreed to
             when purchasing the home

17.   Homeowners in foreclosure sometimes file simultaneously for bankruptcy.   17.____
      The automatic stay is a function unique to bankruptcy.
      An automatic stay is defined as
         A. a large lump sum payment due as the last payment on a loan
         B. an injunction automatically issued by the bankruptcy court when someone
             files for bankruptcy
         C. an optional injunction that requires creditors to call the debtor and seek a
             settlement
         D. another term meaning "to stay a motion" or to hold a request from the
             court temporarily

18.   Dave approaches the clerk's desk and asks how, generally, judges make their   18.____
      decisions on legal matters. The MOST correct answer would be based on
         A. case law, or the body of all court decisions which govern or provide
             precedent on the same legal issue before the judge
         B. case law, personal opinion and oral arguments by attorneys
         C. case law, oral arguments by attorneys, and the defendant's rap sheet
         D. "stare decisis" or that which has already been decided

19. Which hearing below will MOST likely be heard in the Commercial Division
    of the Suffolk County Supreme courthouse?
    A. Divorce petition between Bill and Amy
    B. A custody dispute between Jim and John
    C. A business dispute between ABC Corp. and XYZ, Inc.
    D. A petition for expungement of a stockbroker's record

    19.____

20. Richard may face criminal charges for allegedly embezzling thousands of
    dollars from his company's business account.
    If a grand jury decides there is enough evidence to move forward with criminal
    charges against Richard, they
    A. return an information   B. return an indictment
    C. issue a warrant   D. issue a seizure

    20.____

21. At trial, the prosecutor asks many pointed questions at Richard. The
    prosecutor believes Richard is lying on the stand.
    When an attorney attempts to reduce the credibility of the other side's witness,
    they are said to be trying to _____ the witness on the stand.
    A. objectify   B. anger   C. impeach   D. frustrate

    21.____

22. During a lengthy trial, four jurors conspire with one another to enter votes
    of "not guilty" and hatch a plan to sway other jurors in their favor in an attempt
    to close out deliberations early.
    What is the likely outcome of the trial?
    A. Hung jury   B. Mistrial
    C. Acquittal   D. Defensive charge

    22.____

23. The judge's charge to the jury is also known as
    A. closing statements   B. quid pro quo
    C. jury instructions   D. sua sponte

    23.____

24. Who is the only party responsible for delivering the sentence to the
    convicted?
    A. Bailiff   B. Jury
    C. Judge   D. Jury foreperson

    24.____

25. A motion for directed verdict is made
    A. without the jury present
    B. with only the jury foreperson present
    C. with the entire jury present
    D. with only the alternate jurors present

    25.____

KEY (CORRECT ANSWERS)

1.	C		11.	B
2.	D		12.	B
3.	A		13.	D
4.	D		14.	D
5.	A		15.	B
6.	D		16.	A
7.	D		17.	B
8.	D		18.	A
9.	A		19.	C
10.	C		20.	B

21.	C
22.	B
23.	C
24.	C
25.	A

TEST 2

DIRECTIONS: Each question or incomplete statement is followed by several suggested answers or completions. Select the one that BEST answers the question or completes the statement. *PRINT THE LETTER OF THE CORRECT ANSWER IN THE SPACE AT THE RIGHT.*

1. Juror #12 is a close friend of your brother's, Tom. Tom starts to strike up a conversation with you outside of the courtroom.
How should you respond?
   A. Politely decline to engage, unless he or she is asking for directions
   B. Politely decline to engage, unless he or she would like to talk about the case
   C. Politely decline to engage, unless he or she knows you personally
   D. Engage the conversation remaining mindful of the appearance of bias and immediately ceasing the conversation if the trial at hand comes up

1.____

2. A charge of attempted murder is LEAST likely to accompany a charge of
   A. murder   B. burglary   C. robbery   D. assault

2.____

Questions 3-4.

DIRECTIONS: Questions 3 and 4 are to be answered on the basis of the following fact pattern.

Mary approaches you inside the Albany County Supreme Court and says that she has been served with a lawsuit. She is confused about the entire lawsuit process and is confused as to what area of the courthouse she should be in. She believes, but is not entirely sure, that her sister may be suing her over money she lent her then subsequently lost gambling in the casino.

3. Which of the following is the MOST appropriate response you can provide Mary with regard to her being served?
She should have a copy of the _____ with her and refer to it, which will tell her where she would report within the courthouse.
   A. answer   B. complaint   C. summons   D. information

3.____

4. Mary produces the document and asks you if there is anything she can do to respond to the lawsuit.
What is the MOST appropriate answer?
She should
   A. file an answer, and perhaps seek legal counsel
   B. seek legal counsel
   C. check in at the Preliminary Conference desk
   D. file an injunction, and perhaps seek legal counsel

4.____

5. Who decides whether the jurors are allowed to take notes during the trial?
   A. The judge
   B. The plaintiff's attorney, since they are bringing the case to court
   C. Jurors are always allowed to take notes during trials
   D. Jurors are never allowed to take notes during trials.

5.____

6. During a trial, one of the jurors writes a question for one of the witnesses on a piece of paper and hands it to the court officer.
What is the CORRECT procedure?
The court officer
   A. may, but is not required to, pass the written question to the judge
   B. must pass the written question to the judge, who may or may not ask the witness the question posed
   C. must decline receipt of the written message
   D. passes the written question to the court assistant who may or may not read the question aloud

6.____

7. If questions arise during the jury deliberation process, what is the role of the court officer?
   A. To deliver the written question from the jury foreperson to the judge
   B. To repeat the question orally as told to the court officer by the jury foreperson to the judge
   C. To read the written question in open court with all parties present other than the defendant
   D. To record the written question in the docket

7.____

8. A juror has informed you that she accidentally read information about the case she is serving on while she was at the supermarket last night.
How should you respond to her?
   A. Berate her for not being more diligent in seeking out information about the case
   B. Inform the court officer that the juror should be replaced
   C. Remove the juror from the jury box and replace him or her with an alternate juror yourself
   D. Inform the judge immediately

8.____

9. Which court proceeding takes place CLOSEST in time to an arrest?
   A. Arraignment   B. Sentencing
   C. Trial   D. Jury selection

9.____

10. Which of the following is LEAST likely to occur at the conclusion of a trial?
   A. Sentencing   B. Appeal
   C. Reversal   D. Plea bargaining

10.____

11. You overhear two jurors talking about the case in the hallway during recess. From their conversation, it appears that they are related to one another.
You should
   A. do nothing as it's none of your business
   B. make sure no one else hears them
   C. simply tell them not to discuss the case between themselves
   D. tell the judge

11.____

12. How many jurors typically serve on a trial?   12._____
    A. 12   B. 18   C. 16   D. 6

13. During jury selection, the judge has already excused 25 prospective jurors   13._____
for cause. How many more jurors can be excused for cause before reaching
the excusal limit?
    A. 5
    B. 10
    C. The judge has reached the limit
    D. There is no excusal limit "for cause"

14. Which of the following is the jury usually prohibited from doing during a trial on which   14._____
they are serving?
    A. Visiting the scene of the alleged crime
    B. Read or listen to news about the trial from outside sources
    C. Research case law that applies to the trial
    D. All of the above

15. In New York City, jury trials are conducted at which of the following courts?   15._____
    A. Supreme Court   B. New York City Civil Court
    C. New York City Criminal Court   D. All of the above

16. A trial involving an alleged assault and battery is MOST likely to occur at   16._____
which New York City court?
    A. Town and Village Court   B. New York City Civil Court
    C. New York City Criminal Court   D. County Court

17. In vacating a default, which must the petitioner file FIRST?   17._____
    A. Notice of motion   B. Emergency affidavit
    C. Legal back   D. Injunction

18. Order the steps of a typical trial from first to last.   18._____
    I. Opening statements   II. Jury selection
    III. Deliberations   IV. Oath and preliminary instructions
    The CORRECT answer is:
    A. I, II, III, IV   B. IV, III, II, I   C. I, II, IV, III   D. II, IV, I, III

19. On appeal, three justices hear a case that was already decided in the lower   19._____
courts. The issue before them is a complicated issue involving a determination
of legal guardian.
An opinion from the entire panel of justices is known as a(n)
    A. per curiam decision   B. affirmative decision
    C. stare decisis   D. en banc order

20. One of the judges agrees with the decision of the court, but disagrees with   20._____
the reasoning of the conclusion. This judge decides to write his own opinion.
This is deemed a
    A. dissenting opinion   B. remedial decision
    C. concurring opinion   D. recurrent opinion

21. Suppose that one of the judges disagrees entirely with the ruling.   21.____
How will the judgment be altered because of the disagreement?
The judgment
   A. is unaffected because the majority voted in agreement with the trial court
   B. is unaffected because this judge did not author a dissenting opinion
   C. is unaffected because oral arguments were not made before the panel
   D. will be overturned

22. The appellate court still requires _____, even if it is established by the trial   22.____
court, known as original _____.
   A. domicile; venue   B. venue; jurisdiction
   C. jurisdiction; jurisdiction   D. jurisdiction; domicile

23. The legal theory upon which a case is based is called a   23.____
   A. basis   B. decisis
   C. cause of action   D. precedent

24. Sarah and her friend, Ashley, burglarized a number of homes in Kings   24.____
County over the summer. They were only apprehended after one of their other
friends overheard them talking about their crimes. At the time, both Sarah and
Ashley were 18 and legally minors.
A minor is legally defined as:
   A. In New York, a minor is anyone under the age of 18
   B. Anyone under 18
   C. A legally emancipated individual
   D. An infant or individual under the age of legal competence

25. The BEST place to refer back to the testimony of one witness is   25.____
   A. the docket
   B. the judge's notes which can be obtained freely from chambers
   C. the stenographer's transcript
   D. clerk notes which, in some instances, are available online

KEY (CORRECT ANSWERS)

1.	D	11.	D
2.	A	12.	A
3.	B	13.	D
4.	B	14.	D
5.	A	15.	D
6.	B	16.	C
7.	A	17.	A
8.	D	18.	D
9.	A	19.	A
10.	D	20.	C

21.	A
22.	C
23.	C
24.	D
25.	C

TEST 3

DIRECTIONS: Each question or incomplete statement is followed by several suggested answers or completions. Select the one that BEST answers the question or completes the statement. *PRINT THE LETTER OF THE CORRECT ANSWER IN THE SPACE AT THE RIGHT.*

1. The pre-trial hearing is MOST likely to take place after _____, but before _____.   1.____
   A. arraignment; jury selection
   B. deliberations; closing statements
   C. assignment; adjudication
   D. plea bargain; opening statement

2. During a court recess, you see one of the jurors walking into the judge's   2.____
   chambers. You immediately
   A. halt the juror and demand he or she return to the deliberation room
   B. allow the juror to proceed, but ask the judge about the incident later
   C. allow the juror to proceed and assume they know one another personally
   D. allow the juror to proceed, but inform the court officer of the incident

3. When reading an indictment in court, each charge represents a(n)   3.____
   A. allegation of a crime
   B. proven criminal act
   C. evidentiary plea
   D. legal certainty

4. After a defendant has been acquitted, he or she will likely be   4.____
   A. free to leave the courthouse
   B. remanded to federal prison
   C. detained until further notice
   D. formally sentenced

5. Jeremiah, a defense attorney, has approached you in the hallways of the   5.____
   New York Civil Court. He is concerned that his client, Dave, may become
   violent during court proceedings.
   How do you handle Jeremiah's request to closely supervise Dave while court is
   in session?
   A. Inform the judge of Jeremiah's request and allow proceedings to continue
      as normal
   B. Ask that a court officer be present during court proceedings
   C. Request the judge to sequester the jury while Dave is present
   D. Ignore Jeremiah's request for now, until you see how Dave behaves
      yourself

6. Jury sequestration is   6.____
   A. extremely common given the complex nature of most criminal trials
   B. becoming increasingly common
   C. more common in civil cases than in criminal trials
   D. rare

7. At arraignment, the defendant is MOST likely to   7.____
   A. state his case
   B. convince the judge of his or her innocence
   C. enter a plea
   D. gather information on his or her case from the State's attorney

8. A warrant can be issued for an individual's arrest or for   8.____
   A. search of premises outlined in the warrant itself
   B. testimony
   C. deposition of the arrested individual
   D. evidence found at the scene

9. The responsibility to record notes for the judge and listen to issues of law   9.____
that may need to be researched later are reserved for the
   A. court officer   B. stenographer
   C. judge's clerk   D. jury

10. Information about the charges against the defendant, as well as the   10.____
parties involved in the case, can MOST likely be found in the
   A. judge's notes   B. docket
   C. information   D. discovery report

11. The opening statements in a trial are delivered by the   11.____
   A. defendant   B. plaintiff   C. attorneys   D. judge

12. When the judge sustains the objection of an attorney who is asking a   12.____
question of the witness on the stand, the witness must
   A. answer the question as asked
   B. wait for counsel to re-phrase the question in a proper form or ask another
      question before answering
   C. refuse to answer the question
   D. the witness may step down

13. An expert is permitted to   13.____
   A. review the plaintiff's evidence, draw a reasonable conclusion and give
      testimony to that effect
   B. review the defendant's evidence, draw a reasonable conclusion and
      submit his or her opinion in writing to the judge
   C. give his or her opinion based on the facts in evidence and provide the
      reasoning for that opinion
   D. provide an opinion in open court

14. Prosecutor and defense counsel have both made closing arguments in the trial of   14.____
Samuel Smith Jones. Mr. Jones is being tried for capital murder for the alleged
murder of his mother and sister.
Which party is entitled to a rebuttal in closing arguments?
   A. The prosecutor
   B. The defense
   C. The defense, but only after the plaintiff has given their closing argument
   D. The defense, but only if the plaintiff waives their right to make a closing
      argument

15. When a jury cannot agree on a verdict, a(n) _____ occurs and the result is   15._____
    a _____.
    A. mistrial; acquittal   B. mistrial; hung jury
    C. hung jury; mistrial   D. acquittal; mistrial

16. Nominal damages are   16._____
    A. damages awarded in name only, indicating no substantial harm was done
    B. damages to recompense the injured for the infliction of emotional distress
    C. damages to recompense the initiator of the lawsuit
    D. a reimbursement of filing fees, awarded to the person who can prove they
       are injured

17. The type of recovery being sought by the plaintiff is known as the   17._____
    A. order   B. punishment
    C. remedy   D. issue

18. Robert approaches the clerk's desk in a panic. He says that he filed a   18._____
    lawsuit last week against his cousin, Mike, but neglected to add his cousin's
    friend, Rory, to the suit.
    Robert must _____ the compliant.
    A. amend   B. refile   C. re-serve   D. redact

19. In a foreclosure action, which of the following will the borrower MOST likely   19._____
    be asked about in terms of securing a second or third mortgage?
    A. Business terms   B. Collateral
    C. Damages   D. Remedy

20. Maya has asked you about Article 7A proceedings.   20._____
    Article 7A hearings allow
    A. tenants being foreclosed upon to file a class action against the landlord
    B. at least 1/3 of tenants to ask the court to appoint an administrator to run
       the building in select circumstances
    C. tenants to forego paying the rent when living conditions in the building
       become inhabitable
    D. tenants to book their landlord from collecting rent when living conditions in
       the building become inhabitable

21. The Housing Court, sometimes referred to as Landlord and Tenant Court,   21._____
    is held at the
    A. Town and Village Court   B. New York City Civil Court
    C. New York City Criminal Court   D. County Court

22. Without an attorney, how much money can one sue for in Town or Village   22._____
    Courts, outside of New York City?
    A. Up to $3,000   B. Up to $5,000
    C. Up to $2,500   D. Up to $2,000

23. Judith wants to sue her neighbor, Samantha, in small claims court after Samantha borrowed Judith's lawnmower and refused to return it. Judith has begun a petition in small claims court for recovery of the lawnmower.
How will the case proceed?
   A. The case will not go forward, because only money damages can be sought in small claims court.
   B. The case will not go forward, because small claims court cannot compel Samantha to return the lawnmower.
   C. The case will not go forward, because the lawnmower exceeds the small claims court limit.
   D. Judith will likely prevail.

23._____

24. Daniel wants to file for probate of his father's estate. The filing fee is based on
   A. Daniel's assets
   B. Daniel's age
   C. The size of the estate
   D. The age at which Daniel's father passed

24.____

25. Family court will hear each of the following cases EXCEPT
   A. custody and visitation   B. adoption
   C. juvenile delinquency   D. estate

25.____

KEY (CORRECT ANSWERS)

1.	A		11.	C
2.	A		12.	B
3.	A		13.	C
4.	A		14.	A
5.	B		15.	C
6.	D		16.	A
7.	C		17.	C
8.	A		18.	A
9.	C		19.	B
10.	B		20.	B

21.	B
22.	A
23.	A
24.	C
25.	D

TEST 4

DIRECTIONS: Each question or incomplete statement is followed by several suggested answers or completions. Select the one that BEST answers the question or completes the statement. *PRINT THE LETTER OF THE CORRECT ANSWER IN THE SPACE AT THE RIGHT.*

1. Jason is currently a student at SUNY Buffalo. He is worried that his recent conviction will affect his financial aid package with the college.
How will Jason's conviction of drug possession affect his financial aid?
It will
   A. remain unaffected
   B. remain unaffected as long as Jason is represented by counsel
   C. automatically be cancelled for a period of time
   D. be cancelled indefinitely

   1.____

2. Who is responsible for drafting the Pre-Sentence report that judges use in sentencing convicted defendants?
   A. Defendant's attorney
   B. Probation officer
   C. Court assistant
   D. Judge's law clerk

   2.____

3. Restitution cannot be made for
   A. breach of contract
   B. assault and battery
   C. lost wages
   D. future losses

   3.____

4. In a bench trial, the _____ serves as the ultimate fact finder.
   A. jury   B. judge   C. bailiff   D. law clerk

   4.____

5. The role of the bankruptcy trustee is to represent the
   A. interest of the bankruptcy estate and the creditors of the debtor
   B. debtor against all creditors
   C. largest creditor of the debtor
   D. smallest creditor of the debtor

   5.____

6. The bankruptcy estate typically includes _____ at the time of the filing.
   A. all property of the debtor, including interests in property
   B. the home where the debtor resides
   C. the home and personal vehicle of the debtor
   D. all personal property, but not real property, of the debtor

   6.____

7. When a party to a lawsuit cannot afford the cost of the lawsuit, the Court
   A. may permit that party to proceed without being required to pay for court costs
   B. disallows payment for foreclosure proceeds
   C. does not require that party to pay for filing fees
   D. requires that party to settle the matter in ADR

   7.____

8. An answer is a formal response to which document?   8.____
   A. indictment   B. discovery   C. complaint   D. summons

9. Ishmael sued his former employer, Igor, for loss of wages. Igor lost the case   9.____
   and now wishes to appeal the ruling.
   When Igor appeals the case, he becomes an
   A. appellee   B. appellant   C. respondent   D. defendant

10. Damiano has been sentenced to six years for armed robbery and ten years   10.____
    for grand larceny. He is sentenced to serve his prison terms concurrently.
    What is the MAXIMUM amount of time he will spend behind bars?
    A. Six years   B. Sixteen years
    C. Ten years   D. Four years

11. What does the exclusionary rule exclude in a criminal trial?   11.____
    A. Testimony that is deemed hearsay by a judge in a court of competent
       jurisdiction
    B. Evidence obtained in violation of a defendant's constitutional or statutory
       rights
    C. Depositions that are unsworn or not notarized
    D. Affidavits that are unsworn or not notarized

12. David is being arraigned and needs to enter a plea for the crime he allegedly   12.____
    committed while he was with his friend, Robert. Robert pleads guilty during his
    arraignment yesterday, but David has been advised by his attorney to plead no
    contest, also known as
    A. nolo contendere   B. pro se   C. quid pro quo   D. qui tam

13. Adoptions can be heard in which two courts?   13.____
    A. Family court and surrogate court
    B. Foreclosure court and family court
    C. Family court and commercial court
    D. Family court and court of claims

14. Which party may NOT file a paternity petition?   14.____
    A. The child's mother
    B. The man who believes he may be the father of the child
    C. The child or the child's guardian
    D. The child's teacher or other close associate

15. Amy was married to Bob at the time her child was born. John believes he is   15.____
    the father of Amy's baby.
    Who is presumed to be the father of Amy's child?
    A. Bob
    B. John
    C. Neither can be presumed; a DNA test must be administered in this
       circumstance
    D. Neither can be presumed; each has to petition the court separately

16. Parties that represent themselves during court hearings are referred to as   16.____
    _____ litigants.
       A. qui tam   B. pro se   C. en banc   D. quid quo pro

17. Normally, guardianship petitions must be filed in _____ court.   17.____
       A. family   B. surrogates   C. probate   D. civil

18. At what age can a child's own preference be taken under consideration in   18.____
    guardianship or custody hearings?
       A. 12   B. 14   C. 17   D. 16

19. Civil litigation claims against the State of New York or other State-related   19.____
    agencies are heard exclusively in the
       A. Civil Court   B. Criminal Court
       C. Court of Claims   D. Surrogate Court

20. Preliminary conferences are automatically scheduled by the Court within   20.____
    _____ days after a Request for Judicial Intervention (RJI).
       A. 30   B. 45   C. 50   D. 55

21. There are two junior attorneys that have been sent to cover the preliminary   21.____
    conference of their case *Abe v. Gabe* in part 22 of the court. Both attorneys
    approach the clerk's desk to ask what the "return date" on a motion refers to.
    The return date is the date the
       A. motion will be conferenced and/or orally argued at the discretion of the
          court
       B. attorneys must return for more information
       C. attorneys must return with the clients
       D. attorneys must return to complete discovery

22. Decisions made on motions and pro se litigants must be   22.____
       A. mailed or a copy provided of the decision
       B. made available for photocopy or fax
       C. made available for scan, but not photocopied or faxed
       D. uploaded to the court website so it can be easily accessed online

23. A stipulation of settlement represents a formal agreement between the   23.____
       A. judge and the parties resolving the case
       B. litigants and their attorneys resolving the dispute
       C. clerk and the litigants representing a near end to the dispute at issue
       D. judge and the clerk representing a notation of the resolution

24. A motion to vacate a default in foreclosure part represents an attempt by the   24.____
    homeowner or borrower to
       A. reverse the court's finding of default
       B. reverse the court's finding of dereliction
       C. obtain a new hearing
       D. reschedule a hearing due to a missed court date

25. The Personal Appearance Part in the Civil Court is where which types of   25._____
    cases are heard?
    Cases where
    A. one or both parties are self-represented
    B. the plaintiff is self-represented
    C. the defendant is self-represented
    D. clerk is the fact finder

    _____

KEY (CORRECT ANSWERS)

1.	C		11.	B
2.	B		12.	A
3.	D		13.	A
4.	B		14.	D
5.	A		15.	A
6.	A		16.	B
7.	A		17.	A
8.	C		18.	B
9.	B		19.	C
10.	C		20.	B

21.	A
22.	A
23.	B
24.	A
25.	A

_____

COURTROOM TERMS

A/K/A: Acronym that stands for "also known as" and introduces any alternative or assumed names or aliases of an individual. A term to indicate another name by which a person is known.

Arraignment: The bringing of a defendant before the court to answer the matters charged against him in an indictment or information. The defendant is read the charges and must respond with his plea.

Arrest: Deprivation of one's liberty by legal authority.

Bail: An amount of money set by the court to procure the release of a person from legal custody; this money is to be forfeited if the defendant fails to appear for trial.

Beyond a Reasonable Doubt: The standard of proof required for a finding of guilty in a criminal matter. Satisfied to a moral certainty. This is a higher standard of proof than that required in a civil matter (preponderance of the evidence).

Co-Defendant: Any additional defendant or respondent in the same case.

Confession: A voluntary statement made by a person charged with a crime wherein said person acknowledges his/her guilt of the offense charged and discloses participation in the act.

Controlled Dangerous Substance: That group of legally designated drugs, which, by statute, it is illegal to possess or distribute.

Criminal complaint: The initial written notice to a defendant that he/she is being charged with a public offense.

Due Process of Law: The exercise of the powers of the government with the safeguards for the protection of individual rights as set forth in the constitution, statutes, and common case law.

Felony: A crime of a more serious nature than a misdemeanor, the exact nature of which is defined by state statute and which is punishable by a term of imprisonment exceeding one year or by death.

Grand Jury: A jury of inquiry whose duty is to receive complaints and accusations in criminal cases, hear the evidence presented on the part of the state, and determine whether to indict (see "indictment" below).

Impeach: As used in the Law of Evidence, to call into question the truthfulness of a witness, by means of introducing evidence to discredit him or her.

Indictment: A written accusation presented by a grand jury after having been presented with evidence, charging that a person named therein has done some act, or has been guilty of some omission that by law is a public offense.

Miranda Warnings: The compulsory advisement of a person's rights prior to any custodial interrogation; these include: a) the right to remain silent; b) that any statement made may be used against him/her; c) the right to an attorney; d) the appointment of counsel if the accused cannot afford his or her own attorney. Unless these rights are given, any evidence obtained in an interrogation cannot be used in the individual's trial against him/her.

Misdemeanor: Offense lower than felony and generally punishable by a fine or imprisonment other than in a penitentiary.

Motion to Quash: Application to the court to set aside the complaint, indictment or subpoena due to a lack of probable cause to arrest the defendant, or in matters heard by a grand jury, due to evidence not properly presented to the grand jury.

Motion to Sever: Application to the court made when there are two defendants charged with the same crimes or who acted jointly in the commission of a crime, when their attorneys feel it would be in their best interest if they had separate trials.

Motion to Suppress Evidence: Application to the court to prevent evidence from being presented at trial when said evidence has been obtained by illegal means. It applies to physical evidence, statements made by defendant when not advised by counsel or through wiretapping, prior convictions, etc..

Parole: A conditional release from custody at the discretion of the paroling authority prior to his or her completing the prison sentence imposed. During said release the offender is required to observe conditions of this status under the supervision of a parole agency.

Plea: A defendant's formal answer in court to the charges contained in a charging document.

Guilty: A plea by the defendant in which he acknowledges guilt either of the offense charged or of a less serious offense pursuant to an agreement with the prosecuting attorney. It should be understood, however, that the court may not be obliged to recognize this.

Nolo Contendere: A plea that is admissible in some jurisdictions, in which the defendant states that he does not contest the charges against him. Also called "no contest", this plea has the same effect as a guilty plea, except that it cannot be used against the defendant in civil actions arising out of the same incident which gave rise to the criminal charges.

Not Guilty: A plea of innocence by the defendant.

Not Guilty by Reason of Insanity: A plea that is sometimes entered in conjunction with the "not guilty" plea.

Double Jeopardy: A plea entered by a defendant who has been tried for an offense wherein he asserts that he cannot be tried a second time for said offense, unless he successfully secured a new trial after an appeal, or after a motion for a new trial was granted by the trial court.

Police Report: The official report made by any police officer involved with the incident or appearing after the incident, setting forth the officer's observations and statements of parties and witnesses. It can be used as evidence in a trial.

Pre-Trial Intervention: Utilized in some states when a defendant is accused of a first offense, to divert the defendant from the criminal justice system.

Probation: To allow a person convicted of a minor offense to go at large, under a suspension of sentence, during good behavior, and generally under the supervision of a probation officer.

Prosecutor: The attorney who prosecutes defendants for crimes, in the name of the government.

Search Warrant: A written order, issued by the court, directing the police to search a specified location for particular personal property (stolen or illegally possessed).

Speedy Trial: Mandate by the government that all criminal trials must take place within a specified time after arrest.

Writ of Habeas Corpus: A mandate issued from a court requiring that an individual be brought before the court.

GLOSSARY OF LEGAL TERMS

TABLE OF CONTENTS

GLOSSARY OF LEGAL TERMS

A

ACTION - "Action" includes a civil action and a criminal action.

A FORTIORI - A term meaning you can reason one thing from the existence of certain facts.

A POSTERIORI - From what goes after; from effect to cause.

A PRIORI - From what goes before; from cause to effect.

AB INITIO - From the beginning.

ABATE - To diminish or put an end to.

ABET - To encourage the commission of a crime.

ABEYANCE - Suspension, temporary suppression.

ABIDE - To accept the consequences of.

ABJURE - To renounce; give up.

ABRIDGE - To reduce; contract; diminish.

ABROGATE - To annul, repeal, or destroy.

ABSCOND - To hide or absent oneself to avoid legal action.

ABSTRACT - A summary.

ABUT - To border on, to touch.

ACCESS - Approach; in real property law it means the right of the owner of property to the use of the highway or road next to his land, without obstruction by intervening property owners.

ACCESSORY - In criminal law, it means the person who contributes or aids in the commission of a crime.

ACCOMMODATED PARTY - One to whom credit is extended on the strength of another person signing a commercial paper.

ACCOMMODATION PAPER - A commercial paper to which the accommodating party has put his name.

ACCOMPLICE - In criminal law, it means a person who together with the principal offender commits a crime.

ACCORD - An agreement to accept something different or less than that to which one is entitled, which extinguishes the entire obligation.

ACCOUNT - A statement of mutual demands in the nature of debt and credit between parties.

ACCRETION - The act of adding to a thing; in real property law, it means gradual accumulation of land by natural causes.

ACCRUE - To grow to; to be added to.

ACKNOWLEDGMENT - The act of going before an official authorized to take acknowledgments, and acknowledging an act as one's own.

ACQUIESCENCE - A silent appearance of consent.

ACQUIT - To legally determine the innocence of one charged with a crime.

AD INFINITUM - Indefinitely.

AD LITEM - For the suit.

AD VALOREM - According to value.

ADJECTIVE LAW - Rules of procedure.

ADJUDICATION - The judgment given in a case.

ADMIRALTY - Court having jurisdiction over maritime cases.

ADULT - Sixteen years old or over (in criminal law).

ADVANCE - In commercial law, it means to pay money or render other value before it is due.

ADVERSE - Opposed; contrary.

ADVOCATE - (v.) To speak in favor of;
(n.) One who assists, defends, or pleads for another.

AFFIANT - A person who makes and signs an affidavit.

AFFIDAVIT - A written and sworn to declaration of facts, voluntarily made.

AFFINITY- The relationship between persons through marriage with the kindred of each other; distinguished from consanguinity, which is the relationship by blood.

AFFIRM - To ratify; also when an appellate court affirms a judgment, decree, or order, it means that it is valid and right and must stand as rendered in the lower court.

AFOREMENTIONED; AFORESAID - Before or already said.

AGENT - One who represents and acts for another.

AID AND COMFORT - To help; encourage.

ALIAS - A name not one's true name.

ALIBI - A claim of not being present at a certain place at a certain time.

ALLEGE - To assert.

ALLOTMENT - A share or portion.

AMBIGUITY - Uncertainty; capable of being understood in more than one way.

AMENDMENT - Any language made or proposed as a change in some principal writing.

AMICUS CURIAE - A friend of the court; one who has an interest in a case, although not a party in the case, who volunteers advice upon matters of law to the judge. For example, a brief amicus curiae.

AMORTIZATION - To provide for a gradual extinction of (a future obligation) in advance of maturity, especially, by periodical contributions to a sinking fund which will be adequate to discharge a debt or make a replacement when it becomes necessary.

ANCILLARY - Aiding, auxiliary.

ANNOTATION - A note added by way of comment or explanation.

ANSWER - A written statement made by a defendant setting forth the grounds of his defense.

ANTE - Before.

ANTE MORTEM - Before death.

APPEAL - The removal of a case from a lower court to one of superior jurisdiction for the purpose of obtaining a review.

APPEARANCE - Coming into court as a party to a suit.

APPELLANT - The party who takes an appeal from one court or jurisdiction to another (appellate) court for review.

APPELLEE - The party against whom an appeal is taken.

APPROPRIATE - To make a thing one's own.

APPROPRIATION - Prescribing the destination of a thing; the act of the legislature designating a particular fund, to be applied to some object of government expenditure.

APPURTENANT - Belonging to; accessory or incident to.

ARBITER - One who decides a dispute; a referee.

ARBITRARY - Unreasoned; not governed by any fixed rules or standard.

ARGUENDO - By way of argument.

ARRAIGN - To call the prisoner before the court to answer to a charge.

ASSENT - A declaration of willingness to do something in compliance with a request.

ASSERT - Declare.

ASSESS - To fix the rate or amount.

ASSIGN - To transfer; to appoint; to select for a particular purpose.

ASSIGNEE - One who receives an assignment.

ASSIGNOR - One who makes an assignment.

AT BAR - Before the court.

AT ISSUE - When parties in an action come to a point where one asserts something and the other denies it.

ATTACH - Seize property by court order and sometimes arrest a person.

ATTEST - To witness a will, etc.; act of attestation.

AVERMENT - A positive statement of facts.

B

BAIL - To obtain the release of a person from legal custody by giving security and promising that he shall appear in court; to deliver (goods, etc.) in trust to a person for a special purpose.

BAILEE - One to whom personal property is delivered under a contract of bailment.

BAILMENT - Delivery of personal property to another to be held for a certain purpose and to be returned when the purpose is accomplished.

BAILOR - The party who delivers goods to another, under a contract of bailment.

BANC (OR BANK) - Bench; the place where a court sits permanently or regularly; also the assembly of all the judges of a court.

BANKRUPT - An insolvent person, technically, one declared to be bankrupt after a bankruptcy proceeding.

BAR - The legal profession.

BARRATRY - Exciting groundless judicial proceedings.

BARTER - A contract by which parties exchange goods for other goods.

BATTERY - Illegal interfering with another's person.

BEARER - In commercial law, it means the person in possession of a commercial paper which is payable to the bearer.

BENCH - The court itself or the judge.

BENEFICIARY - A person benefiting under a will, trust, or agreement.

BEST EVIDENCE RULE,THE - Except as otherwise provided by statute, no evidence other than the writing itself is admissible to prove the content of a writing. This section shall be known and may be cited as the best evidence rule.

BEQUEST - A gift of personal property under a will.

BILL - A formal written statement of complaint to a court of justice; also, a draft of an act of the legislature before it becomes a law; also, accounts for goods sold, services rendered, or work done.

BONA FIDE - In or with good faith; honestly.

BOND - An instrument by which the maker promises to pay a sum of money to another, usually providing that upon performances of a certain condition the obligation shall be void.

BOYCOTT - A plan to prevent the carrying on of a business by wrongful means.

BREACH - The breaking or violating of a law, or the failure to carry out a duty.

BRIEF - A written document, prepared by a lawyer to serve as the basis of an argument upon a case in court, usually an appellate court.

BURDEN OF PRODUCING EVIDENCE - The obligation of a party to introduce evidence sufficient to avoid a ruling against him on the issue.

BURDEN OF PROOF - The obligation of a party to establish by evidence a requisite degree of belief concerning a fact in the mind of the trier of fact or the court. The burden of proof may require a party to raise a reasonable doubt concerning the existence of nonexistence of a fact or that he establish the existence or nonexistence of a fact by a preponderance of the evidence, by clear and convincing proof, or by proof beyond a reasonable doubt.

Except as otherwise provided by law, the burden of proof requires proof by a preponderance of the evidence.

BUSINESS, A - Shall include every kind of business, profession, occupation, calling or operation of institutions, whether carried on for profit or not.

BY-LAWS - Regulations, ordinances, or rules enacted by a corporation, association, etc., for its own government.

C

CANON - A doctrine; also, a law or rule, of a church or association in particular.

CAPIAS - An order to arrest.

CAPTION - In a pleading, deposition or other paper connected with a case in court, it is the heading or introductory clause which shows the names of the parties, name of the court, number of the case on the docket or calendar, etc.

CARRIER - A person or corporation undertaking to transport persons or property.

CASE - A general term for an action, cause, suit, or controversy before a judicial body.

CAUSE - A suit, litigation or action before a court.

CAVEAT EMPTOR - Let the buyer beware. This term expresses the rule that the purchaser of an article must examine, judge, and test it for himself, being bound to discover any obvious defects or imperfections.

CERTIFICATE - A written representation that some legal formality has been complied with.

CERTIORARI - To be informed of; the name of a writ issued by a superior court directing the lower court to send up to the former the record and proceedings of a case.

CHANGE OF VENUE - To remove place of trial from one place to another.

CHARGE - An obligation or duty; a formal complaint; an instruction of the court to the jury upon a case.

CHARTER - (n.) The authority by virtue of which an organized body acts;
(v.) in mercantile law, it means to hire or lease a vehicle or vessel for transportation.

CHATTEL - An article of personal property.

CHATTEL MORTGAGE - A mortgage on personal property.

CIRCUIT - A division of the country, for the administration of justice; a geographical area served by a court.

CITATION - The act of the court by which a person is summoned or cited; also, a reference to legal authority.

CIVIL (ACTIONS)- It indicates the private rights and remedies of individuals in contrast to the word "criminal" (actions) which relates to prosecution for violation of laws.

CLAIM (n.) - Any demand held or asserted as of right.

CODICIL - An addition to a will.

CODIFY - To arrange the laws of a country into a code.

COGNIZANCE - Notice or knowledge.

COLLATERAL - By the side; accompanying; an article or thing given to secure performance of a promise.

COMITY - Courtesy; the practice by which one court follows the decision of another court on the same question.

COMMIT - To perform, as an act; to perpetrate, as a crime; to send a person to prison.

COMMON LAW - As distinguished from law created by the enactment of the legislature (called statutory law), it relates to those principles and rules of action which derive their authority solely from usages and customs of immemorial antiquity, particularly with reference to the ancient unwritten law of England. The written pronouncements of the common law are found in court decisions.

COMMUTE - Change punishment to one less severe.

COMPLAINANT - One who applies to the court for legal redress.

COMPLAINT - The pleading of a plaintiff in a civil action; or a charge that a person has committed a specified offense.

COMPROMISE - An arrangement for settling a dispute by agreement.

CONCUR - To agree, consent.

CONCURRENT - Running together, at the same time.

CONDEMNATION - Taking private property for public use on payment therefor.

CONDITION - Mode or state of being; a qualification or restriction.

CONDUCT - Active and passive behavior; both verbal and nonverbal.

CONFESSION - Voluntary statement of guilt of crime.

CONFIDENTIAL COMMUNICATION BETWEEN CLIENT AND LAWYER - Information transmitted between a client and his lawyer in the course of that relationship and in confidence by a means which, so far as the client is aware, discloses the information to no third persons other than those who are present to further the interest of the client in the consultation or those to whom disclosure is reasonably necessary for the transmission of the information or the accomplishment of the purpose for which the lawyer is consulted, and includes a legal opinion formed and the advice given by the lawyer in the course of that relationship.

CONFRONTATION - Witness testifying in presence of defendant.

CONSANGUINITY - Blood relationship.

CONSIGN - To give in charge; commit; entrust; to send or transmit goods to a merchant, factor, or agent for sale.

CONSIGNEE - One to whom a consignment is made.

CONSIGNOR - One who sends or makes a consignment.

CONSPIRACY - In criminal law, it means an agreement between two or more persons to commit an unlawful act.

CONSPIRATORS - Persons involved in a conspiracy.

CONSTITUTION - The fundamental law of a nation or state.

CONSTRUCTION OF GENDERS - The masculine gender includes the feminine and neuter.

CONSTRUCTION OF SINGULAR AND PLURAL - The singular number includes the plural; and the plural, the singular.

CONSTRUCTION OF TENSES - The present tense includes the past and future tenses; and the future, the present.

CONSTRUCTIVE - An act or condition assumed from other parts or conditions.

CONSTRUE - To ascertain the meaning of language.

CONSUMMATE - To complete.

CONTIGUOUS - Adjoining; touching; bounded by.

CONTINGENT - Possible, but not assured; dependent upon some condition.

CONTINUANCE - The adjournment or postponement of an action pending in a court.

CONTRA - Against, opposed to; contrary.

CONTRACT - An agreement between two or more persons to do or not to do a particular thing.

CONTROVERT - To dispute, deny.

CONVERSION - Dealing with the personal property of another as if it were one's own, without right.

CONVEYANCE - An instrument transferring title to land.

CONVICTION - Generally, the result of a criminal trial which ends in a judgment or sentence that the defendant is guilty as charged.

COOPERATIVE - A cooperative is a voluntary organization of persons with a common interest, formed and operated along democratic lines for the purpose of supplying services at cost to its members and other patrons, who contribute both capital and business.

CORPUS DELICTI - The body of a crime; the crime itself.

CORROBORATE - To strengthen; to add weight by additional evidence.

COUNTERCLAIM - A claim presented by a defendant in opposition to or deduction from the claim of the plaintiff.

COUNTY - Political subdivision of a state.

COVENANT - Agreement.

CREDIBLE - Worthy of belief.

CREDITOR - A person to whom a debt is owing by another person, called the "debtor."

CRIMINAL ACTION - Includes criminal proceedings.

CRIMINAL INFORMATION - Same as complaint.

CRITERION (sing.)

CRITERIA (plural) - A means or tests for judging; a standard or standards.

CROSS-EXAMINATION - Examination of a witness by a party other than the direct examiner upon a matter that is within the scope of the direct examination of the witness.

CULPABLE - Blamable.

CY-PRES - As near as (possible). The rule of *cy-pres* is a rule for the construction of instruments in equity by which the intention of the party is carried out *as near as may be*, when it would be impossible or illegal to give it literal effect.

D

DAMAGES - A monetary compensation, which may be recovered in the courts by any person who has suffered loss, or injury, whether to his person, property or rights through the unlawful act or omission or negligence of another.

DECLARANT - A person who makes a statement.

DE FACTO - In fact; actually but without legal authority.

DE JURE - Of right; legitimate; lawful.

DE MINIMIS - Very small or trifling.

DE NOVO - Anew; afresh; a second time.

DEBT - A specified sum of money owing to one person from another, including not only the obligation of the debtor to pay, but the right of the creditor to receive and enforce payment.

DECEDENT - A dead person.

DECISION - A judgment or decree pronounced by a court in determination of a case.

DECREE - An order of the court, determining the rights of all parties to a suit.

DEED - A writing containing a contract sealed and delivered; particularly to convey real property.

DEFALCATION - Misappropriation of funds.

DEFAMATION - Injuring one's reputation by false statements.

DEFAULT - The failure to fulfill a duty, observe a promise, discharge an obligation, or perform an agreement.

DEFENDANT - The person defending or denying; the party against whom relief or recovery is sought in an action or suit.

DEFRAUD - To practice fraud; to cheat or trick.

DELEGATE (v.)- To entrust to the care or management of another.

DELICTUS - A crime.

DEMUR (v.) - To dispute the sufficiency in law of the pleading of the other side.

DEMURRAGE - In maritime law, it means, the sum fixed or allowed as remuneration to the owners of a ship for the detention of their vessel beyond the number of days allowed for loading and unloading or for sailing; also used in railroad terminology.

DENIAL - A form of pleading; refusing to admit the truth of a statement, charge, etc.

DEPONENT - One who gives testimony under oath reduced to writing.

DEPOSITION - Testimony given under oath outside of court for use in court or for the purpose of obtaining information in preparation for trial of a case.

DETERIORATION - A degeneration such as from decay, corrosion or disintegration.

DETRIMENT - Any loss or harm to person or property.

DEVIATION - A turning aside.

DEVISE - A gift of real property by the last will and testament of the donor.

DICTUM (sing.)

DICTA (plural) - Any statements made by the court in an opinion concerning some rule of law not necessarily involved nor essential to the determination of the case.

DIRECT EVIDENCE - Evidence that directly proves a fact, without an inference or presumption, and which in itself if true, conclusively establishes that fact.

DIRECT EXAMINATION - The first examination of a witness upon a matter that is not within the scope of a previous examination of the witness.

DISAFFIRM - To repudiate.

DISMISS - In an action or suit, it means to dispose of the case without any further consideration or hearing.

DISSENT - To denote disagreement of one or more judges of a court with the decision passed by the majority upon a case before them.

DOCKET (n.) - A formal record, entered in brief, of the proceedings in a court.

DOCTRINE - A rule, principle, theory of law.

DOMICILE - That place where a man has his true, fixed and permanent home to which whenever he is absent he has the intention of returning.

DRAFT (n.) - A commercial paper ordering payment of money drawn by one person on another.

DRAWEE - The person who is requested to pay the money.

DRAWER - The person who draws the commercial paper and addresses it to the drawee.

DUPLICATE - A counterpart produced by the same impression as the original enlargements and miniatures, or by mechanical or electronic re-recording, or by chemical reproduction, or by other equivalent technique which accurately reproduces the original.

DURESS - Use of force to compel performance or non-performance of an act.

E

EASEMENT - A liberty, privilege, or advantage without profit, in the lands of another.

EGRESS - Act or right of going out or leaving; emergence.

EIUSDEM GENERIS - Of the same kind, class or nature. A rule used in the construction of language in a legal document.

EMBEZZLEMENT - To steal; to appropriate fraudulently to one's own use property entrusted to one's care.

EMBRACERY - Unlawful attempt to influence jurors, etc., but not by offering value.

EMINENT DOMAIN - The right of a state to take private property for public use.

ENACT - To make into a law.

ENDORSEMENT - Act of writing one's name on the back of a note, bill or similar written instrument.

ENJOIN - To require a person, by writ of injunction from a court of equity, to perform or to abstain or desist from some act.

ENTIRETY - The whole; that which the law considers as one whole, and not capable of being divided into parts.

ENTRAPMENT - Inducing one to commit a crime so as to arrest him.

ENUMERATED - Mentioned specifically; designated.

ENURE - To operate or take effect.

EQUITY - In its broadest sense, this term denotes the spirit and the habit of fairness, justness, and right dealing which regulate the conduct of men.

ERROR - A mistake of law, or the false or irregular application of law as will nullify the judicial proceedings.

ESCROW - A deed, bond or other written engagement, delivered to a third person, to be delivered by him only upon the performance or fulfillment of some condition.

ESTATE - The interest which any one has in lands, or in any other subject of property.

ESTOP - To stop, bar, or impede.

ESTOPPEL - A rule of law which prevents a man from alleging or denying a fact, because of his own previous act.

ET AL. (alii) - And others.

ET SEQ. (sequential) - And the following.

ET UX. (uxor) - And wife.

EVIDENCE - Testimony, writings, material objects, or other things presented to the senses that are offered to prove the existence or non-existence of a fact.

Means from which inferences may be drawn as a basis of proof in duly constituted judicial or fact finding tribunals, and includes testimony in the form of opinion and hearsay.

EX CONTRACTU

EX DELICTO - In law, rights and causes of action are divided into two classes, those arising *ex contractu* (from a contract) and those arising *ex delicto* (from a delict or tort).

EX OFFICIO - From office; by virtue of the office.

EX PARTE - On one side only; by or for one.

EX POST FACTO - After the fact.

EX POST FACTO LAW - A law passed after an act was done which retroactively makes such act a crime.

EX REL. (relations) - Upon relation or information.

EXCEPTION - An objection upon a matter of law to a decision made, either before or after judgment by a court.

EXECUTOR (male)

EXECUTRIX (female) - A person who has been appointed by will to execute the will.

EXECUTORY - That which is yet to be executed or performed.

EXEMPT - To release from some liability to which others are subject.

EXONERATION - The removal of a burden, charge or duty.

EXTRADITION - Surrender of a fugitive from one nation to another.

F

F.A.S.- "Free alongside ship"; delivery at dock for ship named.

F.O.B.- "Free on board"; seller will deliver to car, truck, vessel, or other conveyance by which goods are to be transported, without expense or risk of loss to the buyer or consignee.

FABRICATE - To construct; to invent a false story.

FACSIMILE - An exact or accurate copy of an original instrument.

FACTOR - A commercial agent.

FEASANCE - The doing of an act.

FELONIOUS - Criminal, malicious.

FELONY - Generally, a criminal offense that may be punished by death or imprisonment for more than one year as differentiated from a misdemeanor.

FEME SOLE - A single woman.

FIDUCIARY - A person who is invested with rights and powers to be exercised for the benefit of another person.

FIERI FACIAS - A writ of execution commanding the sheriff to levy and collect the amount of a judgment from the goods and chattels of the judgment debtor.

FINDING OF FACT - Determination from proof or judicial notice of the existence of a fact. A ruling implies a supporting finding of fact; no separate or formal finding is required unless required by a statute of this state.

FISCAL - Relating to accounts or the management of revenue.

FORECLOSURE (sale) - A sale of mortgaged property to obtain satisfaction of the mortgage out of the sale proceeds.

FORFEITURE - A penalty, a fine.

FORGERY - Fabricating or producing falsely, counterfeited.

FORTUITOUS - Accidental.

FORUM - A court of justice; a place of jurisdiction.

FRAUD - Deception; trickery.

FREEHOLDER - One who owns real property.

FUNGIBLE - Of such kind or nature that one specimen or part may be used in the place of another.

G

GARNISHEE - Person garnished.

GARNISHMENT - A legal process to reach the money or effects of a defendant, in the possession or control of a third person.

GRAND JURY - Not less than 16, not more than 23 citizens of a county sworn to inquire into crimes committed or triable in the county.

GRANT - To agree to; convey, especially real property.

GRANTEE - The person to whom a grant is made.

GRANTOR - The person by whom a grant is made.

GRATUITOUS - Given without a return, compensation or consideration.

GRAVAMEN - The grievance complained of or the substantial cause of a criminal action.

GUARANTY (n.) - A promise to answer for the payment of some debt, or the performance of some duty, in case of the failure of another person, who, in the first instance, is liable for such payment or performance.

GUARDIAN - The person, committee, or other representative authorized by law to protect the person or estate or both of an incompetent (or of a *sui juris* person having a guardian) and to act for him in matters affecting his person or property or both. An incompetent is a person under disability imposed by law.

GUILTY - Establishment of the fact that one has committed a breach of conduct; especially, a violation of law.

H

HABEAS CORPUS - You have the body; the name given to a variety of writs, having for their object to bring a party before a court or judge for decision as to whether such person is being lawfully held prisoner.

HABENDUM - In conveyancing; it is the clause in a deed conveying land which defines the extent of ownership to be held by the grantee.

HEARING - A proceeding whereby the arguments of the interested parties are heared.

HEARSAY - A type of testimony given by a witness who relates, not what he knows personally, but what others have told hi, or what he has heard said by others.

HEARSAY RULE, THE - (a) "Hearsay evidence" is evidence of a statement that was made other than by a witness while testifying at the hearing and that is offered to prove the truth of the matter stated; (b) Except as provided by law, hearsay evidence is inadmissible; (c) This section shall be known and may be cited as the hearsay rule.

HEIR - Generally, one who inherits property, real or personal.

HOLDER OF THE PRIVILEGE - (a) The client when he has no guardian or conservator; (b) A guardian or conservator of the client when the client has a guardian or conservator; (c) The personal representative of the client if the client is dead; (d) A successor, assign, trustee in dissolution, or any similar representative of a firm, association, organization, partnership, business trust, corporation, or public entity that is no longer in existence.

HUNG JURY - One so divided that they can't agree on a verdict.

HUSBAND-WIFE PRIVILEGE - An accused in a criminal proceeding has a privilege to prevent his spouse from testifying against him.

HYPOTHECATE - To pledge a thing without delivering it to the pledgee.

HYPOTHESIS - A supposition, assumption, or toehry.

I

I.E. (id est) - That is.

IB., OR IBID.(ibidem) - In the same place; used to refer to a legal reference previously cited to avoid repeating the entire citation.

ILLICIT - Prohibited; unlawful.

ILLUSORY - Deceiving by false appearance.

IMMUNITY - Exemption.

IMPEACH - To accuse, to dispute.

IMPEDIMENTS - Disabilities, or hindrances.

IMPLEAD - To sue or prosecute by due course of law.

IMPUTED - Attributed or charged to.

IN LOCO PARENTIS - In place of parent, a guardian.

IN TOTO - In the whole; completely.

INCHOATE - Imperfect; unfinished.

INCOMMUNICADO - Denial of the right of a prisoner to communicate with friends or relatives.

INCOMPETENT - One who is incapable of caring for his own affairs because he is mentally deficient or undeveloped.

INCRIMINATION - A matter will incriminate a person if it constitutes, or forms an essential part of, or, taken in connection with other matters disclosed, is a basis for a reasonable inference of such a violation of the laws of this State as to subject him to liability to punishment therefor, unless he has become for any reason permanently immune from punishment for such violation.

INCUMBRANCE - Generally a claim, lien, charge or liability attached to and binding real property.

INDEMNIFY - To secure against loss or damage; also, to make reimbursement to one for a loss already incurred by him.

INDEMNITY - An agreement to reimburse another person in case of an anticipated loss falling upon him.

INDICIA - Signs; indications.

INDICTMENT - An accusation in writing found and presented by a grand jury charging that a person has committed a crime.

INDORSE - To write a name on the back of a legal paper or document, generally, a negotiable instrument

INDUCEMENT - Cause or reason why a thing is done or that which incites the person to do the act or commit a crime; the motive for the criminal act.

INFANT - In civil cases one under 21 years of age.

INFORMATION - A formal accusation of crime made by a prosecuting attorney.

INFRA - Below, under; this word occurring by itself in a publication refers the reader to a future part of the publication.

INGRESS - The act of going into.

INJUNCTION - A writ or order by the court requiring a person, generally, to do or to refrain from doing an act.

INSOLVENT - The condition of a person who is unable to pay his debts.

INSTRUCTION - A direction given by the judge to the jury concerning the law of the case.

INTERIM - In the meantime; time intervening.

INTERLOCUTORY - Temporary, not final; something intervening between the commencement and the end of a suit which decides some point or matter, but is not a final decision of the whole controversy.

INTERROGATORIES - A series of formal written questions used in the examination of a party or a witness usually prior to a trial.

INTESTATE - A person who dies without a will.

INURE - To result, to take effect.

IPSO FACTO - By the fact iself; by the mere fact.

ISSUE (n.) The disputed point or question in a case,

J

JEOPARDY - Danger, hazard, peril.

JOINDER - Joining; uniting with another person in some legal steps or proceeding.

JOINT - United; combined.

JUDGE - Member or members or representative or representatives of a court conducting a trial or hearing at which evidence is introduced.

JUDGMENT - The official decision of a court of justice.

JUDICIAL OR JUDICIARY - Relating to or connected with the administration of justice.

JURAT - The clause written at the foot of an affidavit, stating when, where and before whom such affidavit was sworn.

JURISDICTION - The authority to hear and determine controversies between parties.

JURISPRUDENCE - The philosophy of law.

JURY - A body of persons legally selected to inquire into any matter of fact, and to render their verdict according to the evidence.

L

LACHES - The failure to diligently assert a right, which results in a refusal to allow relief.

LANDLORD AND TENANT - A phrase used to denote the legal relation existing between the owner and occupant of real estate.

LARCENY - Stealing personal property belonging to another.

LATENT - Hidden; that which does not appear on the face of a thing.

LAW - Includes constitutional, statutory, and decisional law.

LAWYER-CLIENT PRIVILEGE - (1) A "client" is a person, public officer, or corporation, association, or other organization or entity, either public or private, who is rendered professional legal services by a lawyer, or who consults a lawyer with a view to obtaining professional legal services from him; (2) A "lawyer" is a person authorized, or reasonably believed by the client to be authorized, to practice law in any state or nation; (3) A "representative of the lawyer" is one employed to assist the lawyer in the rendition of professional legal services; (4) A communication is "confidential" if not intended to be disclosed to third persons other than those to whom disclosure is in furtherance of the rendition of professional legal services to the client or those reasonably necessary for the transmission of the communication.

General rule of privilege - A client has a privilege to refuse to disclose and to prevent any other person from disclosing confidential communications made for the purpose of facilitating the rendition of professional legal services to the client, (1) between himself or his representative and his lawyer or his lawyer's representative, or (2) between his lawyer and the lawyer's representative, or (3) by him or his lawyer to a lawyer representing another in a matter of common interest, or (4) between representatives of the client or between the client and a representative of the client, or (5) between lawyers representing the client.

LEADING QUESTION - Question that suggests to the witness the answer that the examining party desires.

LEASE - A contract by which one conveys real estate for a limited time usually for a specified rent; personal property also may be leased.

LEGISLATION - The act of enacting laws.

LEGITIMATE - Lawful.

LESSEE - One to whom a lease is given.

LESSOR - One who grants a lease

LEVY - A collecting or exacting by authority.

LIABLE - Responsible; bound or obligated in law or equity.

LIBEL (v.) - To defame or injure a person's reputation by a published writing.

(n.) - The initial pleading on the part of the plaintiff in an admiralty proceeding.

LIEN - A hold or claim which one person has upon the property of another as a security for some debt or charge.

LIQUIDATED - Fixed; settled.

LIS PENDENS - A pending civil or criminal action.

LITERAL - According to the language.

LITIGANT - A party to a lawsuit.

LITATION - A judicial controversy.

LOCUS - A place.

LOCUS DELICTI - Place of the crime.

LOCUS POENITENTIAE - The abandoning or giving up of one's intention to commit some crime before it is fully completed or abandoning a conspiracy before its purpose is accomplished.

M

MALFEASANCE - To do a wrongful act.

MALICE - The doing of a wrongful act Intentionally without just cause or excuse.

MANDAMUS - The name of a writ issued by a court to enforce the performance of some public duty.

MANDATORY (adj.) Containing a command.

MARITIME - Pertaining to the sea or to commerce thereon.

MARSHALING - Arranging or disposing of in order.

MAXIM - An established principle or proposition.

MINISTERIAL - That which involves obedience to instruction, but demands no special discretion, judgment or skill.

MISAPPROPRIATE - Dealing fraudulently with property entrusted to one.

MISDEMEANOR - A crime less than a felony and punishable by a fine or imprisonment for less than one year.

MISFEASANCE - Improper performance of a lawful act.

MISREPRESENTATION - An untrue representation of facts.

MITIGATE - To make or become less severe, harsh.

MITTIMUS - A warrant of commitment to prison.

MOOT (adj.) Unsettled, undecided, not necessary to be decided.

MORTGAGE - A conveyance of property upon condition, as security for the payment of a debt or the performance of a duty, and to become void upon payment or performance according to the stipulated terms.

MORTGAGEE - A person to whom property is mortgaged.

MORTGAGOR - One who gives a mortgage.

MOTION - In legal proceedings, a "motion" is an application, either written or oral, addressed to the court by a party to an action or a suit requesting the ruling of the court on a matter of law.

MUTUALITY - Reciprocation.

N

NEGLIGENCE - The failure to exercise that degree of care which an ordinarily prudent person would exercise under like circumstances.

NEGOTIABLE (instrument) - Any instrument obligating the payment of money which is transferable from one person to another by endorsement and delivery or by delivery only.

NEGOTIATE - To transact business; to transfer a negotiable instrument; to seek agreement for the amicable disposition of a controversy or case.

NOLLE PROSEQUI - A formal entry upon the record, by the plaintiff in a civil suit or the prosecuting officer in a criminal action, by which he declares that he "will no further prosecute" the case.

NOLO CONTENDERE - The name of a plea in a criminal action, having the same effect as a plea of guilty; but not constituting a direct admission of guilt.

NOMINAL - Not real or substantial.

NOMINAL DAMAGES - Award of a trifling sum where no substantial injury is proved to have been sustained.

NONFEASANCE - Neglect of duty.

NOVATION - The substitution of a new debt or obligation for an existing one.

NUNC PRO TUNC - A phrase applied to acts allowed to be done after the time when they should be done, with a retroactive effect.("Now for then.")

O

OATH - Oath includes affirmation or declaration under penalty of perjury.

OBITER DICTUM - Opinion expressed by a court on a matter not essentially involved in a case and hence not a decision; also called dicta, if plural.

OBJECT (v.) - To oppose as improper or illegal and referring the question of its propriety or legality to the court.

OBLIGATION - A legal duty, by which a person is bound to do or not to do a certain thing.

OBLIGEE - The person to whom an obligation is owed.

OBLIGOR - The person who is to perform the obligation.

OFFER (v.) - To present for acceptance or rejection.

      (n.) - A proposal to do a thing, usually a proposal to make a contract.

OFFICIAL INFORMATION - Information within the custody or control of a department or agency of the government the disclosure of which is shown to be contrary to the public interest.

OFFSET - A deduction.

ONUS PROBANDI - Burden of proof.

OPINION - The statement by a judge of the decision reached in a case, giving the law as applied to the case and giving reasons for the judgment; also a belief or view.

OPTION - The exercise of the power of choice; also a privilege existing in one person, for which he has paid money, which gives him the right to buy or sell real or personal property at a given price within a specified time.

ORDER - A rule or regulation; every direction of a court or judge made or entered in writing but not including a judgment.

ORDINANCE - Generally, a rule established by authority; also commonly used to designate the legislative acts of a municipal corporation.

ORIGINAL - Writing or recording itself or any counterpart intended to have the same effect by a person executing or issuing it. An "original" of a photograph includes the negative or any print therefrom. If data are stored in a computer or similar device, any printout or other output readable by sight, shown to reflect the data accurately, is an "original."

OVERT - Open, manifest.

P

PANEL - A group of jurors selected to serve during a term of the court.

PARENS PATRIAE - Sovereign power of a state to protect or be a guardian over children and incompetents.

PAROL - Oral or verbal.

PAROLE - To release one in prison before the expiration of his sentence, conditionally.

PARITY - Equality in purchasing power between the farmer and other segments of the economy.

PARTITION - A legal division of real or personal property between one or more owners.

PARTNERSHIP - An association of two or more persons to carry on as co-owners a business for profit.

PATENT (adj.) - Evident.

      (n.) - A grant of some privilege, property, or authority, made by the government or sovereign of a country to one or more individuals.

PECULATION - Stealing.

PECUNIARY - Monetary.

PENULTIMATE - Next to the last.

PER CURIAM - A phrase used in the report of a decision to distinguish an opinion of the whole court from an opinion written by any one judge.

PER SE - In itself; taken alone.

PERCEIVE - To acquire knowledge through one's senses.

PEREMPTORY - Imperative; absolute.

PERJURY - To lie or state falsely under oath.

PERPETUITY - Perpetual existence; also the quality or condition of an estate limited so that it will not take effect or vest within the period fixed by law.

PERSON - Includes a natural person, firm, association, organization, partnership, business trust, corporation, or public entity.

PERSONAL PROPERTY - Includes money, goods, chattels, things in action, and evidences of debt.

PERSONALTY - Short term for personal property.

PETITION - An application in writing for an order of the court, stating the circumstances upon which it is founded and requesting any order or other relief from a court.

PLAINTIFF - A person who brings a court action.

PLEA - A pleading in a suit or action.

PLEADINGS - Formal allegations made by the parties of their respective claims and defenses, for the judgment of the court.

PLEDGE - A deposit of personal property as a security for the performance of an act.

PLEDGEE - The party to whom goods are delivered in pledge.

PLEDGOR - The party delivering goods in pledge.

PLENARY - Full; complete.

POLICE POWER - Inherent power of the state or its political subdivisions to enact laws within constitutional limits to promote the general welfare of society or the community.

POLLING THE JURY - Call the names of persons on a jury and requiring each juror to declare what his verdict is before it is legally recorded.

POST MORTEM - After death.

POWER OF ATTORNEY - A writing authorizing one to act for another.

PRECEPT - An order, warrant, or writ issued to an officer or body of officers, commanding him or them to do some act within the scope of his or their powers.

PRELIMINARY FACT - Fact upon the existence or nonexistence of which depends the admissibility or inadmissibility of evidence. The phrase "the admissibility or inadmissibility of evidence" includes the qualification or disqualification of a person to be a witness and the existence or non-existence of a privilege.

PREPONDERANCE - Outweighing.

PRESENTMENT - A report by a grand jury on something they have investigated on their own knowledge.

PRESUMPTION - An assumption of fact resulting from a rule of law which requires such fact to be assumed from another fact or group of facts found or otherwise established in the action.

PRIMA FACUE - At first sight.

PRIMA FACIE CASE - A case where the evidence is very patent against the defendant.

PRINCIPAL - The source of authority or rights; a person primarily liable as differentiated from "principle" as a primary or basic doctrine.

PRO AND CON - For and against.

PRO RATA - Proportionally.

PROBATE - Relating to proof, especially to the proof of wills.

PROBATIVE - Tending to prove.

PROCEDURE - In law, this term generally denotes rules which are established by the Federal, State, or local Governments regarding the types of pleading and courtroom practice which must be followed by the parties involved in a criminal or civil case.

PROCLAMATION - A public notice by an official of some order, intended action, or state of facts.

PROFFERED EVIDENCE - The admissibility or inadmissibility of which is dependent upon the existence or nonexistence of a preliminary fact.

PROMISSORY (NOTE) - A promise in writing to pay a specified sum at an expressed time, or on demand, or at sight, to a named person, or to his order, or bearer.

PROOF - The establishment by evidence of a requisite degree of belief concerning a fact in the mind of the trier of fact or the court.

PROPERTY - Includes both real and personal property.

PROPRIETARY (adj.) - Relating or pertaining to ownership; usually a single owner.

PROSECUTE - To carry on an action or other judicial proceeding; to proceed against a person criminally.

PROVISO - A limitation or condition in a legal instrument.

PROXIMATE - Immediate; nearest

PUBLIC EMPLOYEE - An officer, agent, or employee of a public entity.

PUBLIC ENTITY - Includes a national, state, county, city and county, city, district, public authority, public agency, or any other political subdivision or public corporation, whether foreign or domestic.

PUBLIC OFFICIAL - Includes an official of a political dubdivision of such state or territory and of a municipality.

PUNITIVE - Relating to punishment.

Q

QUASH - To make void.

QUASI - As if; as it were.

QUID PRO QUO - Something for something; the giving of one valuable thing for another.

QUITCLAIM (v.) - To release or relinquish claim or title to, especially in deeds to realty.

QUO WARRANTO - A legal procedure to test an official's right to a public office or the right to hold a franchise, or to hold an office in a domestic corporation.

R

RATIFY - To approve and sanction.

REAL PROPERTY - Includes lands, tenements, and hereditaments.

REALTY - A brief term for real property.

REBUT - To contradict; to refute, especially by evidence and arguments.

RECEIVER - A person who is appointed by the court to receive, and hold in trust property in litigation.

RECIDIVIST - Habitual criminal.

RECIPROCAL - Mutual.

RECOUPMENT - To keep back or get something which is due; also, it is the right of a defendant to have a deduction from the amount of the plaintiff's damages because the plaintiff has not fulfilled his part of the same contract.

RECROSS EXAMINATION - Examination of a witness by a cross-examiner subsequent to a redirect examination of the witness.

REDEEM - To release an estate or article from mortgage or pledge by paying the debt for which it stood as security.

REDIRECT EXAMINATION - Examination of a witness by the direct examiner subsequent to the cross-examination of the witness.

REFEREE - A person to whom a cause pending in a court is referred by the court, to take testimony, hear the parties, and report thereon to the court.

REFERENDUM - A method of submitting an important legislative or administrative matter to a direct vote of the people.

RELEVANT EVIDENCE - Evidence including evidence relevant to the credulity of a witness or hearsay declarant, having any tendency in reason to prove or disprove any disputed fact that is of consequence to the determination of the action.

REMAND - To send a case back to the lower court from which it came, for further proceedings.

REPLEVIN - An action to recover goods or chattels wrongfully taken or detained.

REPLY (REPLICATION) - Generally, a reply is what the plaintiff or other person who has instituted proceedings says in answer to the defendant's case.

RE JUDICATA - A thing judicially acted upon or decided.

RES ADJUDICATA - Doctrine that an issue or dispute litigated and determined in a case between the opposing parties is deemed permanently decided between these parties.

RESCIND (RECISSION) - To avoid or cancel a contract.

RESPONDENT - A defendant in a proceeding in chancery or admiralty; also, the person who contends against the appeal in a case.

RESTITUTION - In equity, it is the restoration of both parties to their original condition (when practicable), upon the rescission of a contract for fraud or similar cause.

RETROACTIVE (RETROSPECTIVE) - Looking back; effective as of a prior time.

REVERSED - A term used by appellate courts to indicate that the decision of the lower court in the case before it has been set aside.

REVOKE - To recall or cancel.

RIPARIAN (RIGHTS) - The rights of a person owning land containing or bordering on a water course or other body of water, such as lakes and rivers.

S

SALE - A contract whereby the ownership of property is transferred from one person to another for a sum of money or for any consideration.

SANCTION - A penalty or punishment provided as a means of enforcing obedience to a law; also, an authorization.

SATISFACTION - The discharge of an obligation by paying a party what is due to him; or what is awarded to him by the judgment of a court or otherwise.

SCIENTER - Knowingly; also, it is used in pleading to denote the defendant 's guilty knowledge.

SCINTILLA - A spark; also the least particle.

SECRET OF STATE - Governmental secret relating to the national defense or the international relations of the United States.

SECURITY - Indemnification; the term is applied to an obligation, such as a mortgage or deed of trust, given by a debtor to insure the payment or performance of his debt, by furnishing the creditor with a resource to be used in case of the debtor's failure to fulfill the principal obligation.

SENTENCE - The judgment formally pronounced by the court or judge upon the defendant after his conviction in a criminal prosecution.

SET-OFF - A claim or demand which one party in an action credits against the claim of the opposing party.

SHALL and MAY - "Shall" is mandatory and "may" is permissive.

SITUS - Location.

SOVEREIGN - A person, body or state in which independent and supreme authority is vested.

STARE DECISIS - To follow decided cases.

STATE - "State" means this State, unless applied to the different parts of the United States. In the latter case, it includes any state, district, commonwealth, territory or insular possession of the United States, including the District of Columbia.

STATEMENT - (a) Oral or written verbal expression or (b) nonverbal conduct of a person intended by him as a substitute for oral or written verbal expression.

STATUTE - An act of the legislature. Includes a treaty.

STATUTE OF LIMITATION - A statute limiting the time to bring an action after the right of action has arisen.

STAY - To hold in abeyance an order of a court.

STIPULATION - Any agreement made by opposing attorneys regulating any matter incidental to the proceedings or trial.

SUBORDINATION (AGREEMENT) - An agreement making one's rights inferior to or of a lower rank than another's.

SUBORNATION - The crime of procuring a person to lie or to make false statements to a court.

SUBPOENA - A writ or order directed to a person, and requiring his attendance at a particular time and place to testify as a witness.

SUBPOENA DUCES TECUM - A subpoena used, not only for the purpose of compelling witnesses to attend in court, but also requiring them to bring with them books or documents which may be in their possession, and which may tend to elucidate the subject matter of the trial.

SUBROGATION - The substituting of one for another as a creditor, the new creditor succeeding to the former's rights.

SUBSIDY - A government grant to assist a private enterprise deemed advantageous to the public.

SUI GENERIS - Of the same kind.

SUIT - Any civil proceeding by a person or persons against another or others in a court of justice by which the plaintiff pursues the remedies afforded him by law.

SUMMONS - A notice to a defendant that an action against him has been commenced and requiring him to appear in court and answer the complaint.

SUPRA - Above; this word occurring by itself in a book refers the reader to a previous part of the book.

SURETY - A person who binds himself for the payment of a sum of money, or for the performance of something else, for another.

SURPLUSAGE - Extraneous or unnecessary matter.

SURVIVORSHIP - A term used when a person becomes entitled to property by reason of his having survived another person who had an interest in the property.

SUSPEND SENTENCE - Hold back a sentence pending good behavior of prisoner.

SYLLABUS - A note prefixed to a report, especially a case, giving a brief statement of the court's ruling on different issues of the case.

T

TALESMAN - Person summoned to fill a panel of jurors.

TENANT - One who holds or possesses lands by any kind of right or title; also, one who has the temporary use and occupation of real property owned by another person (landlord), the duration and terms of his tenancy being usually fixed by an instrument called "a lease."

TENDER - An offer of money; an expression of willingness to perform a contract according to its terms.

TERM - When used with reference to a court, it signifies the period of time during which the court holds a session, usually of several weeks or months duration.

TESTAMENTARY - Pertaining to a will or the administration of a will.

TESTATOR (male)

TESTATRIX (female) - One who makes or has made a testament or will.

TESTIFY (TESTIMONY) - To give evidence under oath as a witness.

TO WIT - That is to say; namely.

TORT - Wrong; injury to the person.

TRANSITORY - Passing from place to place.

TRESPASS - Entry into another's ground, illegally.

TRIAL - The examination of a cause, civil or criminal, before a judge who has jurisdiction over it, according to the laws of the land.

TRIER OF FACT - Includes (a) the jury and (b) the court when the court is trying an issue of fact other than one relating to the admissibility of evidence.

TRUST - A right of property, real or personal, held by one party for the benefit of another.

TRUSTEE - One who lawfully holds property in custody for the benefit of another.

U

UNAVAILABLE AS A WITNESS - The declarant is (1) Exempted or precluded on the ground of privilege from testifying concerning the matter to which his statement is relevant; (2) Disqualified from testifying to the matter; (3) Dead or unable to attend or to testify at the hearing because of then existing physical or mental illness or infirmity; (4) Absent from the hearing and the court is unable to compel his attendance by its process; or (5) Absent from the hearing and the proponent of his statement has exercised reasonable diligence but has been unable to procure his attendance by the court's process.

ULTRA VIRES - Acts beyond the scope and power of a corporation, association, etc.

UNILATERAL - One-sided; obligation upon, or act of one party.

USURY - Unlawful interest on a loan.

V

VACATE - To set aside; to move out.

VARIANCE - A discrepancy or disagreement between two instruments or two aspects of the same case, which by law should be consistent.

VENDEE - A purchaser or buyer.

VENDOR - The person who transfers property by sale, particularly real estate; the term "seller" is used more commonly for one who sells personal property.

VENIREMEN - Persons ordered to appear to serve on a jury or composing a panel of jurors.

VENUE - The place at which an action is tried, generally based on locality or judicial district in which an injury occurred or a material fact happened.

VERDICT - The formal decision or finding of a jury.

VERIFY - To confirm or substantiate by oath.

VEST - To accrue to.

VOID - Having no legal force or binding effect.

VOIR DIRE - Preliminary examination of a witness or a juror to test competence, interest, prejudice, etc.

W

WAIVE - To give up a right.

WAIVER - The intentional or voluntary relinquishment of a known right.

WARRANT (WARRANTY) (v.) - To promise that a certain fact or state of facts, in relation to the subject matter, is, or shall be, as it is represented to be.

WARRANT (n.) - A writ issued by a judge, or other competent authority, addressed to a sheriff, or other officer, requiring him to arrest the person therein named, and bring him before the judge or court to answer or be examined regarding the offense with which he is charged.

WRIT - An order or process issued in the name of the sovereign or in the name of a court or judicial officer, commanding the performance or nonperformance of some act.

WRITING - Handwriting, typewriting, printing, photostating, photographing and every other means of recording upon any tangible thing any form of communication or representation, including letters, words, pictures, sounds, or symbols, or combinations thereof.

WRITINGS AND RECORDINGS - Consists of letters, words, or numbers, or their equivalent, set down by handwriting, typewriting, printing, photostating, photographing, magnetic impulse, mechanical or electronic recording, or other form of data compilation.

Y

YEA AND NAY - Yes and no.

YELLOW DOG CONTRACT - A contract by which employer requires employee to sign an instrument promising as condition that he will not join a union during its continuance, and will be discharged if he does join.

Z

ZONING - The division of a city by legislative regulation into districts and the prescription and application in each district of regulations having to do with structural and architectural designs of buildings and of regulations prescribing use to which buildings within designated districts may be put.